ACCESS TO HIGHER EDUCATION

Oliver Fulton
(Editor)

John H. Farrant   Martin Trow   Alan Gordon

Geoffrey Squires   Ernest Rudd

Maureen Woodhall

SOCIETY FOR RESEARCH INTO HIGHER EDUCATION

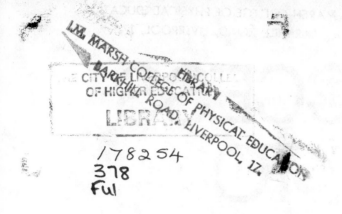
Research into Higher Education Monographs

The Society for Research into Higher Education, at the
University, Guildford, Surrey GU2 5XH

First published 1981

© 1981 Society for Research into Higher Education

ISBN 0 900868 89 9

Printed in England by Direct Printers, Butts Pond
Industrial Estate, Sturminster Newton, Dorset DT10 1AZ

ACCESS TO HIGHER EDUCATION

is to be returned on or b

that the time is ripe for a great national debate. . . .' The present programme is intended to contribute to that debate by offering both a structure within which the main issues can be considered and assessment of the evidence on which future policy should be based.

Gareth Williams
Programme Director

FOREWORD

by Sir Adrian Cadbury

I enjoyed taking part in the discussions at the SRHE/Leverhulme seminar on demand and access and learnt a great deal from them. Although I was not at the seminar to put my views or to represent those of industry and commerce, certain points struck me as particularly relevant to employers. These concern not graduate recruitment, which was dealt with in the first seminar on the labour market, but the demand for and access to higher education as it affects people at work.

As an employer I am above all conscious of the way in which the talents and abilities of people in industry are under-used. I entirely agree with the view that we are excessively cautious in regard to the capabilities of individuals if given the chance; we undervalue them and they undervalue themselves. Within our own company we attempt to draw on this untapped resource by involving people in the activities of the business and giving them the opportunity to contribute to the way it develops. I accept all the limitations of this approach in practice, but my direct contact with employee representatives through our participative system confirms my view that a significant number of people want to have more of a say in the decisions which directly affect them, and have the capacity to do so effectively. As a footnote which also applies to changes in the educational system, if an institution moves to a more open and participative style of management it will be changed in the process: it is not simply an optional extra.

The second aspect of the employment scene which concerns me is our lamentable record of training compared with other European countries. Some fifty per cent of school-leavers take jobs which provide no formal training whatsoever, when the West German figure is more like five per cent. This is not entirely the fault of employers. From the early 1900s young people at Bournville spent a day a week during term-time at the Day Continuation College. This was dropped as a condition of employment in the 1960s, partly because it did not help recruitment, partly because of doubts about the value of compulsory further education. My guess is that as a result fewer school-leavers use this kind of opportunity as an entry point into continuing education.

The third point I would make is that there will be major changes in the way work in manufacturing industry will be organized within our time horizon. Fewer people will be employed and more of them will contract to work so many hours a year or to carry out particular tasks rather than be paid for their attendance at a factory or office; instead of having ancillary services (like computing and design) on our larger sites, we will be buying them in, often from the same people as before, who will be self-employed; improved communication systems will cut down on physical movement and on the number who have to congregate at a fixed place for a fixed time; the production hours required for a given output will be markedly reduced. It adds up to a combination of rapid technological change and more leisure (or time spent not working).

If one accepts the general sense of direction of this analysis, it brings together under-used abilities, lack of training and a world of work where we will not only have more free time but more control over how and when we take it. This brings me down firmly in favour of stimulating the demand for education to provide for missed opportunities and for changes through time in the attitudes of individuals towards education; education will also have an essential role in helping industry itself to cope with the demands of technological change. As an industrialist it seem to me oddly illogical to suppose that a single dose of higher education from 18 to 21 could inoculate you for life. I therefore see the employment scene in the years ahead as supporting an expansion in educational opportunity, and I believe that a rational economic case could be made out for this addition to educational provision, although the social case will stand on its own.

The conclusion that we should encourage an increase in educational demand leads on to the question of access. Here I would concentrate on the ways into the educational system and my objective would be to multiply the points of contact between educational institutions and people at work. One of the roles of the Day Continuation College was in providing just that kind of link and the Open University is now making a contribution in this respect. Alan Gordon (Chapter 4) talks of whetting children's appetite at school; and Geoffrey Squires (Chapter 5) of the DipHE as an easier first step towards a more advanced qualification. The aim must be to widen awareness of what is available, in the belief that more people would take up what is on offer if they thought it was within their reach in all senses. From this point of view I believe that the location of educational institutions is vital — where they are is more important than what they are, so we should build on whatever is to hand. Flexible timetabling of courses is also an essential encouragement to access. Some concern was expressed about fragmentation of the educational system; I am not advocating fragmentation but pluralism. I am sceptical of arguments based on the need for uniformity, common standards and all the rest of it and in favour of as much flexibility and local initiative as we can get away with. Above all though, I want to maximize the ways into the system.

I accept that my references to educational institutions may seem rather cavalier, but my lack of precision is based on imperfect knowledge, and anyway it gives me a freer hand. My impression is that the higher education system as a whole is not geared to meet the demands of pluralism. The universities are too cut off from life at work to find it easy to respond to the wide range of needs of mature students spelled out by Geoffrey

Squires (p.150). They could do more to nourish their roots in the local community and to encourage non-students to use the campus — give them access to lectures, recreational facilities, libraries and so on. The main point is that, whatever the institution, the structure and content of courses should meet the needs of those who want to benefit from them. This is where the sense of the market introduced by Professor Trow (Chapter 3) is so valuable. The market will be very diverse and to meet it will require innovative and creative thinking on the part of the providers of education. Incidentally there must be scope for innovation in teaching methods, building on the distance learning techniques developed by the Open University and on the work of adult educationalists.

The final point is on a different issue altogether and it concerns the current crisis over funding. I want to reinforce strongly the point that full advantage needs to be taken of all opportunities to bring about change in institutions, as they rarely occur. The great difficulty is to persuade people that change is necessary; when institutions accept that change is inevitable we should make the most of it. I have had the disagreeable task of running down parts of a business, which is not as daunting for a variety of reasons as reducing the size of a university. I believe that if you involve in its planning and implementation those affected by this kind of decision, you will be heartened by the constructive nature of their response. Going through the motions of participation, however, will as effectively unite opposition to change as a decision imposed without consultation. The key is to take as positive a view of the ways of meeting cuts as possible.

As to the proposals put forward by Oliver Fulton in Chapter 1, I hope that reaction will not be too pessimistic nor too constrained by finance. If the money is not available centrally for what we think should be done, we should look for other sources of funds. We need to look ahead twenty years. We tend to underestimate people's abilities and we should not make the same mistake in underestimating the degree to which the educational system can be reshaped if we can win support for our views.

Adrian Cadbury
Chairman
7 August 1981

THE LEVERHULME PROGRAMME
OF
STUDY INTO THE FUTURE OF HIGHER EDUCATION

This is the second publication of a programme of study focusing informed opinion and recent research findings on the major strategic options likely to be available to higher education institutions and policy-making bodies in the 1980s and 1990s. The programme has been made possible by a generous grant from the Leverhulme Trust to the Society for Research into Higher Education, and is entirely independent of governmental or other organizational pressure.

The present monograph arises out of a specialist seminar held in June 1981 with Sir Adrian Cadbury in the Chair. I would like to take this opportunity of recording my personal thanks to Sir Adrian for his excellent chairmanship but even more importantly for the invaluable support and advice he has given the programme since its conception.

The most critical issue currently facing higher education is the extent to which consensual arrangements and assumptions that generally worked well during the long postwar period of expansion can cope with the much more stringent conditions likely to prevail in the 1980s and 1990s. Is there sufficient common purpose amongst the various institutions and interest groups that constitute 'the higher education system' to permit the development of viable long-run strategies, or must higher education policy increasingly become the outcome of a struggle for survival and dominance among conflicting interests and ideas?

The fundamental question for the present volume is the extent to which something similar to the 'Robbins principle' of basing higher education provision on student demand can and should continue to be the primary planning criterion in the 1980s and 1990s and if so what adaptations to the basic principle are necessary. The first report of the series[1] has suggested that forecasts of manpower needs do not offer a simple alternative criterion. If this view of the main contender for an alternative criterion is accepted it reinforces the need to re-examine the concept of student demand in the context of the likely conditions of the 1980s and 1990s.

The programme is an experiment in formulating long-term strategies openly, taking into account the best available specialist knowledge about a complex system, the legitimate interests of a wide range of conflicting pressure groups, and wider public interests as perceived by disinterested

---

[1] Lindley, R. (Editor) (1981) *Higher Education and the Labour Market* Guildford: SRHE.

individuals with no direct day-to-day involvement in higher education. The final recommendations will be the result of an iterative process in which proposals are made, then discussed, then revised, then reconsidered. Stage one is to commission research reviews by acknowledged experts in various specialist areas. Stage two is a seminar at which others with detailed knowledge and experience of the area discuss these reviews. Stage three is publication of the reviews together with a report of the discussion and of the policy implications highlighted by it. Stage four is wider debate in the press and in specially convened conferences. Stage five is reconsideration of the policy issues in the light of the wider reaction. Stage six is the preparation of a final report. A seventh stage is of course hoped for, in which public authorities and institutions of higher education will take up the report's recommendations.

Two topics have now reached the third stage: higher education and the labour market (already published); and demand and access (the present volume). There will be six other main areas of inquiry: these are summarized below.

INSTITUTIONAL ADAPTATION AND CHANGE
Whatever measures are taken during the 1980s to relate the higher education system more closely to the needs of society and to the demands of new categories of students, there is a strong probability that before the end of the decade there will be some excess capacity. There is already some evidence of apparent mismatch between the patterns of provision and the demand for places. Unless some careful co-ordination is undertaken the decline in the age groups from 1984 onwards will make this problem very much worse. At the level of individual institutions there will be considerable interest in appropriate strategies for survival and growth; while for the system as a whole there needs to be a concern for some measure of rationalization, so that any reduction in capacity that does occur does as little harm as possible to the essential fabric of higher education. A single seminar obviously cannot produce a detailed plan for rationalization, institution by institution. However, it should be possible to consider and make recommendations about the principles which need to be followed when the decline in the birthrate begins to make itself seriously felt in the late 1980s.

THE RESEARCH FUNCTION
Universities are institutions whose function is teaching and research. In pursuing parity of esteem, many polytechnics have claimed equal treatment with regard to funding for research. However, there is ambiguity concerning the relationship that does exist, and that ought to exist, between research and teaching in higher education institutions. There is considerable disagreement, for example, about whether in practice research is competitive with, or complementary to teaching, in the activities of academic staff. The actual and desirable relationship between 'research', 'scholarship', and

consultancy activities is not at all clear. An unspecified proportion of the UGC grant to universities is normally deemed to be for research and scholarship. At the same time earmarked funds for scientific research are made available through the research councils. Increasingly, universities and polytechnics have undertaken contractual research for both public and private sector activities. An attempt at rationalizing the public finance of research was made by the Rothschild Report in 1971, but its recommendations have largely been ignored. A careful examination is needed of the place and organization of research in higher education institutions.

THE ROLE OF THE ARTS

The Robbins Committee, while recognizing that music has a place in the universities, was somewhat doubtful about the other 'arts'. Nevertheless, many universities have developed courses in the fine arts and the performing arts, while at the same time many arts colleges have come formally within the compass of higher education. However, the treatment of the arts in higher education has for the most part remained within the confines of academic subject specializations. There have been very few attempts to integrate the arts into more general curricula. The aim of this seminar will be to examine the role of higher education both in providing training for professional arts and performers and in the teaching of the arts as part of our general cultural heritage.

THE TEACHING FUNCTION

The largest task of higher education institutions is the teaching of students. The scope of this activity ranges from training in specific vocational skills to the provision of opportunities for self-development in a wide range of general analytical and creative activities. Since 1960 there has been a huge increase in the curricular content of higher education; at the same time considerable attention has been devoted to the improvement of teaching, particularly through the use of new educational technologies. However, with rather few exceptions, of which the Open University is the most outstanding example, there has been little change in the ways in which the teaching function has been carried out. During the 1980s new problems are likely to emerge, particularly as a result of the aging of the stock of teachers and the lack of opportunities for mobility within higher education and out of it. The existence of a healthy higher education system in the 1990s is likely to depend at least as much on the attention that is paid to the content and methods of teaching as on external circumstances. This seminar will therefore give consideration to what is taught and how it is taught. It will give rise to two published volumes in the present series.

MECHANISMS OF FINANCE

There are two levels of discussion about financial policy for higher education which ought to be brought together. The first is consideration of radical changes in the financial arrangements, such as greater dependence on private finance of various kinds and the replacement of student grants by loans. The second is about whether the existing financial mechanisms for disbursing public funds do in fact ensure an allocation of resources which is consistent with public policy objectives. The tension between academic freedom and public accountability is one which needs to be kept constantly under review.

STRUCTURE AND GOVERNANCE

The Robbins Report recommended the establishment of what was in effect a unitary system of higher education dominated by the universities. Almost immediately, a binary system was established in which government policy set up a competitive sector (the polytechnics) with parity of esteem with the universities and financed through the local authorities. Subsequently, largely as a result of the reduction in the demand for teachers, many colleges of education have been turned into a third sector purportedly catering for a rather different clientele from the second. There is also, of course, the Open University, and there remain a number of further education colleges, outside the polytechnics, which offer degree-level work. Furthermore, the forthcoming decline in the size of the age group which normally enters higher education is likely to encourage each category of institution to attempt to move into new areas. In the light of this kind of consideration the government has proposed the establishment of a new national body to control public sector higher education. A careful review of this and other options for long-term development is opportune. In particular the government proposals increase the need for a careful consideration of the relationships between the university sector and public sector higher education.

The last of these research-based seminars will take place in late summer 1982. The material produced in the course of debate on their separate topics will be brought together at one further seminar. A final report setting out the conclusions and policy recommendations of the programme as a whole will be published in 1983.

The scope of the Leverhulme Programme is very wide. The need for a major review of higher education has been recognized for some time and has been given special impetus by the publication during 1980 and 1981 of major reports having strong implications for its future: those of the Committee of Enquiry into the Engineering Profession (*Engineering our Future*), and the House of Commons Education, Science and Arts Committee (*The Funding and Organisation of Courses in Higher Education*), and the recent government Green Paper on the Organization of Public Sector Higher Education. The House of Commons Committee acknowledges the initiative behind the present programme and in the closing remarks of its report states: 'We believe that higher education is at a watershed in its development and that the time is ripe for a great national debate. . . .' The present programme is intended to contribute to that debate by offering both a structure within which the main issues can be considered and assessment of the evidence on which future policy should be based.

Gareth Williams
Programme Director

FOREWORD

by Sir Adrian Cadbury

I enjoyed taking part in the discussions at the SRHE/Leverhulme seminar on demand and access and learnt a great deal from them. Although I was not at the seminar to put my views or to represent those of industry and commerce, certain points struck me as particularly relevant to employers. These concern not graduate recruitment, which was dealt with in the first seminar on the labour market, but the demand for and access to higher education as it affects people at work.

As an employer I am above all conscious of the way in which the talents and abilities of people in industry are under-used. I entirely agree with the view that we are excessively cautious in regard to the capabilities of individuals if given the chance; we undervalue them and they undervalue themselves. Within our own company we attempt to draw on this untapped resource by involving people in the activities of the business and giving them the opportunity to contribute to the way it develops. I accept all the limitations of this approach in practice, but my direct contact with employee representatives through our participative system confirms my view that a significant number of people want to have more of a say in the decisions which directly affect them, and have the capacity to do so effectively. As a footnote which also applies to changes in the educational system, if an institution moves to a more open and participative style of management it will be changed in the process: it is not simply an optional extra.

The second aspect of the employment scene which concerns me is our lamentable record of training compared with other European countries. Some fifty per cent of school-leavers take jobs which provide no formal training whatsoever, when the West German figure is more like five per cent. This is not entirely the fault of employers. From the early 1900s young people at Bournville spent a day a week during term-time at the Day Continuation College. This was dropped as a condition of employment in the 1960s, partly because it did not help recruitment, partly because of doubts about the value of compulsory further education. My guess is that as a result fewer school-leavers use this kind of opportunity as an entry point into continuing education.

The third point I would make is that there will be major changes in the way work in manufacturing industry will be organized within our time horizon. Fewer people will be employed and more of them will contract to work so many hours a year or to carry out particular tasks rather than be paid for their attendance at a factory or office; instead of having ancillary services (like computing and design) on our larger sites, we will be buying them in, often from the same people as before, who will be self-employed; improved communication systems will cut down on physical movement and on the number who have to congregate at a fixed place for a fixed time; the production hours required for a given output will be markedly reduced. It adds up to a combination of rapid technological change and more leisure (or time spent not working).

If one accepts the general sense of direction of this analysis, it brings together under-used abilities, lack of training and a world of work where we will not only have more free time but more control over how and when we take it. This brings me down firmly in favour of stimulating the demand for education to provide for missed opportunities and for changes through time in the attitudes of individuals towards education; education will also have an essential role in helping industry itself to cope with the demands of technological change. As an industrialist it seem to me oddly illogical to suppose that a single dose of higher education from 18 to 21 could inoculate you for life. I therefore see the employment scene in the years ahead as supporting an expansion in educational opportunity, and I believe that a rational economic case could be made out for this addition to educational provision, although the social case will stand on its own.

The conclusion that we should encourage an increase in educational demand leads on to the question of access. Here I would concentrate on the ways into the educational system and my objective would be to multiply the points of contact between educational institutions and people at work. One of the roles of the Day Continuation College was in providing just that kind of link and the Open University is now making a contribution in this respect. Alan Gordon (Chapter 4) talks of whetting children's appetite at school; and Geoffrey Squires (Chapter 5) of the DipHE as an easier first step towards a more advanced qualification. The aim must be to widen awareness of what is available, in the belief that more people would take up what is on offer if they thought it was within their reach in all senses. From this point of view I believe that the location of educational institutions is vital — where they are is more important than what they are, so we should build on whatever is to hand. Flexible timetabling of courses is also an essential encouragement to access. Some concern was expressed about fragmentation of the educational system; I am not advocating fragmentation but pluralism. I am sceptical of arguments based on the need for uniformity, common standards and all the rest of it and in favour of as much flexibility and local initiative as we can get away with. Above all though, I want to maximize the ways into the system.

I accept that my references to educational institutions may seem rather cavalier, but my lack of precision is based on imperfect knowledge, and anyway it gives me a freer hand. My impression is that the higher education system as a whole is not geared to meet the demands of pluralism. The universities are too cut off from life at work to find it easy to respond to the wide range of needs of mature students spelled out by Geoffrey

Squires (p.150). They could do more to nourish their roots in the local community and to encourage non-students to use the campus — give them access to lectures, recreational facilities, libraries and so on. The main point is that, whatever the institution, the structure and content of courses should meet the needs of those who want to benefit from them. This is where the sense of the market introduced by Professor Trow (Chapter 3) is so valuable. The market will be very diverse and to meet it will require innovative and creative thinking on the part of the providers of education. Incidentally there must be scope for innovation in teaching methods, building on the distance learning techniques developed by the Open University and on the work of adult educationalists.

The final point is on a different issue altogether and it concerns the current crisis over funding. I want to reinforce strongly the point that full advantage needs to be taken of all opportunities to bring about change in institutions, as they rarely occur. The great difficulty is to persuade people that change is necessary; when institutions accept that change is inevitable we should make the most of it. I have had the disagreeable task of running down parts of a business, which is not as daunting for a variety of reasons as reducing the size of a university. I believe that if you involve in its planning and implementation those affected by this kind of decision, you will be heartened by the constructive nature of their response. Going through the motions of participation, however, will as effectively unite opposition to change as a decision imposed without consultation. The key is to take as positive a view of the ways of meeting cuts as possible.

As to the proposals put forward by Oliver Fulton in Chapter 1, I hope that reaction will not be too pessimistic nor too constrained by finance. If the money is not available centrally for what we think should be done, we should look for other sources of funds. We need to look ahead twenty years. We tend to underestimate people's abilities and we should not make the same mistake in underestimating the degree to which the educational system can be reshaped if we can win support for our views.

Adrian Cadbury
Chairman
7 August 1981

CONTENTS

SEMINAR PARTICIPANTS

Access to Higher Education
Sir Adrian Cadbury (Chairman)
Prof. David Beswick, University of Melbourne
*Prof. Tessa Blackstone, University of London Institute of Education
Dr Donald Bligh, University of Exeter
Miss Sheila Brown, Department of Education and Science
Mr Geoffrey Caston, Committee of Vice-Chancellors and Principals
Mr R.J. Cormack, The Queen's University, Belfast
Dr Edwin Cox, Goldsmith's College, University of London
Mr W. Done, Cheshire County Council Further Education Unit
Mr J. Dunning, Napier College of Commerce and Technology
Prof. Noel Entwistle, University of Edinburgh
+ Mr John Farrant, University of Sussex
Mr Oliver Fulton (Convenor), University of Lancaster
Mme Dorotea Furth, Organisation for Economic Co-operation and
    Development
Dr Ian Gibbs, Combined Colleges Research Group
+ Mr Alan Gordon, University of Bristol
*Prof. A.H. Halsey, University of Oxford
*Dr Richard Hoggart, Goldsmiths' College, University of London
Dr Edwin Kerr, Council for National Academic Awards
Prof. Naomi McIntosh, Channel Four
Mr J.A.M. Mitchell, Scottish Education Department
Mr Guy Neave, European Institute of Education
Prof. Sir Brian Pippard, University of Cambridge
+ Dr Ernest Rudd, University of Essex
Mr David Stanton, Department of Employment
Mr Peter Scott, The Times Higher Education Supplement
Mr Michael Shattock, University of Warwick
+ Mr Geoffrey Squires, University of Hull
Miss Lesley Sutherland, National Union of Students
Mr John Thompson, Department of Education and Science
Mr H. Tomlinson, Birley High School, Manchester
+ Prof. Martin Trow, University of California at Berkeley
Prof. Leslie Wagner, Polytechnic of Central London
Mr Phillip Whitehead, MP
*Prof. Gareth Williams, University of Lancaster
+ Miss Maureen Woodhall, University of Lancaster
Miss Olga Wojtas, The Times Higher Education Supplement

+ Author of paper   *Discussant

INTRODUCTION AND ACKNOWLEDGEMENTS

This volume, a product of the Society for Research into Higher Education's Leverhulme Programme of Study into the Future of Higher Education, originated in the invited seminar which took place at Middleton Hall, Gorebridge, Midlothian on 29 June - 1 July 1981. The book contains seven chapters. In Chapter 1 I draw on the seminar papers and discussions to analyse the medium- and long-term policy issues concerning the demand for and access by British residents to higher education at undergraduate level, and make a series of recommendations which are then summarized. The remaining chapters are six commissioned papers, earlier versions of which were prepared for the Middleton Hall seminar; Chapters 6 and 7, on the special topics of demand for and access to postgraduate courses and demand and access by overseas students, are preceded by brief introductions.

THE CONTEXT
The assigned task of this stage of the Programme is to assess probable future trends in demand for higher education, to propose medium- and long-term policies for responding to or influencing these trends, and to examine the accessibility of higher education to different groups in society — in other words, to undertake a radical re-examination of the basis on which higher education should be supplied. The aim of the Programme as a whole is to examine the policy issues in a completely open-minded spirit. Nevertheless, in mid-1981, three considerations inevitably constrain the mood, if not the judgement, of anyone concerned with demand and access to higher education.

The first is the long-term trend in demand and access. The 1970s have seen a sharp reversal in the perceived success of higher education in achieving the objectives set for it eighteen years ago by the Robbins Committee. During the 1960s the total demand for higher education raced ahead of the Robbins projections (although these had at first been regarded as optimistic), until by 1970 it seemed reasonable to expect that for the foreseeable future far greater expansion than Robbins had proposed would be needed to cope with the combination of a rising birthrate and a rising rate of participation. Since that time the age participation rate, far from rising, has stagnated, then declined; and this trend, if continued, will combine with the impending sharp fall in the number of 18-year-olds over the next few years to imply a substantial contraction in the size of the higher education system by the 1990s. So much is clearly stated in the paper prepared by John

Farrant (Chapter 2).

During the 1970s it also became apparent that the expansion of higher education has not of itself led to either of the two main consequences for which the Robbins Committee had hoped. The first of these — economic growth resulting from the 'human capital' created through education — was the topic of the first volume in this series (Lindley, R. (Editor) (1981) *Higher Education and the Labour Market* Guildford: SRHE) and need not be discussed at length. Although that report concludes by giving higher education moderately good marks for its response to economic needs and puts at least part of the blame for economic problems on constraints and failures elsewhere, there is still no doubt that the implied promise of Robbins, naïvely though it may have been interpreted, has not been fulfilled. Certainly the economic case for substantial public finance of higher education can no longer be merely assumed.

Robbins' other expectation — the achievement of a greater measure of social equality — is a central concern of this volume. Here again, the prima facie evidence (as discussed by John Farrant (Chapter 2) and Alan Gordon (Chapter 4), indicates that expansion did not result in reduced class inequality. The participation of working-class students in universities has recently shown a marked decline, and although hard data are lacking for public sector higher education, it seems clear that the polytechnics, at least, have not retained all of the attractiveness to working-class children which their predecessor colleges had, and for which the originators of the binary policy had hoped. Although women's participation in university and polytechnic courses has increased, there is good reason to believe that this development owes more to wider social change than to the expansion of opportunities within higher education: and it has been substantially counter-balanced by the sharp decline in the supply of places in teacher-training courses, where women comprise the vast majority of students.

To this gradually dawning failure to achieve much of Robbins' hopes the summer of 1981 added the more immediate prospect of enforced contraction. The seminar ended on the eve of the notorious 'UGC letter', in which a reduction of 8 per cent in government grant to the universities was translated into reduced student targets and proposed staff redundancies — the first decline in the supply of places in the memory of any staff now working in universities. Such a decline (which was intended to be accompanied by similar reduction in the public sector) was announced well before the decline in student numbers anticipated later in the decade. It has therefore been widely interpreted as a repudiation of the 'Robbins principle', that it should be government policy to provide places to meet expected demand, and that qualified candidates should not be turned away from higher education. Recent government statements have in fact confirmed the view that the Robbins principle is no longer considered sacrosanct.

The third sobering influence was that of the previous seminar, on higher education and the labour market. This had not, perhaps, pre-empted the discussion of demand and access as thoroughly as might have been feared: far from proposing a planning criterion based on labour market needs to replace the Robbins principle, Robert Lindley, its convenor, had concluded that any such hope '. . . is an illusion. It reflects a lack of understanding about the way the labour market works' (Lindley 1981). Moreover, a system wherein students react spontaneously to perceived changes in labour market conditions and institutions respond to these changes, seems to be at least as effective in responding to economic needs as a more directly 'steered' system might be. Thus the Robbins principle is by no means discredited in advance. But the labour market seminar also passed on the very clear view that the demand for higher educaton is strongly influenced by labour market conditions; and that it is excessively optimistic to hope for a major expansion in the size of the pool of graduates in the face of the uncertainty of likely labour market prospects over the next few years.

None of these considerations was passively accepted by most participants in the demand and access seminar. Farrant's conclusion that an absolute decline in demand was to be expected, ceteris paribus, was disputed. Robbins' hopes of economic growth and social equality were analysed, argued over, and restated, with the addition of other uses for higher education and with explanations for what went wrong. The Robbins principle was defended, and governments attacked. And the primacy of the labour market in the minds of 18-year-olds and of older students was also hotly disputed. Nevertheless, the discussion took place against a background of public scepticism about the value of higher education, a scepticism which had its proponents inside the seminar.

Press reports of the seminar (*Times Higher Education Supplement* No. 454, 17 July 1981) claimed to detect a 'defensiveness' in the discussion. If so, the mood was a natural and appropriate response to the challenge of these external events and to the 'hard liners' in the seminar who persisted in asking awkward questions. As a result, the first part of Chapter 1 is devoted to a brief discussion of the economic, social and political value of higher education. It is emphatically not intended as a comprehensive 'defence' of higher education — which would be absurd in a few pages — but simply as a sketch of some appropriate lines of argument. Much of the recent discussion in Britain has been ridiculously narrowly conceived. Higher education cannot and should not be judged solely for its short-run ability to meet such criteria as can be most easily quantified. All that can be done here is to propose some alternative — but far from nebulous — criteria which could help to restore the balance.

What follows in Chapter 1 is a personal interpretation of the issues, drawing on the papers printed here and on the two days of discussion. Participants will recognize many of their own ideas; many will also disagree with some of what follows. Probably none of the recommendations would command their unanimous agreement: some might not even be acceptable to the majority. If so, my defence is that they seem to me to follow naturally from the trend of discussion and the logic of external circumstances. Nevertheless, the conclusions and recommendations of this chapter are my responsibility and commit none of the other participants to them. I am of course most grateful for participants' help during the seminar; I thank them also, in advance, for their toleration of my interpretations, misinterpretations and occasional wilful neglect or disagreement.

ACKNOWLEDGEMENTS
As convenor of the demand and access section in the SRHE's Leverhulme Programme I have been greatly helped by a large number of colleagues. Gareth Williams, Director of the programme, and Sir Adrian Cadbury, Chairman of the demand and access seminar, have been unfailing sources of advice, support and encouragement. Colleagues in the Programme's Research Advisory Group provided help and advice at the planning stages. Participants in the seminar not only contributed their ideas to Chapter 1 but gave me an extensive hearing for my own. In particular I owe a great deal to the authors of Chapters 2 to 6 and to Tessa Blackstone, A.H. Halsey, Richard Hoggart and Gareth Williams, who acted as 'discussants' of some of these papers at the seminar. A draft of Chapter 1 has been read, and much improved, by Lynne Alexander, David Beswick, Sir Adrian Cadbury, Lord Fulton and Gareth Williams. None of them, however, are responsible for the faults that remain; nor should they be taken as committed in any way to the opinions and recommendations, which remain my own.

I would like to use this opportunity to thank all of these people for their help. Thanks are also due to Deirdre Brown and Pat Parrott, who typed and retyped Chapter 1 under considerable pressure; to Betsy Breuer, the Programme's efficient and patient administrator; and to the staff of SRHE, especially Sally Kington who edited the final manuscript.

Oliver Fulton
Editor
Matterdale, Cumbria
August 1981

1

PRINCIPLES AND POLICIES

by Oliver Fulton

OUTLINE
This chapter is divided into three sections. In the light of the economic, social and political benefits which higher education is said to confer, the first poses the fundamental question whether the participation rate in higher education in Britain is, though low by international standards, adequate for our needs. It is concluded that the participation rate is undesirably low. The second section turns to the more specific problem of how to respond to stagnant demand and an 18-year-old population which will shortly begin to decline. It is argued that the participation rate is not entirely dependent on factors external to higher education. Higher education itself can and should adapt in ways which will encourage greater participation. The third section of the paper proposes a number of specific policies aimed at increasing demand and improving access. In the course of the chapter a series of explicit policy recommendations are made, and further recommendations for research and information needs. These are summarized on pages 36-38.

THE ROBBINS PRINCIPLE AND ITS ASSUMPTIONS
The 'Robbins principle', on which higher education planning has been based from 1963 until very recently, states that 'courses of higher education should be available to all who are qualified by ability and attainment to pursue them and who wish to do so.' Apparently forthright and positive, its strength is, paradoxically, largely negative (see also Chapter 2, p.45). By focusing on student demand, it rejects alternative criteria for providing courses, such as the needs of the labour market, or the resources available. But if uninterpreted, the statement's positive usefulness is weak. It gives little guidance in principle on the way in which planning should respond to demand.[1] And it is based on a set of assumptions which are no longer valid.

One assumption is fundamental. It seemed in 1963, whether one judged by short-term or long-term historical trends in Britain or by comparison with other advanced Western societies, that the trend of demand for higher education was inexorably upward. The basic policy issue was whether or not the supply of places should be expanded to meet this naturally growing demand — and the committee gave a clear answer. Now that the growth has apparently halted we can see that demand is not autonomous but can itself be an object of policy. In other words, the statement that higher education should be available to all who wish to undertake it disguises the contingent nature of such a wish. The demand for higher education depends in part on what kind of higher education is on offer, and on what terms. There is of course considerable dispute about the degree of elasticity of demand and what, if any policies could really increase it. For the moment, the point is simply that the Robbins principle gives no guidance to governments (or institutions) as to whether they should attempt to stimulate or to restrain the expression of demand; it prescribes only that they respond to a particular type — 'qualified demand' — at whichever level it is expressed.

In the changed circumstances of the 1970s and 1980s, policy making for the future cannot avoid this issue. We need to ask whether the present and likely future participation rate is satisfactory, too high or not high enough. The answer to this question, which will tell us whether we should aim to stimulate or to restrain demand, logically precedes any question about how to respond to demand as expressed. And in order to answer it, we need to ask fundamental questions about the value of higher education in modern Britain.

The discussion which follows tackles this issue directly. It should be made clear that it is the *participation rate* which is our concern when discussing the amount of higher education that is desirable, and not the *number* of students in the system or of graduates produced. The participation rate, or the proportion of persons of a given age who have the opportunity to obtain higher education, is the most useful criterion for historical and international comparison, and provides the best measure of achievement in most of the respects discussed below. It is important to be clear about this, since the impending demographic decline means that even a quite sizeable increase over the next fifteen years in the participation rate of 18-year-olds, or older students, does not imply an increase in the total numbers in higher education (see Chapter 2).

ASSESSING THE PARTICIPATION RATE

The Economic Issues

It is generally agreed that the theories of the 1950s and 1960s which related economic growth to investment in education were at best over-optimistic. Certainly there has been so far little obvious and direct pay-off to the economy from increased expenditure on higher education; and further doubts have been rasied by the rise of 'credentialist' theory in sociology and economics (Collins 1979) which would assert that increased educational expenditure is at best a symptom not a cause of economic growth, and may be totally unconnected to it. However, the belief that education contributes to economic growth is a theory which will not lie down. Even in the labour market seminar, attended mainly, it seemed at times, by professional sceptics who knew very well the lack of hard evidence to associate educational expenditure with economic growth, there was a persistent feeling that Britain's poor economic performance must be connected somehow with its comparatively low production and utilization of highly qualified manpower.

In the present seminar, economists were in shorter supply, and this particular ground was not gone over again. The 'real' needs of the economy are distinctly chimerical, after all, and it would be over-ambitious even to attempt to assess them at present, let alone predict their nature up to twenty years from now (Lindley 1981). On the much narrower front of likely labour market trends, however, there was a degree of qualified optimism (from an expansionist point of view). The evidence still suggests that in the long run the 'qualification spiral' is irreversible. Once graduates have been forced down the labour market in search of new jobs, these jobs continue to recruit graduates. In the short run, such jobs may pay less and carry less prestige than more traditional graduate careers — and even in the latter, salaries may well fall as a result of the temporary over-supply, so helping to cause a slow-down in the growth of demand for higher education. But in due course, salary differentials in favour of graduates tend to re-establish themselves and provide the impetus for a further wave of expansion (Freeman 1981 for evidence from the USA). Because the graduate labour market is, comparatively, one of fairly free international movement, this cycle may provide part of the explanation for the almost universal experience of expansion in the 1960s followed by stagnation in the 1970s (Williams 1974). It therefore seems reasonable to expect that the present stagnation will be followed by renewed growth in demand for graduate labour — at a time when, in Britain, the pool of young people[2] of college age is declining. Thus the warning that the graduate labour market might act as a brake on expansion was partly accepted, but also turned on its head in the argument that it might in due course act as a powerful accelerator for renewed growth.[3]

The labour market is not the concern of this volume. But the economic accounting of higher education does not start and finish here. One of the most powerful and coherent defences of investment in higher education was published in 1977 by the Carnegie Council on Policy Studies in Higher Education (Bowen 1977). It used a major research review in an attempt to enumerate and as far as possible to quantify all the possible benefits which might accrue to individuals and to societies as a result of expenditure on higher education. Some of these benefits are highly speculative; some can only be translated into economic terms with great difficulty. But what remains is still a formidable list.

American evidence reviewed by Bowen suggests that the credentialist attack on higher education is overstated. This is a major concern of the labour market volume in this series (Lindley 1981) and need not be discussed at length here. In brief, however, it seems that aside from specifically job-related skills and knowledge, students can be shown also to gain general skills, capacities and dispositions, which are lasting, and which to a considerable degree vindicate the practice of many employers of recruiting 'good' graduates, regardless of course content. There is no comparable wealth of research on the outcomes of British higher education: the assumption of a common 'gold standard' of degree performance has tended to focus research more on comparative success and failure than on average levels of achievement. Research of the latter kind is clearly needed, as well as research not so much on employers' behaviour and expectations in recruiting graduates, as on graduates' subsequent job performance. Conventional 'rate of return' studies have not answered all the questions.

More unexpected, however, are those outcomes of higher education which are not job-related but still have economic consequences. Bowen's review of research reveals a series of benefits from higher education which have been under-emphasized or ignored even by the noisiest of propagandists for American colleges and universities. As a result of their general level of education (not of health education specifically) American graduates lead healthier and longer lives: indeed, it is claimed that 'investment in *general* education would be more effective in reducing mortality than investment in improved medical care' (Grossman 1975, cited in Bowen 1977). As far as the family is concerned, college education appears to lead to 'a perceptible narrowing of traditional differences between the sexes' (Bowen 1977, p.190) and hence, amongst other effects, to greater labour force participation by women. It leads to later marriage and to marginally lower divorce rates; and to lower and more rational patterns of fertility in which, it is claimed, college-educated parents 'trade quality for quantity in their total outlays for children' (ibid, p.194). Most notably, 'one of the most important outcomes of higher education is the favourable effect of parents' education on the intelligence and achievement of children' (ibid, p.198) — even taking into account the effects of correlates of higher education such as higher income levels. It can thus be argued that higher educational investment is subject to a 'multiplier' effect over successive generations. There is an obvious analogy to Bourdieu's (disapproving) claim (1977) that investment in education constitutes for individual families an accumulation of 'cultural capital', off which succeeding generations can then live. If this can be distributed more widely and more equitably, the whole society can benefit.

The result of Bowen's review of research is a long list (from which I have given only a small selection) of the apparent benefits of American higher education to the economy of the United States,[4] concluding that in the period up to 1970 investment in higher education produced a huge net benefit. Of course there are obvious questions to be raised about the applicability of any such findings to British higher education, which cannot be answered without a careful review of the functions of both higher and secondary education in the two societies. What is clear is that any assessment of the economic benefits of higher education which is confined to examining conventionally measured rates of return is seriously deficient. Certainly no economic case can be made for restricting the supply of higher education which has not weighed up the wider factors briefly described above. A similar review is now needed for British higher education.

Research and Information Recommendation 1
A wide-ranging review should be undertaken, comparable to that by Howard Bowen for the Carnegie Council on Policy Studies in Higher Education (Bowen 1977), of available evidence on the direct and indirect value of investment in British higher education; where primary research evidence is not available, such research should also be undertaken.

Before turning to considerations of social policy, two economic counter-arguments must be considered. The first concerns available finance. Sceptical governments presumably need to be convinced not only that higher education is a good investment, but that it is better than alternative claimants on public resources. Clearly the evidence is not yet available. I return to the issue of finance later in this chapter, and one of the later volumes in this series will be devoted to it. For the moment, all that needs to be said is that this constraint is broadly accepted, though for different reasons. The aim of the proposals in this chapter would be to try to increase participation without necessarily demanding a greater share of public resources in the long term.

A second objection concerns the dangers of graduate unemployment, which has again been put forward in 1981 as a reason for contracting the supply of places. I have already argued that a longer view suggests that this danger is exaggerated. (Even in the short run, unemployment rates for graduates are lower than those for earlier leavers.) The danger of a shortage of graduates when economic recovery takes place is at least equally serious, and we cannot afford to wait until then to find out, since it would take a minimum of five years to increase the output. In any event, if the broad economic arguments given above are correct, it is as true of the 18-21 as it is of the 16-18 age group, where it is more generally accepted, that it is better for the state to pay out education and training subsidies than unemployment benefit.

Social and Political Issues

The Consequences of Reduced Participation   There is a wide range of social policy arguments concerning the rate of participation in higher education. One way into them is to look first at the arguments for and against a level of participation below what exists at present. Participation could presumably be reduced in either of two ways: in theory it might be possible to make higher education so unattractive that demand is further reduced; but in practice the simplest method, which has apparently been adopted by the present government, is to abandon the Robbins principle and agree to reject 'qualified' applicants. Here the social argument is entirely one-sided. It is extremely unlikely that any such contraction can be achieved without adverse effects on such equality of opportunity as now exists.

There is of course disagreement, in higher education policy as well as in social policy in general, about the kind of social equality which is desirable: a 'strong' concept (Halsey 1972), in which policies are assessed by their effectiveness in achieving equality of *results*, may have costs (for example in the necessity of practising positive discrimination at entry) which not everyone is prepared to pay. But a 'weak' concept, of equality of opportunity or of treatment, is generally agreed on as a minimum standard to which a democratic society should aim. It should be clearly understood that to enforce contraction of higher education below the level which demand would justify, will tend to damage equality of opportunity.

Reductions in opportunities will not affect all applicants equally: it will be 'marginal' applicants who will be rejected. One kind of marginality is that perceived by individual admissions officials faced with difficult choices. If they behave like employers and recruiters in times of recession, they may be tempted to reject the candidates they define as socially marginal: women, mature students and others whose claim to admission they may see as slightly less legitimate than eighteen-year-old males — future 'breadwinners'. Moreover, they will avoid risk when distributing scarce resources. Candidates with unusual qualifications, and those from schools or colleges with little experience of preparation for higher education (and this means disproportionately those from relatively deprived areas, including not only working-class children but ethnic minorities) will tend to be rejected in favour of safer choices.

Secondly, contraction will encourage institutional, as well as bureaucratic conservatism. Experiments with new courses, new admissions procedures, and so on will have to compete with established and apparently successful arrangements and are likely to lose (see Williams 1981). Even if established, they will be given less time to prove themselves. Without these experiments, 'conventional' (that is young, middle-class, male) applicants are most likely to be attracted to apply and will be most likely to succeed (see also footnote 6 below). Not only will opportunity be reduced, but demand itself will probably decline. After the wave of new ideas in the 1960s, this process may have been partly responsible for the decline in the 1970s in the proportion of working-class students.

Thus a deliberate rejection of the Robbins principle, implying a refusal to meet qualified demand, would have undesirable social consequences. Even a policy of nominally retaining the principle while trying to reduce demand would have similar consequences, since reductions would have to come both from restrictions on innovation and responsiveness and from a financial squeeze on students. These too are likely to have a disproportionate effect on marginal candidates.

However, the most convincing argument against restricting access is the simplest. The right to education, whether as a means to other goals or simply as an end in itself, is one of the rights of citizenship in modern democratic societies. It should simply not be conceivable that some citizens should be bluntly refused any chance of education, at any level including higher education, if they can benefit from it. To set rigid quotas for admission to publicly funded higher education, regardless of demand, when there is no viable private alternative, would be to do just this. Fortunately, it is politically quite unlikely that such a policy could be maintained for long.[5]

The conclusion from this discussion of the likely consequences of a contraction in the supply of places below that indicated by the 'qualified demand' for higher education is the following *minimal* recommendation.

Policy Recommendation 1
Courses of higher education should (continue to) be available to all those who are qualified by attainment to pursue them and who wish to do so.

Arguments for Increased Participation   In the past, the fundamental social policy motive for expanding higher education was the search for social equality. Just as with economic arguments, that hope was excessively naïve and has not been attained in the form in which it was promised. So much is clear — although it should not be forgotten that the general increase in participation has affected members of the working class too. Class differentials[6] have not improved (see Chapter 2) and relative opportunities of mobility have not been enhanced, but still it is now considerably less unusual for a child of manual workers (skilled manual workers, at least) to attend a university or polytechnic than it was fifty, twenty-five or even fifteen years ago. The sense of exclusion, short of 'sponsorship' via grammar school selection and university scholarship, with all the psychological costs which that implied for the successful, is probably now less total. But it is still strong, as Gordon documents (Chapter 4). There is a basic and unacceptable inequity in the preservation of an expensive, privileged and privilege-conveying educational and social experience for a socially unrepresentative élite.

The question for us, however, is whether increased participation will lead to wider social representativeness, given its failure to do so in the recent past. The short answer is probably no. Expansion of opportunity is at best a necessary condition, and certainly not a sufficient one, for greater equality of access. Expansion on the same lines as in the 1960s would probably not attract working-class children in disproportionate numbers; but the likelihood, as I shall argue shortly, is that it would probably not attract anyone at all. The point is that if expansion is to attract a new clientele, it must be designed to do so, and not simply consist of more of the same, in the hope that others, previously unattracted, will come.

But whether or not students are equitably recruited, the total level of participation is itself a problem. Whatever allowances are made for the level of achievement represented by a degree, for the content of the curriculum and its relation to subsequent employment, or for the character of secondary education, the British participation rate in higher education is now very low in comparison with most other advanced industrial countries (Cerych and

Colton 1980). Some of the quantifiable benefits which higher education conveys to individual graduates and to their society have already been discussed. Others include the opportunity for personal self-discovery and development, the development of a sense of responsibility for others, the development of political and social effectiveness, the 'refinement of taste, conduct and manners' and even the likelihood of greater happiness and self-fulfillment (Bowen 1977). If higher education brings all of this, should it be confined to so few? Add to this that a society with a higher proportion of graduates appears to gain a population which is socially cohesive, more committed to the use of reason and argument in the resolution of conflict, more respectful of individual differences, and more aware of its cultural and artistic heritage (Bowen 1977) then higher education becomes not a luxury but an irresistible necessity.

The point can be partly illustrated by re-examining the common fear of 'under-employment' of graduates in jobs previously considered as demanding lower levels of skill and training. If higher education does in fact convey even a modest selection of the benefits claimed for it, any category of job is likely to change dramatically when graduates are recruited into it for the first time. Such changes may include gains in productivity, but will range much wider. To take one example, the huge increase in graduate recruitment into the civil service in recent years undoubtedly means that bureaucratic functions previously performed in a routine and formalized way are now being undertaken by workers who have been taught to use their imaginations and not to yield their judgement entirely to the rulebook. The consequences for the internal organization of the civil service may be interesting: but the public, especially in client relationships, is likely to be the one to benefit. Similar examples could be found in almost any type of employment.

Thus it can be argued that there are strong social policy grounds for increasing participation in higher education and, in doing so, for improving access for groups at present under-represented. A.H. Halsey pointed out at the seminar that the comparative ineffectiveness of educational expansion in improving opportunity in recent years had been masked by the very high rate of occupational change which had in any case taken place. When that rate slows, as it will, educational opportunity will become a vital safety-valve. The obverse of that argument is that if higher education continues to be seen as small, exclusive and privileged there is likely to be a populist reaction of which the first signs are already visible.

So far, higher education has been treated as a single homogeneous activity. It has to be admitted that not all students in all institutions acquire all of the benefits listed above, partly because of personal or institutional inadequacies, but partly also because institutions' and courses' aims vary widely (Ramsden 1981). Some of the most difficult questions about the provision of higher education, which have been obvious ever since the Robbins Report, concern not the overall size of the system but its shape: where and how should higher education be provided? It is impossible in the space available here to answer either the curricular questions or even the broad issues of structure or organization which they imply. But it will be a central argument of this chapter that the present structure and organization has reached its limit: if participation is to be increased, higher education will have to change. It may be objected that the kinds of change which we propose, especially if they result in substantial expansion, would weaken the capacity of British higher education to achieve all of the benefits now claimed for it. It is impossible to answer such a speculation: the present functions of the system would undoubtedly be changed by substantial growth in participation (see Trow 1974). But the American evidence cited above was derived from a diversified 'mass' system with a much higher participation rate. It is unlikely that all of the benefits would vanish if we began to follow suit.

Any proposal to attract new students into higher education needs to face two commonplace criticisms. The first is that no-one else wants higher education, and the second that no-one else is clever enough to benefit from it. The first of these is often presented as too obvious to need discussion. The age participation rate has not reached anywhere near the level forecast in the early 1970s, has begun to decline, and looks unlikely to rise dramatically (Chapter 2); and the remarkable growth in overseas student numbers (see Chapter 6) is evidence of excess capacity at present: places have been available but unused. But all that this tells us is that the existing product, at its current price (in entry standards as well as economic costs) has not attracted new customers — which is not at all to say that there is no unsatisfied demand of any kind. Contrary evidence is provided by surveys of school-leavers, showing that a much larger number of 15-year-olds (of the order of 30 per cent: see Fulton and Gordon 1979) aspire to higher education than eventually participate in it (see also Gordon in Chapter 4); or by the experiences of urban communities in the United States in which participation has doubled in a year after opening a new community college (Trow in Chapter 3); or by the successful 'gamble' of the Open University which has found 50,000 applicants a year for ten years now (Squires in Chapter 5). The seminar learned too that higher education is looked to even by deprived members of ethnic minorities as a vital social institution which could provide them with a lifeline — a responsibility of which most institutions in Britain are completely unaware. This is in sharp contrast to the reaction of universities and colleges in the United States, which have made great efforts to welcome ethnic minorities by special admission programmes and by encouraging studies of minority culture and history. There are, in fact, many reasons to believe that a different kind of higher education could find a large pool of aspiring students.

The objection that the 'pool of ability' has been exhausted is even more directly contradicted by research. It is true that the 'pool' of 'qualified leavers' — those who have achieved two 'A' level passes, in the Robbins interpretation — is limited, and that higher education cannot hope to recruit many more students if it insists on this qualification for most of its entrants while the numbers achieving it in secondary education are stagnant. But there is no question at all that (leaving the adult population entirely aside) the number of young people intrinsically capable of benefiting from higher education far exceeds the number who at present do so.

A large-scale survey of fifteen-year-olds in 1977 found that, whereas 70 per cent of boys of high measured verbal ability intended to enter higher education if their fathers held non-manual occupations, the proportion of 'highly able' sons of manual workers was almost exactly half, at 36 per cent: comparable figures for girls were 61 per cent (non-manual) and 38 per cent (manual) (Fulton and Gordon 1979). Considering that some middle-class children of quite moderate measured verbal ability levels succeed in entering higher education, it is safe to assert that even a doubling of the proportion of the age group who attend higher education need have no adverse effect on average levels of ability (see also Chapter 4, pp.123-6). The argument put forward so forcefully by the Robbins Committee and by Douglas (1964) that this untapped pool constitutes not only a social injustice but also a severe wastage of scarce talent which the nation can ill afford is still entirely valid.

The result of this review of arguments on the level of participation in higher education is the following recommendation

Policy Recommendation 2
It should be the aim of government and of higher education institutions to achieve a substantial increase in the participation rate in higher education.

Practical Implications in the Face of Stagnant Demand and Future Demographic Decline   In Chapter 2, John Farrant combines the evidence of recent trends in demand with the future size of the 18-year-old age group to outline the immediate problem facing policy makers. He concludes that '. . . within the limits of policy initiatives likely to be taken by either the present Government or its successor, there is little prospect of averting a decline in the total size of the higher education system by 1990' (p.64 below). If this is indeed the case, the future for higher education for many years will be a continuation of the present exercise of contraction. Such a prospect was no more palatable to members of the seminar than it is proving to be to employees of higher education at large, and an attack was mounted on it from several directions.

Most of the lines for such an attack have already been hinted at. Economic explanations of demand, while leading some people to pessimism, encouraged others to expect cyclical recovery to a higher plateau, after the labour market had adjusted to new uses for graduates. Others questioned the primacy of economic models and pointed to the counter-evidence of, for example, the growth in women's participation, or of sharp regional variations, neither of which can be fully explained by economic theories,[7] to the key roles of lower and upper-secondary education in creating or stifling educational aspirations, and to a series of other potential agents of change. The convincing evidence of a substantial pool of ability means that whatever its prophetic accuracy no-one concerned with higher education should be content that Farrant's forecast comes about by mere default. Nevertheless, there was a general, if reluctant, agreement that short of new policy initiatives, the forecast of contraction *is* reasonable. It is a commonplace that any detailed forecast may not — indeed will not — be fulfilled as it stands; but this broad prediction is the appropriate starting point for policy formulation.

The key question then is whether the 'likely . . . policy initiatives . . . of this Government or its successor' are as immutable (or doomed to be as ineffectual) as this forecast implies. In immediate terms, the choice for higher education policy makers is not the theoretical choice posed and answered in the first part of this chapter — namely what is the desirable level of participation; but the practical one of how to respond to the present prospect of contraction. Here the choice is threefold: (i) to follow the graph of demand down as it falls (or even to anticipate it, as present government policy appears to be); (ii) to continue on a level course in the hope that students will turn up; or (iii) to change direction and try some 'unlikely' policy initiatives.

The present political battle seems to be confined to the first two alternatives. The natural tendency of higher education institutions, especially of the universities, is to favour option (ii) and choose inaction. They argue that contraction will be painful and damaging and can usually be shown to cost more than the likely short-run savings; there is always enough doubt about future forecasts to justify a little longer delay; and, if things do go badly wrong, the universities at least can pick up extra students at the expense of public sector higher education.

Governments, however, of whatever political complexion, will undoubtedly choose option (i) if option (ii) is the only alternative. Policies are always based on likelihood, not certainties. The immediate cost of contraction may be high; but it is unreasonable to incur the certain short-run cost of empty places in the quite uncertain hope of future benefits. The recent history of central planning of higher education numbers is one of regularly undershot targets (Williams 1974). There was even a three per cent decline student numbers entering in 1980 from the forecast as late as 1978 (DES 1978, Central Projection). When decline does occur the prospect of universities 'poaching' from the local authority sector will not be politically tolerable. If these two options are the only alternatives, contraction in both sectors is likely — under any government.

The third option, of a real change of direction, has much more to commend it, if it can achieve an increase in participation in line with Policy Recommendation 2. It has the considerable advantage of making use of the substantial resource built up in the British system of higher education, rather than allowing it to be dissipated. This is an argument which should commend itself to those policy makers and administrators responsible for building up the resource over the past twenty years. But they will need to be convinced that new and deserving students can be found. Simply hoping for a miraculous upturn, or embarking on a frantic search for 'warm bodies' like some American colleges and universities (see Chapter 3) are tactics which are unlikely to be approved by higher education's paymasters.

The question then is what kind of policies can help to increase participation. It is often said that most young people make their decision whether or not to aim for higher education before they reach the minimum school-leaving age. This is perfectly true of those who decide firmly against it; it is very difficult for anyone who has left full-time education for work, or embarked on a non-'A' level course, to change direction back towards qualifying for higher education. But it does not follow from this, as is often asserted, that their decision is influenced only by the schools. It is true, as Gordon shows in Chapter 4, that many young people leave school at sixteen because they resent the non-adult status of full-time pupils or students, or dislike academic study, or are not attracted by the particular options available to them. It is therefore quite likely that different practices and different opportunities, in either lower or upper-secondary education or both, might increase the attractiveness of staying on for an 'A' level course and so increase the pool of 'qualified' applicants from which higher education at present draws. But such proposals are not the primary concern of this volume: they should develop out of a general scrutiny of the aims of secondary education, of which qualifying for higher education is only one part — and not necessarily the most important.

We are concerned here with ways in which higher education itself might become more attractive and more receptive. I shall argue that the evidence provided by Trow, Gordon and Squires in Chapters 3-5 suggests a wide range of possibilities. In any case, we should not lose sight of the political dimension. Higher education institutions and their staff can easily be accused of self-interest when they argue that they should be protected from the prospect of contraction. They will carry much more conviction if they accept some of the responsibility for their present limited attractiveness and show that they are prepared to make substantial changes in their behaviour, rather than continuing as before and expecting other institutions to adapt to their needs.

Thus our choice among the options listed above is the third: to try new policy initiatives to increase participation from among those who are not at present attracted, or accepted, by higher education. And a major element in these initiatives must involve changes in higher education itself.

Policy Recommendation 3
In response to the likely decline in demand from its traditional clientele, the British higher education system should be encouraged to adapt in order to increase participation rates.

Despite the power of Government purse-strings, higher education is relatively autonomous and democratic; autonomous democratic institutions require convincing evidence if they are to change direction. It will be particularly important in the next few years to ensure a flow of relevant information for wide distribution and discussion. The volumes of *Statistics of Education* have their critics; but the present government's decision to abandon their publication in their present from is ominous, although the University Grants Committee will continue to publish statistics for universities previously contained in Volume 6. There is certainly a need, not covered by any present publication, for good data on demand and access to the public sector of higher education.

Research and Information Recommendation 2
(a) *The collection and dissemination of information on demand for and access to higher education should be maintained and where possible enhanced in forms accessible to the widest possible audience.*
(b) *The collection of information on access to public sector higher education in particular should be improved at least to a level comparable with that on access to universities, if necessary by specially commissioned research.*
(c) *Documents such as the DES 'Brown' and 'Grey' papers (DES 1978 and 1979) and DES Statistical Bulletin 12/80 are especially useful and should be published at regular intervals as early as practicable. The DES should explore the possibility of providing direct access for qualified specialists to the relevant computer tapes, possibly through the SSRC Survey Archive.*

RECONSTRUCTING THE ROBBINS PRINCIPLE
One way to divide up the policy issues is to re-examine the various components of the Robbins principle. The principle contained five elements, each of which needs an operational interpretation. Thus:
    'Courses of higher education': the *supply* of courses
    'Should be available': the Robbins *principle*
    'To all': *access* issues
    'Who are qualified by ability and attainment to pursue them':
        preparation, qualification and admission
    'And who wish to do so': the *demand* for places
To these should be added a sixth policy principle, that enunciated by the Anderson Committee of 1962: the principle that subject to residence and other relatively minor reservations of eligibility, all students on full-time degree or 'equivalent' courses should receive a means-tested maintenance grant and (as it now stands) the full amount of their fees. *Finance* is the sixth key element in reconstructing policy.

Some of these elements have been discussed already. The Robbins principle in its original limited interpretation as applying to those with two

'A' levels has been re-affirmed as a minimal recommendation (Policy Recommendation 1). The demand for places and appropriate responses to it have been discussed in general terms in Recommendations 2 and 3. In the sections which follow I look in turn at the other four areas: the supply of courses, preparation, qualification and admission, finance and access.

The Supply of Courses
In general, official policy has until very recently been that an adequate supply of places in higher education should be provided to meet the demand from those with two 'A' levels. But there is nothing in this policy to say what kinds of places are provided. No government could be expected to arrange an indefinite expansion of high-cost subjects such as medicine or technology if demand were to increase dramatically and persistently. In fact the Robbins principle has never been taken as implying any attempt at one-for-one provision of subject places in line with applications whatever their fluctuations. (Chapter 2 shows persistent differences — though also some sharp changes — in competition rates for different subjects.) The question is whether there may be a latent demand from potential applicants who cannot find the course they would like, or are excluded from it, and so from higher education altogether, by highly competitive entry requirements. Would new courses attract new students?

The evidence is suggestive but not conclusive. On the one hand, there is some flexibility: candidates who fail to obtain medical school places seem to settle for related subjects such as pharmacy, or for other fields still further from their original choice; and certainly candidates who fail to get into universities go to polytechnics and elsewhere (Fidler 1979). These apparent mismatches between supply and original demand do not seem to force out of British higher education many candidates who have begun the process of searching for a place (overseas, or directly into employment).

But there is a larger case to answer. I referred above to the primary pieces of evidence for unsatisfied demand — the pool of untapped ability and the ambitions, however naïve, of fifteen-year-olds. To what extent is the supply of courses responsible for the fall-off of able or ambitious school-children who do not even take 'A' level courses? Part of the blame for the low and stagnant participation rate can be ascribed to the rigidities of the British higher education system, with its choice of a high-standard, high-cost, three-year full-time, heavily subsidized degree, a part-time variant whose lower fees scarcely compensate the student for years of effort (and no maintenance grant), or practically nothing.

In Chapter 3, Martin Trow identifies the British dilemma that the insistence on 'nothing but the best' for every student carries with it the price associated with 'élite' quality. This quality, he argues, is exemplified in all the elements we have just identified: not only high quality (of teaching and of graduate output) but also a 'collegiate' model implying a preference for full-time study, restricted admission, high cost per student, socially biased access, and low demand. He also warns that these elements are interconnected in such a way that they cannot necessarily be altered piecemeal. Nevertheless, the lure of structural reform is too strong to resist, and the seminar was tempted by a number of proposals. Most of them have merit a priori: there are obvious attractions in '2 + 2' schemes for higher education (eg Pippard 1969; Bragg 1980) in which a student spends the first two years in a broad general course, and the second two in more specialized, vocational study, perhaps after further selection[8] — or for that matter in similar schemes on a different timetable: '1 + 3', or '1 + 2', and so on. The Scottish variant — 3 + 1 (three years for an Ordinary degree and an extra year for Honours) — attracted considerable favourable comment, with its added attraction, from any student's point of view, that Scottish pupils can obtain their entry qualifications and go on to higher education after only one year in the school sixth form. The fact that Scotland has a somewhat higher participation rate than England and Wales (Chapter 2) led to considerable speculation about whether its degree structure was the main inducement. (There are however other factors which probably contribute to Scotland's participation rate: the economic, with the extra year and the early start increasing the rate of return; the admissions-related, with five Scottish 'Higher' grades instead of two or three 'A' levels; and the cultural.)

However, it is extremely difficult to choose between alternative, apparently attractive schemes for reshaping the map of learning. Sober voices warned against major structural change. The problem is that the present rigid structure of control, through student finance as well as course approval and validation, the 'gold standard' of Honours degrees, and institutional finance, makes experiments of this kind nearly impossible for single institutions to undertake on their own. The position of the DipHE as the single structural innovation of the past ten years attests to this. As a result, any test of restructuring would need to be on an alarmingly large scale, and the British evidence is not yet there to justify it, despite suggestions from experience overseas. It is certainly too early for a central decision on a major change of this kind: the financial cost alone of structural change on such a scale could be prohibitively high unless for large and guaranteed benefits.[9] Finally, some non-British participants in the seminar began to draw back in alarm, pointing out that many countries actually still admire and envy the present structure of British higher education. Some overseas experience, especially in Europe, suggests that our success in expanding élite higher education should not be thrown away lightly.

But if major structural reforms are premature, it is still easy to suggest needs which are not met by the present range of courses. A number of proposals were made at the seminar, mainly concerned with alternative modes of study. For example, it was suggested that the opportunity to construct one's own programme combining periods of full-time study, part-time study, and work, might meet the needs of older students and perhaps tempt some of them gently back into education. At a minimum they might be given a wider choice of mixed mode or sandwich courses. One can also imagine new curricular needs: the growth in the number of sixth-formers taking combinations of science and non-science 'A' levels suggests a great potential for similar interdisciplinary courses at degree level, as well as for science-based but less specialized courses, of which only a few are now available — courses which use a scientific discipline primarily as the basis for general educational development rather than as specifically vocational training.

The conclusion, then, must be that rather than a wholesale and centrally dictated reform of existing opportunities, what is needed is far greater diversity and freedom to experiment. The case for diversity has been argued before, and well summed up in a recent article by Silver (1980). Once again, we return to the rigidities of the present system, and what Silver and others have described as its domination by the values of the university sector. So long as single-subject three-year Honours graduates are what high prestige universities provide, they will be what employers prefer to recruit, and schools prefer to prepare for. The high status and high competition rates of this kind of university course devalue any alternatives and in fact create a vicious circle whereby their prestige is self-perpetuating.[10] Without central intervention, can the circle be broken? If successful universities do not change of their own will (and why should they?) the only leverage can be in the markets at entry or exit from higher education. Lindley (1981) makes proposals for finer discrimination by employers at exit; our point of attack must be at entry. What is proposed is to alter the currency in this market. At present we have a market in academic qualifications, primarily 'A' levels. There are, as I shall argue, other good reasons for trying to weaken their dominance by adding or substituting other types of qualification. But we can also add a new currency, that of finance. By giving greater financial leverage to the student and widening the range of acceptable qualifications, institutions may be persuaded to adapt more readily to new needs.

Market mechanisms are untidy and unpredictable. Taken to the extremes of competition they can produce highly unattractive results of which Trow (Chapter 3) suggests a few. But the fear which is most commonly expressed is that of a demeaning hierarchy, whereby institutions (and their graduates) are regarded as inferior, not because of real differences in quality, but because of the accident of their market position, determined by a combination of mythology, ancient history, and the devious manoeuvres of an 'élitist' establishment of dons, largely no doubt to be found in the more ancient universities. Whether justified or not, it is a real fear, and the slogan of 'nothing but the best' which Trow coins for Britain, exemplified in the objectives of 'parity of esteem' of the binary policy, and of the 'gold standard' of degrees maintained by the CNAA and the external examining system, has the honourable aim of circumventing it.

The sad fact, however, is that these objectives have never been fully achieved. In the eyes of intending students and of employers there is already a hierarchy. The market is subject to central controls, but these controls tend to serve the interests of long-established market leaders and perpetuate existing patterns. Any movement to reflect changing value is restricted. The choice for the future, therefore, is not so much between enforced conformity and hierarchical diversity, as Silver puts it, but between a possible hierarchical diversity and the present enforced and unresponsive hierarchy.

There are obvious temptations for policy makers to keep their controls. A fully fledged market system would mean that central government is bound to pay whatever price is needed, however high participation goes. Indeed, the price per head is increased, since at present the supply of places can in theory be matched accurately to demand, whereas the market implies an oversupply of places: without the threat of a shortfall and the attraction of advantages from extra recruitment, institutions would have no need to experiment. It would be hard, too, to dismantle the present controls over course content, and to accept that the hidden hand of student choice can assess national needs better than the accumulated wisdom of policy making. Freedom to experiment will mean freedom to make mistakes. As will be seen, we are not proposing a full market system on the American model; even so, the case will need to be made and demonstrated that reduced central control does lead to greater participation, and that greater participation brings advantages to outweigh the dangers.

If this case is accepted in principle, there may still be resistance to applying it throughout the system. Should we risk unleashing market forces on every institution? The universities might continue as they are, pursuing 'excellence' and subject to long-term planning, while public sector institutions fight the battle for new students. The disadvantages of such a policy, however, are not hard to see. First, few universities should be content with it, since it implies concentrating on performing the traditional role for a steadily dwindling number of traditional students. Nor, in any case, should the public sector be expected to carry all the risks of experimentation.

But more importantly, such a response would not have the desired effect of increasing total demand or improving access. In Chapter 2, Martin Trow offers an alternative slogan — 'something is better than nothing' — to replace 'nothing but the best'. Whatever that 'something' may be, it should not be rigidly separated from 'the best'. In particular, entry qualifications should differ only in degree, not in kind. Otherwise, the consequence of preserving an élite, competitive and high-entry-standard sector of universities, while encouraging other institutions to change drastically, would be to push streaming back even further down the secondary school. The divisive choices of 'academic' 'O' and 'A' levels or 'non-academic' alternatives would be perpetuated; students taking 'non-academic' courses would know that they would only qualify for 'second best' higher education. As at present, many would choose not to compete. Such a policy would of course also continue to exert the present social class bias.

What is being proposed is quite limited: not necessarily (and certainly not in the short or medium term) a grand merging and restructuring of higher education into 'comprehensive' institutions. There will inevitably continue to be a different role for universities, but the difference should be marked, as in countries with higher participation rates, more by universities' emphasis on research and postgraduate work than by a distinctive contribution to, and exclusive selection for, undergraduate teaching.

But if there is to be no sharp dividing line between the universities and the public sector, the same logic should apply at the present lower boundary of 'advanced' further education. The biggest achievement of the past fifteen years has been the promotion (in both senses of the term) of institutions in the public sector — the polytechnics into academically 'respectable', indeed often distinguished degree-granting bodies, and the colleges and institutes of higher education into multi-purpose institutions, with the commitment to two-'A' level entry to teacher training as a symbol of their high standards. The effect, however, has been to increase the social as well as academic selectivity of the public sector (see Chapter 2) and to leave the rest of advanced and non-advanced further education as a very poor relation outside these institutions.

The distinction between 'advanced' and 'non-advanced' courses now has much more to do with administrative convenience (for resource allocation to institutions, courses, staff salaries and student grants) than it does with academic quality or level. The aim should be to create a much more flexible and porous network of courses and institutions throughout public sector higher and further education; indeed, rationality suggests that all of further education should eventually be governed by the same regulations and conditions as higher education, and indeed that 'further' education should begin at the minimum school-leaving age. Certainly, policies for access and demand should *not* differ between the non-advanced and advanced sectors.

Policy Recommendation 4
The same broad principles of response to demand and provision for access should apply to universities, to public sector higher education and to non-advanced further education. The sharp administrative and academic distinction between 'advanced' and 'non-advanced' courses should be abandoned.

Selection and Admission Policy

First Admission   Discussion of admission policies in higher education is frequently less clear than it might be. In particular, the aims which policies and procedures are intended to serve are too often taken for granted. The Robbins criterion 'qualified by ability and attainment' implies a competitive meritocratic entry system based on the attainment of standard qualifications, and was certainly interpreted by the committee itself in that light. However, this aim can be attacked on three levels.

The first and commonest attack is to point out that 'A' levels are only moderately correlated with degree results. (While true, this claim blurs the fact that there is a quite reasonable correlation in some subjects, notably the sciences, languages and mathematics, and a very low one in many others.) This suggests that large shifts in the 'A' level entry threshold would only produce comparatively small changes in the end result, in terms of degree class distributions. If so, depending on the taste of the critic, the selection system either is basically indefensible, since it results in a large number of inequitable mis-selections (similar criticisms are made of 11-plus selection) or needs improving by the use of alternative predictors. The difficulty with the first position is the quite satisfactory correlation in some subjects; the second founders on the difficulty of finding suitable alternatives.

A more radical line of criticism points out that the primary aim of higher education should be actually to create merit, and not merely to certify or to process those who already possess it. What matters, in other words, is the quality of graduate output and not that of the intake. Indeed, as institutions with comparatively low entry requirements are fond of asserting, there is more merit in achieving a high proportion of 'good' degree classes (firsts and upper seconds) from a poor intake than from a highly selected one. (There is, however, a certain hypocrisy in some such institutions which nevertheless persist in trying to raise the 'A' level standard of their recruits.) The aim of these critics is still to select students who will have the best results at the end of their course. But at least the net is cast wider; if necessary, special teaching methods or preparatory programmes can be used to bring out the best in ill-equipped entrants.

The third line of attack, however, questions the idea even of a meritocratic output. In its original form, this is a quite traditionalist position, for example, justifying the search for a 'balanced' entry in Oxford and Cambridge colleges, so as to include those with talents such as for sport or debating, and criticizing the values of a 'forcing-house for scholarly talent at the expense of the other benefits of education. It has fallen into some dis-repute, not from its assumptions but because it can too easily be used as a cover for favouritism. Nevertheless, it serves to remind us of the multiple purposes of higher education; and it can also lead perfectly logically to positive discrimination in favour of the underprivileged or those previously discriminated against. The aim of a socially and ethnically more equal society is not something with which higher education need be unconcerned.

All of these positions are fairly widely held in higher education, although in universities at least it is largely the advocates of 'A' levels, or of improvements to or replacements for them, who dominate policy. It is surely time, here as elsewhere, not to abandon meritocracy and the search for high standards, but to accept a plurality of goals for higher education.

There are good reasons for not abolishing the ability to admit through standardized criteria such as GCE 'A' level or its 'equivalents'. These criteria have obvious advantages to admissions officers on one hand and schools on the other: they are a standard currency, and it is not easy to operate a market system, however restricted and imperfect, without the use of money. Despite schools' frequent complaints about the 'tyranny' of the 'A' level syllabus, it provides a useful degree of predictability on which sensible advice can be given to potential applicants, and an incentive for academic work in late adolescence. This is not at all to argue for the retention of 'A' levels in their present form — merely for a broadly similar type of examination. To attempt to do away with the present examination entry system would provoke enormous hostility in schools and in those academic disciplines in higher education for which 'A' levels provide a genuinely useful guide to future performance, as the interminable debate about their replacement shows. In any case, there is nothing to suggest that any of the proposed alternatives (such as aptitude tests), if simply substituted for 'A' levels, would improve the 'accuracy' or legitimacy of selection (Choppin et al. 1973; Entwistle and Wilson 1977).

Secondly, possibly the chief attraction of the 'A' level criterion to the Robbins Committee was its usefulness as a planning device. Without a standardized criterion, either of achievement or of aptitude as in the United States, much of the detailed information we now possess on the demand for higher education would be lost, as a glance at the kind of data presented in Chapter 2 will show. It would be extremely difficult to monitor opportunities for access and ensure that demand is satisfied if there were no national examination system.

At the same time, there is no good reason why 'A' levels or their equivalent should continue to be the only permissible route (as they are for very many departments in many universities), or perhaps even the major route, to admission to higher education. It is widely agreed that they are not especially well suited to the needs of many, or even most older students: arguably the same could be said of many younger ones. As Gordon shows in Chapter 4, for many sixteen-year-olds, especially those from working-class families, the prospect of two more years in a school environment is not attractive. It should not be necessary to insist on this. The simplest alternative (already widely used as additional evidence to supplement 'A' levels), is to use 'O' level performance. In most subjects which are not studied before the first year of higher education, an eighteen-year-old who demonstrated his or her general academic ability and motivation two years earlier, but has spent the intervening years at work would be at no significant disadvantage to one who has studied a different subject in the sixth form. Indeed, many teachers in higher education might prefer to deal with students who have gained some maturity outside education, rather than spending time, in the common complaint, undoing the bad learning habits of 'A' level preparation.

This, then, is one possible entry route, but with two difficulties. The first is that 'O' levels are liable to some of the same problems as 'A' levels, in that they can lead to bias in favour of candidates from experienced schools with large sixth forms or 'O' level streams. Second, since many admissions tutors balk at using CSE passes (with less discrimination at the top) instead of GCE 'O' levels, schools which prefer to concentrate on CSE are effectively handicapping their pupils — until the arrival of an integrated examination. Further alternatives are needed; and these should include aptitude tests (by no means a total failure in the large-scale trial (Choppin 1973)), the assessment of prior or 'experiential' learning — for eighteen-year-olds as well as older students — and individual contracts for independent study and project work.

These last would be particularly useful for those disciplines where the 'A' level grade is used as a measure not only of academic ability but also of preparation for the degree-level course — the second of the difficulties mentioned above. The sequential structure of the curriculum in such subjects is undoubtedly one of the main reasons for the larger predictive value of 'A' levels. Any substitute must cope with this problem, and the solution will require flexibility on the part both of the institution and the under-prepared student. Higher education — especially, but not only, high-prestige university departments — is excessively prone to invoke the preservation of high standards as a defence against any experiment — and the present policies of contraction, with their emphasis on these same 'standards' are likely to encourage them to do so.

It is normal for a chemistry department, for example, to insist that its entrants have taken 'A' level courses not only in chemistry but also in mathematics and another relevant science such as physics. But in doing so it is protecting not so much its standard as the level at which it teachers. The huge increase in recent years in the proportion of 'A' level candidates who take 'mixed' combinations of subjects (ie both science and non-science) means that this insistence actually reduces the pool of highly able applicants from which it can draw. Employers are often criticized by higher education staff for their preference for 'good' graduates, regardless of degree subject, over those with apparently relevant degrees. It is worth asking whether this preference is so indefensible, and whether higher education might not learn from it.

There are precedents for a more relaxed attitude — notably the universities' success in coping with large numbers of under-prepared students after the Second World War. Flexibility in the curriculum and, if necessary, remedial teaching, brought them up to acceptable degree standard — alongside other, younger students who were, on paper, considerably better qualified. There will undoubtedly be a need for extended provision of 'remedial' or access courses, not necessarily to be provided by the same institution. Most such courses at present are designed for mature returners to education, and tend to emphasize study skills, personal confidence and so on, more than academic content. But further education colleges do provide preparatory courses, often linked to particular institutions, and these will be increasingly needed if our proposals are accepted. But they should be used, not for the assessment of suitability, but strictly for preparation: students should be provisionally admitted to higher education prior to taking the course, with admission conditional on achieving a standard pass mark, and not on further competition.

To summarize, the Robbins criterion of two 'A' levels or 'equivalent' is no longer adequate as a norm which all but highly exceptional applicants should achieve. The following recommendation encapsulates the general philosophy which we believe is appropriate for admission to courses of post-compulsory education at every level.

Policy Recommendation 5
Courses of higher and further education should be available to all those who can benefit from them and who wish to do so.

Interpretation: the 'A' level qualification or its 'equivalent' should continue to be the primary criterion, but all admitting units (departments or larger units, as appropriate) should admit at least 25 per cent of their students using other criteria. A range of possible criteria have been described: they include aptitude tests, 'O' level or CSE grades, assessments of prior learning, personal 'learning contracts', and so on.[11]

Such a change can be implemented by the institutions themselves, and requires no government action. The original two-'A' level requirement of the grant regulations recommended by the Anderson Committee was modified in 1974, so that there is no restriction on that score. The CNAA, which monitors entry requirements in the public sector, already permits a large intake on non-traditional criteria (CNAA 1980), and many institutions take advantage of this freedom. It is mainly universities which would be affected by the proposal for a 25 per cent minimum. Even here, 12 per cent of new entrants in 1980 did not have 'A' levels (Table 2.11, p.79) — although many of these doubtless held 'equivalent' qualifications such as ONC/D.

Once again, the question will be asked whether it is appropriate to require universities, even those with the highest conventional admission standards, to change them. Critics will presumably include those concerned to preserve the universities' élite status, and those who want to keep a special role for the public sector. The former is understandable, since in the absence of many of the other discriminators found in other national systems (salaries, staff-student ratios, and resources, all of which the authorities attempt to equalize across the British system) admissions standards have become perhaps the chief currency of academic prestige for employers and for academics themselves. This is precisely why the proposal should be applied across the board, to avoid sharpening the hierarchy which already exists. Polytechnics, however, while welcoming the removal of a status difference, may fear that their best candidates, and a distinctive part of their role, are being 'poached' by the universities. The answer is that the two sectors have sufficient other claims to distinctiveness to attract their own candidates, that a commitment to non-traditional entry by universities would in return increase the pool of traditional entrants available to the public sector, and that the aim is to increase the total pool of candidates by making higher education as a whole, not just low-status higher education, visibly less exclusive, rather than benefiting one sector at the expense of another.

How much the total pool will be increased by such methods is far from clear. There are those who believe that they would in fact make little difference to the willingness of school-leavers or older students to participate. If so, they can scarcely damage teaching standards seriously. But the balance of evidence suggests that, combined with other measures proposed in the next section, they might create new demands for higher education — and largely from the able but unqualified pool. In any case, as the experience of the public sector shows, this is not an overwhelmingly risky strategy for institutions. Where necessary, suitable remedial or preparatory courses can protect the level of their teaching.

It is in fact the students themselves who are in danger if such measures are not backed up with special attention[12] once they arrive. In the long run, however, the easier credit transfer which we next propose should reduce the disgrace of 'drop-out' to the sensible decision to 'transfer'. Indeed, a general shift from strict selection before entry with very high retention rates thereafter to fairly easy access combined with higher exclusion rates after a year would help to ease the general problem of matching students to courses and preserving the high standards of the degree.[13] This is a policy which deserves further examination as more diversified types of courses are developed: it could be formalized in the kind of '2 + 2' or '1 + 3' course structures mentioned earlier.

Credit Transfer   Credit transfer is one of the easiest reforms to propose, and one of the hardest to implement within the standard three-year Honours degree package. The difficulties chiefly stem from its potential consequences for the curriculum, which are substantial, and are perceived by many academics as totally insurmountable. Curricular problems are well beyond the remit of this stage of the programme. But it is at least arguable that there is no other single reform entirely within the control of higher education institutions which could have such an effect on demand levels. Coupled with reasonably generous grant eligibility, credit transfer would open up enormous possibilities for recurrent and continuing education, and make even the conventional first degree less formidable as an ambition for those without three full-time years to spare, or with other ideas on how to spend their late adolescence.

I have suggested that the curricular obstacles are extremely serious. They mostly concern what to do with a new arrival, the 'immigrant' with credits which do not match the accumulated credits of conventional students. Perhaps the risks would seem more worth taking if we began by thinking about the 'emigrant': the student who leaves his or her first institution after completing only part of the course. At present such a person is a 'drop-out' or a 'failure' — an example of 'wastage' regardless of anything he may have achieved — stigmatized and indeed penalized on the job market and potentially by the grant-giving authority. But if three years' study conveys so many advantages, it would be odd if one or two years' were to convey none. It should be possible to make clear what has been achieved, to devise positive and respected certificates for part-completion, not consolations for failure or disguises for idleness. Such certificates would give not an automatic right of return but at least the opportunity to compete for advanced standing at another institution, and a credential of some use in the job market. If so, they would be a desirable aim for some of those unattracted by three full years.

Rather than struggling to invent completely new qualifications such as the DipHE, and rather than worrying unduly about what to do with credits from elsewhere, we propose that institutions begin by asking what certification they would be prepared to give to students who have completed only part of their full degree courses. Once enough of such certificates are in circulation, methods for responding to them will almost inevitably arise, as the value of Open University units on the educational and job markets already demonstrates.

Credit transfer, and all that it implies for the curriculum through delayed or recurrent entry, is a powerful but double-edged weapon. If tightly controlled and rigidly interpreted, it could act as a brake on diversification by insisting on a 'gold standard', not just for the degree but for its component elements, the year or even the course unit. But it could also be a means of shifting the balance in the market for educational qualifications away from the supplier and towards the consumer. A student who is essentially committed to completing a course, subject to severe penalties, even before embarking on it, has far less influence over the course content than one who can take his or her fees, per-capita allowances and so on elsewhere if the course fails to meet expectations. Indeed, it is at least arguable that it is the credit system which has really made possible the unique, consumer-orientated quality of American higher education (see Chapter 3).

Policy Recommendation 6
The universities and the CNAA should devise certificates of partial completion of degree courses, to be awarded after appropriate assessment.

Finance
A future seminar will be devoted to all aspects of the finance of higher education, including the funding of research, and the use of financial leverage for goals such as the encouragement of innovation and change or the protection of specific functions. Here, obviously, we are concerned primarily with the relationship to demand and access of the financing of higher education, and especially the financing of students.

The first general point to make is that on the available, admittedly very crude figures British higher education is not, in international terms, under-financed. In 1975 1.2 per cent of GNP was devoted to higher education, compared with 2.2 per cent in the Netherlands, but 1.0 per cent in Belgium, 0.9 per cent in Austria, 0.8 per cent in Germany and Sweden, 0.7 per cent in Italy, and 0.5 per cent in France (Jallade 1980). On the other hand, the participation rate in higher education is lower in Britain than in most of these countries (Cerych and Colton 1980). The purpose of the comparison is not to berate British higher education teachers for idleness or prodigality: indeed, foreign observers at the seminar, as well as those who might be expected to be partial, argued that it was a sign of the high quality and standards of such higher education as is provided in Britain. But the question must inevitably arise, not whether the country 'can afford' the higher expenditure on higher education which a higher participation rate would, other things being equal, imply, but whether it makes political sense to try to extract higher finance from the state. Any political party, whatever its disposition, will have other candidates for new expenditure, whether these are defence and 'law and order' or other levels of education (with which many supporters of higher education would find it hard to disagree). And, to put it no higher, the price of greater support from the state, if forthcoming, would be likely to be greater state control. It thus becomes necessary to consider whether there may not be a price which is worth paying *within* higher education for increased demand and improved access. Martin Trow, in Chapter 3, draws our attention with some delicacy to exactly this question.

The problem is not only that increased participation will require greater expenditure on student maintenance[14] but that many of the measures proposed as ways to increase demand also involve extra costs, whether these are the comparatively small sums involved in administering special admissions and credit transfer schemes, or in providing better counselling and guidance to potential students, or the larger amounts needed for more equitable financing for part-time courses, non-degree courses and indeed for 16-18 year-olds (see below).

The higher education maintenance grant served an important purpose in enabling the post-Robbins expansion to take place. Now, however, its role has, arguably, reversed, and it may act more as a constraint than as a stimulus to expansion. Its real value has been allowed to drift down (and its value compared to 18-21 year-old wages had dropped more stongly still) until at best it no longer provides a substantial added incentive to participation. (It is, however, by no means clear how important the level of the maintenance grant is: Pissarides (1981) shows that for the population as a whole it is less significant than relative salary levels for graduates and non-graduates.) It may be, therefore, that the continued insistence of higher education staff and students on retaining a maintenance grant is an unnecessary hostage to fortune.

The reason for this apparently paradoxical statement is that so long as the higher education maintenance grant consumes so much expenditure, it is hard to imagine a satisfactory level of maintenance being implemented for those on courses other than the present list for mandatory grants. The most obvious omission is strongly emphasized by Gordon in Chapter 4: whereas 18-21 year-olds receive a very substantial grant, grants for 16-18 year-olds in full-time education depend on local discretion and are never generous. When they are compared not only with the prospects of juvenile earnings, but even with unemployment or social security benefit, and especially with the various available forms of training grant for young people, they create a positive disincentive to staying on at school. There is some doubt about the extent to which a substantial educational maintenance allowance for 16-18 year-olds in full-time education would in fact increase staying-on rates — Gordon's evidence is necessarily hypothetical — but it can be strongly argued that this anomaly in educational support is simply inequitable, as between different sectors of education, different age groups and — in effect if not in intention — between social classes. Proper support for the 16-18 age group in education should be very high on the policy agenda for education as a whole.

Secondly, even for older age groups, the distinction between 'higher' and 'non-advanced further' education is, as I have argued, increasingly untenable. As course provision grows more complex, it will probably become unworkable. And there are some well-known, quite specific anomalies which are, once again, indefensible in equity — and may well depress demand. Examples are the difficulties faced by students who wish to take a degree course after a (grant-aided) Higher National Diploma; or the merely 'discretionary' eligibility for grants of 'access' courses for mature students.

Finally, part-time education and continuing education for adults all appear to be desirable for reasons of educational and economic policy: but would-be students are now likely to face sharply increasing fees as well as the other more familiar disincentives. These considerations all lead to the following recommendation.

Policy Recommendation 7
The present grant system should be replaced with a system of 'educational entitlement', whereby every citizen is entitled to support for his or her education or training, regardless of its level. Such support would comprise an age-related maintenance grant and remission or reimbursement of fees, for a maximum of four years full-time or its part-time equivalent *after the compulsory school-leaving age of sixteen. This entitlement should be supplemented with a system of state-supported loans, available for further periods of education or training as desired. It neither precludes nor implies any system of grant support for other courses beyond the four-year minimum (such as postgraduate research or teacher training).*

Detailed regulations for any such entitlement would need to be carefully worked out. For example, it would be necessary to insist that it was claimed for the *first* four years of education after sixteen, thus preventing parents from supporting their children during the relatively cheap sixth-form years and then claiming the grant for four years of higher education. Transitional arrangements for all those over sixteen at the time of introduction would also need to be thought about carefully. The grant should be age-related, so as not to provide a disincentive for adults; it would be equitable if, as far as possible, it were adjusted so as to be neutral as between different ages in terms of foregone earnings. The precise boundary between education or training in an educational institution and training provided within a job would also cause difficulties. (Here the experience of other countries might be helpful in designing regulations.) But the grant should be available to support any form of bona fide education or training, whether provided by public or private institutions and whether or not leading to a recognized qualification.

The direct advantages of this proposal derive from the arguments given above. Indirect advantages include the transfer of an increase in consumer power to the individual student, who would be entitled to claim the grant regardless of the institution attended, or of the course level, or of any transfers he or she might make from one institution to another. This should have the effect of increasing the responsiveness of institutions to individual needs. In particular, the transferability between full and part-time education should encourage the provision of part-time and mixed-mode courses, where this meets the needs of students. A four-year entitlement, implying one year less than the present two-plus-three years (in England and Wales) required for an Honours degree, is the price to be paid for extending support to the 16-18 age group and beyond 'higher' education. However, it is likely that it would increase the pressure on institutions to provide two-year degrees, or early entry, or entry after limited or no sixth-form attendance, all of which would be desirable developments from the point of view of improving access.

This proposal will doubtless be criticized for its failure to support the full two-plus-three pattern as at present. However, a single year's loan, even if covering fees (which could continue to be set well below 'full-cost' rates) as well as living expenses, is not an enormous burden to be incurred, and would probably not act as a deterrent to those already on courses. In any case, loans, despite the opposition of student groups and many academic staff, not only are desirable in equity, as potentially reducing the subsidy to high-earning graduates at the expense of non-participants, but also permit a much greater degree of flexibility than the present system in the means of student support. Repayments can be geared to subsequent earnings through the tax system, or can be reduced, postponed or remitted altogether to suit personal circumstances or those entering jobs for which it is hoped to increase the supply; interest rates can be subsidized to different extents; they can be used, in other words, to increase the influence of government in ways which interfere less crudely with individual freedom than outright direction. The loan system, once instituted, could also be used to supplement the 'entitlement' grant if it were financially necessary to set the latter at a bare 'subsistence' level.[15]

Access Policies

Young People As Gordon (Chapter 4) shows clearly, the acutest problems of demand and access for young people arise at the point of entry not to higher education but to post-compulsory education at the minimum school-leaving age. Our concern is not primarily with demand at that stage, and although members of the seminar were tempted to analyse policies and propose new ones for schools and non-advanced further education these could not be given the same scrutiny as policies bearing more directly on higher education. Thus, despite the attractiveness of recommending major reforms (tertiary colleges, for example, or new examinations at sixteen, or universal education and training for the 16-18 age group) or of criticizing lower secondary schools, these will be resisted here.

Instead, in discussing access for young people we shall concentrate on what higher education itself can do, or what can be done with policies which affect the whole 16-21 age group. Most of these have already been discussed — policies aimed, for example, at widening the range of entry qualifications, providing financial support for the 16-18 age group, increasing the responsiveness of higher education to (new) consumer needs, and blurring the boundaries between institutional types and between advanced and non-advanced courses. All of these policies would, it is hoped, have the effect of increasing the attractiveness of higher education not only to the population in general, but to groups at present under-represented, such as working-class children, members of ethnic minorities, residents of regions with low participation rates, and women (see Chapter 2). They have the merit of defusing the argument, proposed in part provocatively at the seminar, that there is considerable arrogance in supposing that higher education is really what these groups need and trying to 'drag them in off the streets against their better judgement'.[16] If they come in off the streets, it will be because they see something inside which attracts them.

However, there are certain other policies which may also be necessary. Some are low-cost and low-risk, but might be quite effective on a local scale. One example is the cultivation of links between local institutions at different levels: connections between a university or polytechnic and a school or further education college in its immediate region can be extremely helpful in encouraging marginally unconvinced candidates to apply, or in selecting from under- or unusually qualified applicants. As more than one participant pointed out, it is a fallacy to suppose that nationally applied policies can always help in the extraordinarily wide range of local circumstances: the factors which induce a working-class girl from the immediate region to attend (or not to attend) Glasgow University will be quite different from those that apply to the Polytechnic of Central London, or Charlotte Mason

College, Ambleside. It will be necessary for individual institutions to develop suitable 'outreach programmes' for their own particular circumstances, as some already do.

Amongst those programmes, however, should be serious experiments with 'affirmative action'. This differs from the kind of admissions policy proposed above for using alternative entry routes, some of which may also be more attractive to under-represented groups. Here the proposal is to admit members of such groups deliberately at a lower 'standard' than the majority. It is a dangerous policy for two reasons, as American experience has shown: first because it can be perceived as unfair to well-qualified candidates who are excluded, especially in courses for which competition is severe, and secondly because it can be unfair to the specially admitted student, arriving with high expectations but left to compete with better-prepared contemporaries. (And the need for affirmative action is probably greatest on highly competitive courses, where admissions tutors are most likely to recoil from the idea for just these reasons.) Nevertheless, it is of great importance that opportunities should be seen to be available in highly selective institutions as well as in those which may be seen as having less to lose, and therefore less than the best. There have been, it is true, experiments on a very small scale (such as the Oxford-ILEA and Cambridge-ILEA Science Admission Schemes (Spice 1981)); but these scarcely deserve the name since candidates have to jump so many selective hurdles that they have hardly had their passages eased — indeed, many of them would probably have achieved entry by ordinary routes. What is proposed is something simpler and more systematic — a much wider acceptance of the necessity to temper admissions criteria to the circumstances of the individual, with the deliberate aim of increasing the representation of certain groups, *even at the expense of academic standards*. This is entirely compatible with the notion that universities and public sector higher education alike have social as well as academic responsibilities.

Policy Recommendation 8
All institutions, and especially those with highly competitive entry requirements, should undertake significant experiments with positive discrimination in favour of candidates whose circumstances — personal, social or educational — may have prevented them from competing for entry on equal terms with the majority of applicants. When admitted, such students will need special support similar to that given to students entering on 'non-traditional' admissions criteria (Recommendation 5).

These experiments might be included under the 25 per cent quota reserved for non-traditional applicants (Recommendation 5). The groups to be chosen for special treatment should include a wide range, but may vary according to the type of institution and course. For example, it would be appropriate for many science and technology courses but not for most social science courses to apply positive discrimination to women applicants. There are very few courses for which discrimination in favour of ethnic minorities or applicants from inner-city schools, would not be justified. The criterion to be used will ultimately be that proposed in Recommendation 5 — the ability of the individual to benefit — but this can legitimately be supported by the particular responsibilities of an institution to its immediate community, and the desirability of a social balance in the academic community itself.

Older People   In Chapter 5, Geoffrey Squires describes the varied special needs of adult students, and provides a broad justification for acceding to and indeed stimulating the interest of adults in returning to education. As he points out, there are excellent reasons for doing so. These include the legitimate wishes of adults themselves to continue their own self-development (often leading to higher motivation and better performance than that of younger students); economic arguments deriving from the changing labour market and the speed of technological change (strongly pressed at the first seminar in this series (Lindley 1981)); and equity arguments resulting from the imperfections of selection during compulsory education and the enhanced opportunities which the present generation of young people has acquired as a result of the post-Robbins expansion.

The recommendations proposed earlier, especially Recommendation 7 to provide an entitlement to support regardless of age, should serve to increase the accessibility of higher and further education to older students — indeed many of them are proposed with mature students especially in mind. To formalize the position the following policy is proposed.

Policy Recommendation 9
It should be the policy of government and of higher education institutions to encourage the participation of adults in courses of further and higher education at all levels, and to make appropriate provision for their special needs.

Once again, this is a commitment which institutions and courses of *all* kinds should be encouraged to make. There is considerable reluctance to admit older people to some courses, on the grounds that their success rate in the past has not been high. Providers of these courses should ask themselves whether this may have more to do with their own expectations and assumptions than with the supposed defects in older minds. Arranging special support is not cost-free; nor is adapting a whole course to fit a wider range of aptitude and experience. But the benefits described by Squires outweigh the costs.

CONCLUSION
The 'defensiveness' which was referred to in the Introduction, whether justified or not, inevitably takes its toll. Viewed in comparative terms, or

indeed in the perspective of history, there is nothing that could be described even as daring, let alone radical, in the recommendations put forward above. But it is hard to avoid the suspicion that some of them will be seen as much more sweeping than present circumstances should permit. It is worth reiterating that the task of the programme of studies of which this volume is a part is defined as proposing policies for the next twenty years. Proposals such as the abolition of the advanced/non-advanced distinction are put forward not as additional provocations to hard-pressed administrators but as aims towards which policy making might move over the next ten years.

Nevertheless, it may be useful to speculate about some of the likely kinds of opposition to such proposals. There will certainly be criticisms from those who believe that the recommendations are not justified by the evidence. These will need to be met head on. I believe that the recommendations are justified, but the best test will be to subject them to thorough analysis.

Other criticism will be on financial grounds. As has been emphasized, the seminar was thoroughly aware of financial constraints: and one of the strongest general bases for our recommendations has been an unwillingness to demand large shifts of expenditure towards higher education at the expense of other sectors.[17] But this does not altogether settle the matter. To accept that constraint means that any new resources to be claimed will have to be found in large part by reductions elsewhere in post- compulsory education. In a crucial sense, we are arguing that the promotion of a higher participation rate and the improvement of access are so important that sacrifices need to be made for it.

Such sacrifices, as is obvious from these proposals, include giving up the guaranteed full maintenance grant for all three years of higher education, and accepting the possibility of shorter courses as well as loss of students after only one or two years. If the real level of resources spent on higher education does not grow, as it probably will not, they may well also imply a smaller 'unit of resource' and higher student/staff ratio. It is for later seminars to discuss the implications of these resource consequences, but we must be clear that they are likely to occur.

They will also be resisted. A recurring latent theme in the present discussions was the problem of change, the topic of the third seminar. It is not my job to anticipate this next seminar's conclusions, but it is clear that resistance to change will come from inside and outside the academic world. Many academics — especially those in certain universities with less to fear from contraction — will regard the defence of their discipline as more important than the improvement of access, and will resist proposals which may result in a loss of status within the present institutional hierarchy. Our proposal to use market mechanisms as a lever may not work, will have undesirable effects as well as the good ones we claim for it, and certainly needs further discussion. But if the alternative is a reliance on centralized direction, whether by government or other bureaucracies or by the academic guild itself, we believe that the necessary changes will not take place.

At the same time, resistance from outside academia may be substantial. The present social structure, reflected in if not reinforced by educational divisions from primary to postgraduate level, has obvious powers of regeneration. It is at least arguable that the postwar expansion of higher education, far from creating new opportunity, served to re-establish the traditional social hierarchy in new forms. British higher education undoubtedly serves in part to civilize and co-opt the future 'service' class not only into the skills but also into the manners and way of life appropriate to an élite. As that class expanded, it was, on this view, necessary to ensure its proper socialization. Whether the next twenty years will see a further expansion in this class is more doubtful; if not, resistance can be expected (and may already be beginning) to further expenditure on what could turn out to be, for the first time, a new kind of student.

On the other hand, I have also argued that those excluded from higher education cannot be expected indefinitely to support its continued existence on what can easily be made to seem unduly favourable terms. There will certainly be those who will criticize the recommendations made here as insufficiently radical. The constituency which supports higher education in its present form is dangerously small: however desirable in their own right, our proposals are also intended to enlarge it. Whether they will do so remains to be seen.

As one seminar member put it, we need a 'political economy' of higher education which might begin to analyse these questions more systematically. In the meantime, those of us, relics of the 1960s no doubt, who hope to use higher education as an agent, not a creature of change, will certainly take it as a sign of failure if our proposals create no opposition.

RECOMMENDATIONS

Policy Recommendations
1   Courses of higher education should (continue to) be available to all those who are qualified by attainment to pursue them and who wish to do so.
2   It should be the aim of government and of higher education institutions to achieve a substantial increase in the participation rate in higher education.
3   In response to the likely decline in demand from its traditional clientele, the British higher education system should be encouraged to adapt in order to increase participation rates.
4   The same broad principles of response to demand and provision for access should apply to universities, to public sector higher education and to non-advanced further education. The sharp administrative and academic distinction between 'advanced' and 'non-advanced' courses should be abandoned.
5   Courses of higher and further education should be available to all those who can benefit from them and who wish to do so.

Interpretation: The 'A' level qualification or its 'equivalent' should continue to be the primary criterion, but all *admitting units (departments or larger units, as appropriate) should admit* at least 25 per cent *of their students using other criteria, including aptitude tests, 'O' level or CSE grades, assessments of prior learning, personal 'learning contracts', and so on.*

6   *The universities and the CNAA should devise certificates of partial completion of degree courses, to be awarded after appropriate assessment.*

7   *The present grant system should be replaced with a system of 'educational entitlement', whereby every citizen is entitled to support for his or her education or training, regardless of its level. Such support would comprise an age-related maintenance grant and remission or reimbursement of fees, for a maximum of* four *years full-time* or its part-time equivalent *after the compulsory school-leaving age of sixteen. This entitlement should be supplemented with a system of state-supported loans, available for further periods of education or training as desired. It neither precludes nor implies any system of grant support for other courses beyond the four-year minimum (such as postgraduate research or teacher training).*

8   All *institutions, and especially those with highly competitive entry requirements, should undertake significant experiments with positive discrimination in favour of candidates whose circumstances — personal, social or educational — may have prevented them from competing for entry on equal terms with the majority of applicants. When admitted, such students will need special support similar to that given to students entering on 'non-traditional' admissions criteria (Recommendation 5).*

9   *It should be the policy of government and of higher education institutions to encourage the participation of adults in courses of further and higher education at all levels, and to make appropriate provision for their special needs.*

Research and Information Recommendations

1   *A wide-ranging review should be undertaken, comparable to that by Howard Bowen for the Carnegie Council on Policy Studies in Higher Education (Bowen 1977), of available evidence on the direct and indirect value of investment in British higher education; where primary research evidence is not available, such research should also be undertaken.*

2   (a)   *The collection and dissemination of information on demand for and access to higher education should be maintained and where possible enhanced in forms accessible to the widest possible audience.*

    (b)   *In particular, the collection of information on access to public sector higher education should be improved at least to a level comparable with that on access to universities, if necessary by specially commissioned research.*

(c) *Documents such as the DES 'Brown' and 'Grey' papers (DES 1978, 1979) and DES Statistical Bulletin 12/80 are especially useful and should be published at regular intervals as early as practicable. The DES should explore the possibility of providing direct access for qualified specialists to the relevant computer tapes, possibly through the SSRC Survey Archive.*

NOTES

1   This is no criticism of the Robbins Committee: much of their report is in fact devoted to an operational interpretation of the principle. But the interpretation is now inevitably outdated: for example, it did not anticipate the binary policy for higher education.

2   The labour market seminar made a strong economic case for expanding opportunities for older students both on first degree courses and as part of a scheme of recurrent education, as a way of improving the speed and flexibility of the response of higher education to the labour market (Lindley 1981).

3   Here, of course, the number of graduates *is* more significant than the participation rate. But if the actual number is to increase from its present level, the participation rate will have to rise quite sharply, especially in the 1990s (Chapter 2).

4   In fact the book continues with an equally thorough, though occasionally more speculative, review of non-economic benefits both to the individual and to American society and the political system.

5   It is generally conceded that one of the major aims of the Robbins Committee was to 'sell' to those who were unconvinced of its inevitability the politically necessary policy of acceding to demand for higher education. Among the unconvinced were many of the academic staff thmselves (see Halsey & Trow 1971). Even in Eastern Europe attempts to operate rigid limits on higher education in accordance with national plans have had to be modified in response to popular pressure in recent years (Fulton et al. 1980).

6   Sex differentials have improved. But this improvement has not resulted from the policy of expansion as such. Indeed, it has occurred to some extent *despite* official policy: the current supposed 'over-emphasis' on arts and social science has chiefly benefited women — and any disproportionate cutback in places in these subjects is likely to damage women's opportunites correspondingly.

7   The relatively high participation rate in Scotland (see Chapter 2, p.63) can be partly explained by the higher subsidy implied by four years in higher education after a single (unmaintained) year at school; in the case of Wales, however, this option does not exist.

8   There are parallels between these proposals and the American option (or requirement in a few states) of two years at a community college, with

the option of a terminal qualification, followed, if desired, by two years in the 'upper division' of a college or university.

9   In particular, the idea, attractive to several participants, of adopting the full Scottish pattern of one year in the sixth form followed by four years of higher education would increase costs substantially, cause grave political difficulties with schools and non-advanced further education and (if the causes for high Scottish participation are cultural or in any way non-generalizable) might well not increase participation commensurately.

10   The connection is direct: employers prefer to recruit, almost regardless of content, from courses with high entry standards (understandably — but absurdly if the standard of output is as uniform as is claimed); while 'good' students naturally aspire to places on courses with high entry standards and high attractiveness to employers (Lindley 1981).

11   They might also include 'A' level standards *markedly* lower (eg lower points scores or one pass instead of two or three) than those required of the 'conventional' intake. See below on *positive discrimination*, under access policies.

12   It is undeniable that these proposals will involve certain costs: the additional cost of selection, which will become less routine for the special entry component; and the cost of extra tutorial support and counselling if necessary during the first year or for even longer.

13   Whereas the correlation of 'A' level grades with degree results is fairly low, that of first-year examinations is considerably higher (Entwistle and Wilson 1977).

14   If the participation rate were to grow to keep exact pace with demographic decline, precisely filling the places otherwise vacant, there need be no net increase in expenditure. However, in other areas of education the relevant figure is expenditure per head of population; and there will be plenty of alternative costs (such as expenditure on a growing retired population) as the 18-year-old population declines.

15   For example, the entitlement might be based on costs for home-based students: those wishing to attend a residential institution could then find the extra cost through the loan system.

16   The obvious retort is that whatever young people may or may not *need*, higher education is what many of them in fact say they want — but which they then find themselves excluded from. See above, p.13.

17   This is of course no defence against a government determined to cut public expenditure for its own sake and regardless of the consequences — but no such defence exists.

REFERENCES
Bourdieu, P. and Passeron, J.-C. (1977) *Reproduction in Education, Society and Culture* London: Sage

Bowen, H.R. (1977) *Investment in Learning: the individual and social value of American higher education* San Francisco: Jossey Bass
Bragg, S. (1980) Inverting the system. In Evans (1980)
Cerych, L. and Colton, S. (1980) Summarising recent student flows *European Journal of Education* 15 (1)
Choppin, B.H.L. et al. (1973) *The Prediction of Academic Success* Slough: NFER
Collins, R. (1979) *The Credential Society* New York: Academic Press
Council for National Academic Awards (CNAA) (1980) *Extension of Access to Higher Education* CNAA (unpublished)
Department of Education and Science (DES) (1978) *Higher Education into the 1990s: a discussion document* DES Information Division
Department of Education and Science (DES) (1979) *Future Trends in Higher Education* DES Information Division
Douglas, J.W.B. (1964) *The Home and the School* London: McGibbon and Kee
Entwistle, N.J and Wilson, J. (1977) *Degrees of Excellence: the academic achievement game* London: Hodder and Stoughton
Evans, N. (1980) *Education Beyond School: higher education for a changing contest* London: Grant MacIntyre
Fidler, F.B. (1979) *Sixth-Formers' Choice of Higher Education Institutions* University of Lancaster, MA dissertation
Freeman, R.B. (1981) Response to change in the United States. In Lindley (1981)
Fulton, O. and Gordon, A. (1979) The British pool of ability: how deep, and will cash reduce it? *Educational Studies* 5 (2)
Fulton, O., Gordon, A.G. and Williams, G.L. (1980) Higher education and manpower planning: a comparison of planned and market economies *Education Policy Bulletin* 8 (1)
Grossman, M. (1975) The correlation between health and schooling. In N.E. Terleckyj (Editor) *Household Production and Consumption* New York: Columbia University Press (cited in Bowen 1977)
Halsey, A.H. and Trow, M. (1971) *The British Academics* London: Faber and Faber
Halsey, A.H. (Editor) (1972) *Educational Priority Volume 1: Problems and Policies* London: HMSO
Jallade, J.P. (1980) Expenditure on higher education in Europe: past trends and future prospects *European Journal of Education* 15 (1)
Lindley, R. (1981) *Higher Education and the Labour Market* Guildford: SRHE
Pippard, A.B. (1969) The educated scientist *Physics Bulletin* 20
Pissarides, C.A. (1981) *From School to University: the demand for post-compulsory education in Britain* London School of Economics, Centre for Labour Economics, Discussion Paper No. 70

Ramsden, P. (1981) Student learning: a neglected policy issue *Education Policy Bulletin* 9 (1)

Silver, H. (1980) Enforced conformity or hierarchical diversity? In Evans (1980)

Spice, J.E. (1981) *The ILEA-Oxford and ILEA-Cambridge Science Admissions Schemes* Preparatory Paper, Imperial College Education Forum, 11 March

Trow, M.A. (1974) Problems in the transition from élite to mass higher education, In OECD *Policies for Higher Education* (General Report, Conference on Future Structures of Post-Secondary Education, 1973) Paris: OECD

Williams, G.L. (1974) *Higher Education and the Stable State* University of Lancaster, inaugural lecture

Williams, G.L. (1981) The main policy issues facing higher education in the 1980s and 1990s *Education Policy Bulletin* 9 (1)

2

TRENDS IN ADMISSIONS

by John H. Farrant

INTRODUCTION

This paper looks at recent trends in the number and characteristics of people qualifying for entry to, and embarking on, courses of higher education in England and Wales. It is concerned only with 'home' students (that is, UK residents) and not with 'overseas' students, howsoever the categories are defined for the statistics used, and only with higher education funded by Parliament's Education Vote. The focus is on people starting a course of higher education for the first time, so courses for which successful completion of another higher education course is a normal prerequisite are not considered.

Anyone looking at admissions to higher education goes back to the monumental surveys for the year 1961/62 commissioned by the Robbins Committee and published with its report (HE 1963, App. 1 and 2) and asks a host of questions about what has changed over the two decades since. All too often the questions simply cannot be answered from the published statistics, whether routine or from special surveys, on which this paper has had to rely. The committee stated: 'we should be failing in our duty if we were to close this chapter without emphasizing with all the force at our command that the erection and continuation of an adequate statistical service is an essential condition of the successful working of all the machinery we have recommended' (p.256). Major changes have been made in the method of collecting statistics, particularly in creating a computer-based record for each student in further and higher education. But the potential of these huge data files finds little reflection in the published statistics which, if anything, are more limited and less timely than ten years ago and which the present government's policy towards the Statistical Service is scarcely likely to improve.

The Varieties of Higher Education and the Routes to Them

'Higher education' conventionally denotes courses above the standard required for the Advanced ('A') Level of the General Certificate of Education (GCE) (England and Wales), the Higher Grade of the Scottish Certificate of Education, or the Ordinary National Certificate/Diploma (ONC/D). Included by this definition are two categories of students who are not mentioned hereafter. These are 'private study' students, mostly studying for legal, accountancy, banking and surveying qualifications, often by correspondence course, or for University of London external awards; and students, mostly full-time, at institutions which are funded by the government other than through the Education Vote (eg HM Armed Services colleges) or which are wholly privately funded (eg theological colleges). The Robbins Committee found that these groups comprised about one tenth of all initial entrants to higher education (HE 1963, App. 1, p.33; App.2(A), p.4). Probably today the proportion is much less.

The main streams of higher education with which we are concerned are:

1   Full-time study for first degree in universities (other than the Open University); very small numbers of students are part-time at this level or are working for first diplomas.

2   Full-time study in maintained or grant-aided colleges (with various titles including polytechnic, college or institute of higher education, technical college, and college of further education; collectively called the public sector), the majority of entrants now embarking on first degree courses, with the redesignation of the Diplomas in Technology and in Art and Design as degrees of the Council for National Academic Awards (CNAA), and with the phasing out of Certificate courses for intending teachers. Others work for the Higher National Diploma (HND — which hereafter includes the awards of the Business and Technical Education Councils which are replacing it) or for qualifications awarded by professional institutions.

3   Part-time study in maintained or grant-aided colleges, in most cases for the Higher National Certificate (HNC — likewise including BEC and TEC awards) or for professional qualifications. It is usual to distinguish between students attending during the day and those attending in the evening only.

2 and 3 together comprise Advanced Further Education (AFE).

4   Part-time study for a first degree of the Open University (OU).

The route into full-time degree courses is predominantly through GCE 'A' level, with at least two passes, that being also the requirement for a mandatory maintenance grant between 1962 and 1974. Almost 90 per cent of home candidates admitted to British universities are so qualified (Table 2.11(A), p.79), as are some 80 per cent to the public sector, now that two 'A' levels are the normal requirement for teacher training courses (CUA 1978, Table 5; Whitburn et al. 1976, Table 4.5; CNAA Annual Report 1980, Table 3, with allowance for part-time and overseas students). By contrast only about half the full-time students on non-degree courses come by the two-'A' level route; some of the remainder have one 'A' level (the minimum for the HND/C), but OND/C is probably the most significant alternative to 'A' levels. Among part-time students in AFE, those holding two 'A' levels are in a minority. In 1961/62, only 10 per cent did so, but in polytechnics eleven years later it was 30-35 per cent. Again, OND/C may be the major route (HE 1963, App. 2(B), p.132; Whitburn et al. 1976, Tables 6.6, 4.6). The Open University has no formal entry requirements, but of the 1977 entrants

48 per cent had a higher education qualification, a further 12 per cent had two or more 'A' levels (or equivalent) and 4 per cent OND/C (OU 1980, Table A.4.4).

Total Numbers of Students
In Table 2.1 (p.69) are the numbers of full-time home and part-time students in selected years since 1962/63 (the part-timers include a small number who were 'overseas'; postgraduates are also included). In 1962/63 there were 305,000, and in 1978/79 710,000, or 133 per cent more. The annual growth rate of about 8½ per cent in the 1960s was not maintained in the 1970s, but even so, thanks to the Open University, was still around 4 per cent a year up to 1978/79. Without the Open University, the number of full-time students increased faster than part-time; the latter comprised 38 per cent of the total in 1962/63, only 27 per cent seven years later and 30 per cent in 1978/79. The Open University has, however, brought the proportion up to 37 per cent. But the resurgence in the part-time proportion is also due to the fact that in 1977 and 1978 the absolute number of full-timers dropped for the first time since 1952. Even so, if the part-time students are converted to full-time equivalents, they comprised only about 14 per cent of the total load on institutions in 1962/63 and 16 per cent in 1978/79, the small increase being also due to the move from evening to day courses.

A more detailed analysis of the figures for one year, 1978/79 (Table 2.2 p.70) serves to emphasize points already made about how the qualifications aimed for differ with the mode of study and sector. Most part-timers in universities were postgraduates. Sixty-nine per cent of AFE full-timers were on degree or teacher training courses, but only 6 per cent of part-timers. Thirty-seven per cent and forty per cent respectively of part-time (day) students were seeking the HNC and professional qualifications. But among part-time (evening) students only 11 per cent were on HNC coureses, and 55 per cent on professional courses. Of the students embraced by Table 2.2 (p.70), those with whom this paper is particularly concerned are those who, in 1978/79, crossed the threshold of higher education for the first time — that is, the initial entrants. Despite the emphasis placed by the Robbins Committee on initial entrants, as both a record of past progress and a basis for future planning, their number cannot be determined from the published statistics. A surprisingly large proportion of students in the first year of a course which is not postgraduate have previously enrolled on another higher education course. Among full-time degree students the proportion is relatively small, confined mainly to those already holding an HND/C, or those who dropped out of the earlier course. But among those taking non-degree courses the position is very different. In 1961/62, the proportions who already held qualifications obtained in higher education were about 11 per cent among full-time non-degree students in AFE; 19 per cent of part-time day and 33 per cent of part-time evening students (HE 1963, App. 2(B), pp.118-9, 142-3). The 1972/73 study of polytechnics yields figures of 14 per cent and 40 per cent for all full-time and part-time students (Whitburn et al. 1976, Table 4.6). The principal reasons seem to be that many final professional examinations are taken in two or more parts and the courses leading to parts beyond the first are treated as different courses rather than the continuation of the first; and that graduates in 'non-vocational' subjects who seek a professional qualification are unlikely to be full-time students. Table 2.3 (p.71) is therefore liable to mislead; indeed it is doubtful whether the different sources should be combined into totals. What it gives is an analysis by age of (1) university entrants *excluding* transfers between universities; (2) new OU undergraduates; and (3) AFE first-year students. The total of full-time students, 127,600, seems to be about 7000 in excess of 'initial entrants'. How far the number of part-time students, 90,000, exceeds the initial entrants is not known. But, faute de mieux, the table will have to serve for several purposes below.

The Robbins Principle and the Age Participation Rate
The Robbins Committee, in its report of 1963, assumed as an axiom that 'courses of higher education should be available for all those who are qualified by ability and attainment to pursue them and who wish to do so' (HE 1963, para. 31), and until 1980 governments have endorsed and acted upon this axiom as the primary factor in planning the provision of places in higher education. But the 'Robbins principle' is not of itself a formula which gives a target of places. It is notable for marking the rejection of manpower planning as the primary factor in favour of social (or free, or private) demand; but the distribution of places to different subjects has been influenced by manpower considerations, strongly in relation to doctors and school teachers, and less so, though still significantly, in relation to scientists and technologists. Furthermore, 'social demand is not the natural expression of preference by (mainly) young people. It is a function of the conditions created under which students are able to obtain academic qualifications — conditions which are determined by government policy' (R.M. Lindley, in *Fifth Report* pp.457-8), and is also influenced by the standard of the state's provision for higher education, most obviously in relation to maintenance grants, but also to physical amenities and teaching. Finally, the principle has been interpreted restrictively, in part under the influence of the Anderson Committee's formulation of the regulations for mandatory maintenance grants, as applying in the main to people aged under 21 with at least two 'A' level passes (or three Scottish Highers).

Nevertheless, the Robbins principle did lead the committee to devise a means of projecting the future demand for (full-time) higher education from home students:

a   Look at the size of the age groups relevant to higher education
b   Estimate what proportions of these age groups are likely to reach the level of attainment appropriate for entry
c   Make assumptions on how many of those so qualified will enter;

how many will try to enter higher education (the application rate); and what proportion of applicants with given attainments should be given places (the degree of competition)

d   Decide on assumptions about the future length of study

As regards c, Robbins did not have adequate information on applicants and resorted to the result of the interaction of the two variables, namely the proportion of all school-leavers with given qualifications who had entered higher education, and postulated increases over time in that proportion.

The Department of Education and Science has used this method, with a number of modifications, both to monitor actual numbers and to produce projections. The aggregates used are: population in the relevant age group; number staying on after the minimum school-leaving age; number achieving two or more 'A' levels (or three or more Highers) at school or FE colleges ('qualified leavers'); young home entrants (aged under 21 years), mature home students (aged 21 years and over), and overseas entrants, the sum of these three being 'total initial entrants'. The effective length of stay converts entrants to total numbers. In recent years, postgraduates have normally been projected through a separate flow model, rather than through the length of stay of initial entrants (DES 1978, App. II; CUA 1977, pp.37-38). The key ratios used relate to the majority group, namely young home entrants, and are:

1   The Qualified Leaver Rate (QLR)
$$= \frac{\text{Qualified leavers}}{\text{Single relevant age group (18-year-old)}} = \frac{\text{APR}}{\text{QPR}}$$

2   The Qualified Participation Rate (sometimes called the Opporunity or Willingness Rate) (QPR) $= \dfrac{\text{Young home initial entrants}}{\text{Qualified leavers}}$

3   The Age Participation Rate (APR)
$$= \frac{\text{Young home initial entrants}}{\text{Single relevant age group (18-year-old)}}$$

These rates can, with the relevant data, be calculated historically and extrapolated into the future for each sex, for various levels of qualification (eg two 'A' levels, scores greater than nine on three 'A' levels), for countries, and for sectors of higher education. The published projections of young entrants were probably built up from several subsidiary projections. To these were added projections, on necessarily different methodologies, for mature home entrants, overseas entrants, and, if not already included, postgraduate students.

YOUNG HOME FULL-TIME ENTRANTS
Full-time students who entered higher education when aged under 21 comprised two-thirds of the FTE home student load in Table 2.2, (p.70) so the longest section of this chapter is devoted to them. Table 2.4 gives the

various ratios defined in the preceding section.

Between 1960 and 1970, the Age Participation Rate for young home entrants doubled, roughly from 7 per cent to 14 per cent. It peaked at 14.2 per cent in 1971, but fell to 12.4 per cent in 1978 and remained steady for three years. The Qualified Participation Rate was as high as 103 per cent in 1967-69 but fell thereafter to 82 per cent in 1978, rising by only one or two per cent since then. But the APR (and the corresponding QPR) thus presented are not firm evidence of a declining interest of 18- to 20-year-olds in entry to higher education. In the QPR's formula, the numerator includes young home entrants who, neither in the given year nor any other year, are included in the denominator, because they have less than two 'A' levels and so are not 'qualified leavers' (hence why the QPR has exceeded 100). This would not matter if their number were small and their proportion were consistent, but until the mid-1970s many entrants to teacher training in England and Wales were 'unqualifed' in this sense. Indeed, they comprised 15-16 per cent of all young entrants in the late 1960s. But the contraction of teacher training and then the raising of the normal entry requirements to two 'A' levels reduced their number to zero in 1980. Recently published APR's excluding such entrants show a much smaller drop during the 1970s, from 12.3 per cent in 1972 to no lower than 12.0 per cent with recovery to 12.5 per cent in 1980. The QPR on this basis went no higher than 88 per cent in 1969, and no lower than 80 per cent in 1978. If the figures were amended further in recognition that 'unqualified' entrants have been progressively excluded from other courses (professional courses, for example) the ratios might show negligible or no clear decline, only a plateau. Even so, a static participation rate is contrary to educationalists' predictions: the working assumption for the past generation has been of continually rising demand for education, at least until it reached the level already achieved in other advanced countries. The reasons for this levelling off in admissions (and by implication in demand) must be a major concern of this paper. But it is important not to be blinded by the contrast of 1962-72 against 1972-80, for the earliest period stands in contrast to the years before: the APR was stagnant in the late 1950s and early 60s. By looking at participation rates for the 50 years from 1922 to 1972, Williams (1974) has detected a series of 10- to 12-year cycles in the long-term trend rate of growth, with a down-swing of about 4 to 6 years being followed by an up-swing of 5 to 8 years. The current down-swing has already lasted longer than the previous ones and can be expected to continue for several years, but we do not yet know whether it is a minor departure from the long-term trend (with growth being resumed in due course) or whether it marks a fundamental break with the past.

The following paragraphs look at trends in the main factors used in the DES's projections: size of age groups; staying-on at school; and qualified leavers and their destinations.

Size of the Age Group
The number of people aged between 17 and 20 — normally represented by the number of 18-year-olds — is usually held as relevant to the size of the intake to higher education rather than to the participation rate. Nevertheless, it is noticeable that the APR increased most rapidly in the years when the 18-year-old group fell in size from a peak in 1965 to a trough in 1972. It is tempting to suggest that reduced competition afforded more students their first preference as to subject or institution, and induced more to enter higher education. But as the QPR also fell, this argument cannot be sustained: a rising population of qualified leavers was the dominant factor in pushing up the APR rate. There does seem, though, to be some association between the size of the age group and the proportion staying on at school: this is mentioned below. What is in no doubt is that the 18-year-old age group peaks in 1982 and will fall over 13 years by 34 per cent rising again only in 1996. This compares with the fall of only 17 per cent over eight years from the 1965 peak to the 1972 trough. Its long duration reflects the decline in fertility between 1965 and 1977, but 'there are good grounds . . . for assuming higher average fertility in the longer term than experienced over recent years' and OPCS's current projections imply an increase of some 40 per cent in the 18-year-old group from 1996 to 2009 (OPCS 1980; *OPCS Monitor*, 1980 Population Projections 80/1).

Staying on at School
Full-time schooling is compulsory until the age of 16 (15 between 1947 and 1972). Entry to higher education lies, in England and Wales, at least two years beyond the minimum leaving age. As for most people formal education, certainly as a full-time activity, is continuous from the age of five until entry to employment (or is interrupted only for short periods while entry to the next stage of education is sought), the number and proportion of school children who elect to stay in education after the school year in which they reach the age of 16 is at present a, perhaps the, major determinant of the number of entrants to higher education. Indeed, Williams and Gordon (1975) concluded that 'in general, the decision about going on to higher education at 18 appears very much a subsidiary of the earlier decision at 16, despite the fact that staying on (after 18) means a change of institution.' They found, as have many other researchers, that family background had a significant influence on subsequent educational intentions at age 16, but not at age 18 (this point is considered further in the section below on 'social class).

The point at which to start, though, is the numbers who achieve the traditional prerequisite for entry to 'A' level courses in the sixth form, namely five passes at 'O' level: 97 per cent in 1968 and 94 per cent in 1977 of school-leavers with two or more 'A' level passes also had at least five passes at 'O' level or CSE grade 1 (SE 1968, Vol, 2, Table 10; 1977, 2, Table 6). Since the raising of the school leaving age in 1972, it has not been necessary to stay beyond the minimum leaving age to sit 'O' levels. The percentage of the age group who gain five or more 'O' levels in or before the fifth year of secondary schooling is not published, but Table 2.5 (p.73) gives the percentage so qualified by the date of their leaving and is probably a sound guide to what has happened in the fifth form. Overall, the proportion leaving with five or more 'O' levels rose from 15.3 per cent in 1960/61 to 22.1 per cent in 1970/71, but thereafter moved up more slowly, only to 23.7 per cent in 1976/77 and no further by 1978/79. In addition more of those so qualifying have left school before entering the sixth form. In terms of Table 2.5(A) (England and Wales), those leavers aged 15 to 16 were 23.8 per cent of all qualified leavers in their cohort in 1968/69 and 25.3 per cent in 1974/75; in terms of Table 2.5(C) (England only), those leavers were 19.0 per cent in 1974/75 and 22.4 per cent in 1976/77. At most only a quarter of them in 1977 left to take full-time 'A' level courses at FE colleges (SE 1977, Vol. 2, Table 1).

The 17-year-olds at December/January in any academic year embrace most of those who are in the second year of a 'A' level course in school or further education and may qualify for higher education. Table 2.6 (p.74) gives the percentages of that age group in various forms of education up to 1976/77, and Table 2.7 (p.75) gives more recent figures for the 16-18 year-olds. The proportion still in school rose continuously for 26 years from 1946/47, passed 12.5 per cent in 1962/63 and peaked at 20.8 per cent in 1972/73; it dropped slightly for three years and has since held steady at around 21 per cent. Full-time attendance at FE colleges (which include the few tertiary colleges) continued to rise — though possibly because of a shift from part-time study (which is falling) rather than from school. Indeed, the increase in 16-18 year-olds on full-time NAFE courses has, at least since 1973/74, been on the non-GCE courses which in that year catered for 4.7 per cent of those age groups and 7.0 per cent in 1978/79: the proportion on full-time 'A' levels in both schools and FE colleges moved from 15.5 to only 16.0 per cent over the same period (Table 2.7).

Qualified Leavers
Hence it is no surprise that the proportion of the relevant age group gaining two or more 'A' level passes doubled during the 1960s from 6.9 per cent in 1960/61 to 13.9 per cent in 1970/71, was steady for the next four years, rose to 14.8 per cent in 1976/77 (Table 2.8(A) p.76) and remained constant for at least three years (Table 2.8(C)). The Qualified Leaver Rate, QLR, is a measure of the same phenomenon for Great Britain, the figures for the same years as above being 6.6, 14.2 and 15.2, followed by 15.0 for 1979/80 (sources as for Table 2.4, p.72). The proportion of those qualifying who did so at FE colleges also doubled in the 1960s and continued to rise until 1977/78.

If we look at the destination of the school-leavers with two or more 'A' levels, we find that a growing proportion of them has been entering employment rather than full-time further or higher education. In 1967, 21 per cent did so; and ten years later, 29 per cent (Table 2.9, p.77). The trend has been even more marked among the leavers with 'good' certificates, that is, with at least grades CCC or the equivalent: the proportion entering employment rose over the same period by two-thirds, from 9 to 15 per cent. These figures include leavers intending to re-enter full-time education thirteen or more months later, but some of that growing number do not take up the places held over for them and in fact enter permanent employment; anyway, the picture is basically the same if they are excluded.

Discussion
On the evidence so far presented, three main trends can be seen behind the declining proportion of the age group entering full-time higher education since 1972: first, the proportion of the age group who, during compulsory secondary schooling, achieve the normal qualification for 'A' level courses has levelled off; secondly, the proportion of those who stay on and pass two or more 'A' levels but who leave for employment rather than remain in full-time education has risen; and thirdly, young people with less than two 'A' level passes have had their opportunity of entry to higher education diminished. The last arises directly from the curtailment of teacher training and the raising of the entry standards to those and other courses. The Robbins Committee assumed that the proportion of school-leavers entering higher education with each level of GCE qualification from five 'O' level passes upwards would rise to the same degree (HE 1963, App. I, p.132). As the Committee did not expect much change in the proportion of those with five or more 'O' levels who went on to gain 'A' levels, its projections implied a roughly stable distribution of entrants from schools with each level of qualification (p.108). By 1970 the DES seems to have abandoned this aim: as teacher training contracted it did not expect places for all the 'displaced' school-leavers with less than two 'A' levels to be provided elsewhere in higher education. On the projection published at the time, the proportion of school-leavers with one 'A' level who entered higher education would drop from 48 per cent in 1967/68 to 35 per cent in 1976/77, and with five or more 'O' levels from 10 per cent to 5 per cent (DES 1970, p.7 and Table A). What exactly has happened to these leavers cannot be detected with any accuracy from the published statistics.

Three lines of explanation for the other two trends will be discussed: first, policies and practices in secondary schooling; secondly, the competing attractions of employment; and thirdly, whether the gap has widened between what qualified leavers may be seeking in higher education and what is available.

In looking at secondary schooling we may start by reverting to the effect of the size of the age group. Halsey et al. (1980, p.119) have noted, for 1945 to 1970, a marked inverse correlation between the total number of male school-leavers and the proportion who stayed on until at least the age of 16.

What this may indicate is that teachers seek to deter marginal candidates from continuing their education when the cohort gets larger and encourage them to continue when it shrinks. The relationship is less in evidence for 17-year-olds, perhaps because most of these are in the second year of the sixth form and the marginal candidates are likely to be those who are only retainable for one year. Even so, though the proportion of 17-year-olds in school rose steadily right through the large age groups of the mid-1960s, its levelling off has roughly co-incided with the trough of 1969-70 and the renewed rise in the age group's size (Table 2.6, p.74). A similar effect might be expected in the proportion gaining five or more 'O' levels. Even though the fifth year of secondary schooling is compulsory, the staff in a comprehensive school may well not expand the 'O' level stream in proportion to the greater size of the cohort; certainly in a bipartite system the grammar school places are likely to be effectively a constant number irrespective of the short-term fluctuations in the age group. Indeed, the proportions of leavers with 'O' levels inscribe a line parallel to that for staying on (Table 2.5, p.73).

It would be reasonable to expect the raising of the school-leaving age in 1973 to increase the proportion gaining good 'O' level certificates and staying on beyond the minimum age, because the point of decision is now delayed until after the first public examinations. In fact the aggregate statistics show no appreciable increase, nor are there any special studies suggesting that the 'O' level and staying-on rates might have been lower but for the leaving age being raised.

The major structural change in secondary schooling in the past fifteen years has been its reorganization on comprehensive lines. The consequences for higher education are discussed in Gordon's chapter in this volume. Suffice it here to say that reorganization was expected to increase demand for higher education, particularly by working-class children (eg Neave 1975, p.17); that as yet there is no conclusive evidence of this happening; and that the co-incidence of reorganization and the levelling-off in staying-on, etc., has given rise to the argument (by the present Secretary of State for Education, for example) that the former is responsible for the latter (*Fifth Report*, p.528).

The competing attractions of employment as against continued education have been examined statistically by Pissarides (1981a,b) who has presented regression analyses of 16-year-old staying-on rates and of qualified leaver rates against the initial earnings and the present value of lifetime earnings of manual workers, against unemployment rates for graduates, and against consumer expenditure. His conclusions are that the main reason for the slow-down in staying-on in 1969-72 was the increase in the ratio of youth manual earnings to new graduates' earnings, but that in 1975-78 the most important variable for boys was the decrease in real consumer expenditure and for girls was a fall in the relative demand for qualified women; and that the same factors in general serve to explain the reduced demand for higher education two years later. Some raw data on gross incomes are given in Table 2.10 (p.78), and show that between 1965 and 1980 for young people they rose by a factor of 7.5, for adult men in manual jobs by 5.9. for adult men in non-manual jobs by 5.5, for graduates on entering employment by 5.0, and for students (in the form of the maintenance grant) by 4.2. The acceleration of juvenile wages has in part come through trade union pressure to eliminate 'cheap labour'. The relative decline in graduates' starting salaries is presumably explicable by the great increase in the stock of highly qualified manpower. The number of such people available for work has been predicted to increase by 64 per cent between 1971 and 1981, but the number of jobs, of the kind held by them in 1971, to increase by only 31 per cent (Butler 1978). The resulting movement of graduates into new areas of employment has undoubtedly been faster in recent years, particularly into 'lower' grade jobs, with depression of average starting salaries. Gordon's chapter in this volume cites evidence of how 16-year-olds have clear (if not necessarily accurate) perceptions of the higher earnings associated with higher qualifications. Pissarides (1981a) concludes that rising registered unemployment has encouraged staying-on at school, but Gordon in this volume suggests that unemployment benefits and payments under (eg) the Youth Opportunities Programme can act as a positive incentive to leave.

The third explanation to be considered is whether the gap has widened between what qualified leavers may be seeking in higher education and what is available. In one form this question is the obverse of the question of whether reorganization in secondary schooling has contributed to the levelling off of the APR: has higher education failed to adapt itself sufficiently to the changes in the form and content of secondary schooling? Discussion of that question, which is explored by Fulton in Chapter 1, lies beyond the quantifying approach of this chapter, which will be confined to the more mundane question of whether entry has become easier or harder.

The 'degree of competition' over time can be measured only in terms of the 'A' level scores of successful applicants for, by and large, universities only. Over the last twelve years (Tables 2.11(A) and 2.13, pp.79 and 81), scores rose from 1968, dropped in 1974, and have recovered since then. For instance the proportion of 'A' level entrants with only two passes was down to 13.8 per cent in 1972, rose to 15.6 per cent in 1974, but fell back to 14.1 per cent in 1980, while those with scores of nine or more on three passes were 62.9, 58.4 and 61.7 per cent. Given that on average 'A' level entrants to universities have better grades than entrants to AFE (CUA 1978, p.17) and that the universities have in recent years taken a growing share of all new entrants to higher education (Table 2.11(B)), university entrants' grades might have been expected to fall. But as at the same time the 'O' level/one 'A' level entrant has been progressively excluded, the proportion of all home entrants with two or more 'A' levels has risen. Hence an assertion that entry has become more competitive (for qualified leavers) cannot be founded on this evidence. Indeed, an analysis as yet covering only the years 1977 and

1978, of the percentage of those who passed 'A' level in a given subject and were accepted for admission to university, showed that the percentages went up in most main subjects, and down in none, between the two years (Standing Conference on University Entrance, paper 80/14).

If overall it is not more difficult to enter higher education, are there mismatches between supply and demand by subjects and types of courses? The demand for subjects at degree level has its roots in the schools where important subject choices are made from age thirteen onwards affecting the courses in higher education for which a pupil will be qualified. The simplest indicator of changes in subject choice at school is trends in the distribution of 'A' level passes. The figures show the continuous decline in mathematics, physics and chemistry (together 43.7 per cent in 1960, and 29.0 per cent in 1977), of French, German and Latin (12.5 per cent and 7.2 per cent), and the rise of social science and vocational subjects (mainly accounting) (10.4 per cent and 25.5 per cent). The combination of 'A' levels passed by qualified school-leavers show that 50 per cent of male leavers in 1964 were science specialists but only 41 per cent in 1976. Over the same period, though, the proportion of boys passing both science and non-science subjects rose from 11 per cent to 21 per cent (Table 2.12(B), p.80). One of the significant points about the swing away from science is that a consistently larger proportion of science specialists enter higher education than do students taking other combinations of 'A' levels — in 1976, 73 per cent as against 55 per cent, with the students taking both science and non-science subjects tending to follow their non-science colleagues (Table 2.12(A)). The trend towards mixed 'A' levels may be one consequence of secondary school reorganization creating larger sixth forms offering more subjects (Neave 1975). Institutions may have failed, or been unwilling, to adapt their entry requirements and courses sufficiently, particularly in the science, to attract this new clientele.

The trends at 'A' level do not translate themselves directly into trends in subject choice at entry to higher education. The picture here is complicated by the appearance of subjects not studied at school, the various combinations of 'A' level subjects possible for entrance to a particular degree subject, and the supply of places. Nevertheless, most entrants probably embark on courses within the same broad subject field as their 'A' levels (SE 1977, Vol. 2, Table 14). Table 2.13 attempts to show whether it has become easier or harder to enter a given subject relative to all subjects. The 'competition factor' is the ratio of the percentage of three 'A' level entrants in the subject with a grade score of nine or more to this percentage for all subjects (CUA 1978, pp.32-35). Thus, for universities in 1980, the percentage was 72 per cent (= 1.0), for medicine and dentistry 88 per cent (competition factor, 1.23), and for engineering and technology 64 per cent (0.89).

The changes since 1968 in the rankings of the five groups of subjects which can be analysed are striking. Medicine and dentistry have moved up from 0.86 to 1.23, and social studies down from 1.14 to 1.02; arts was at 1.00 in 1968 and at 1.03 in 1980, but was leading the field in 1969-73 at about

1.15; engineering and technology has moved up from a low point of 0.77 in 1972, and science has been consistently between 0.91 and 0.95. The medical group has seen a radical transformation in its competitive position, and has widened the spread of the competition factors. But it admitted only 8 to 9 per cent of the 'A' level entrants to the five groups, and the spread of the factors across the other four groups (which take over 85 per cent of all three 'A' level entrants) has narrowed over the years, suggesting a better match of supply against demand. 'Competition factors' for entrants to CNAA first degree courses, available only for 1970-74, tended to move in sympathy with those for universities (CUA 1978, Table 20).

What the competition for the medical group reflects is the growing demand in the 1970s for entry to 'vocational' subjects, and what happens when the number of places is rigorously controlled by factors other than applicant demand. Table 2.14 (p.82) gives the competition factors for individual vocational subjects which can be identified in the UCCA statistics and also the extent to which home admissions rose over ten years. Apart from the medical subjects and architecture, all increased their intake more than the national average, and all became relatively more competitive. That they did so may be taken as further evidence of school-leavers' awareness of the labour market, though in some cases they must also reflect the rise in required qualifications for entry to the profession concerned. Nevertheless, aside from the medical subjects and law, the proportion of entrants with high scores on three 'A' levels was, even in 1980, below the overall figure. Meanwhile in AFE the provision in most of the same fields has expanded: in the five years to 1978/79 by 51 per cent in business studies, accountancy and law, and by 25 per cent in professional and vocational studies, when the total of full-time students fell by 7 per cent (*Fifth Report*, p.10).

The closing section offers some speculation as to how the various factors reviewed above may operate in the next few years to affect the Age Participation Rate. This section may conclude by emphasizing that no clear picture can be drawn from the available data of the flow of young people through education in the five or so years following the minimum leaving age, at least not in sufficient detail to make informed predictions about flows into higher education; and by hoping that the fourth follow-up of the National Child Development Study's 1958 cohort will be asking the appropriate questions.

MATURE FULL-TIME STUDENTS
Whereas entrants to higher education who are aged under 21 on 31 December following are, in official parlance, 'young', older entrants are 'mature'. The implicit assumption in the DES's method for projecting numbers is that the young entrants arrive on the wave running through the educational system from the schools and FE colleges, but that entrants who have passed the old age of majority are sufficiently distant from their compulsory and sixth-form education for them *not* to be viewed as delayed

entrants from their respective 18-year-old cohorts. With the increasing availability of 'A' level courses in FE colleges, this assumption that a student can only 'lose' two years without being detached from the main stream may be less sound than it was 10 to 15 years ago; indeed studies particularly concerned with mature students have taken 25 as the age limit (Whitburn et al. 1976, p.122; Wynne 1979). But we do not know, for instance, what proportions of mature entrants obtained the qualifications on which they are admitted when they were aged 16-19, or when they were no longer of school age, or are admitted without the normal qualifications. (A small sample of degree students in 1970-71 yielded proportions of roughly 50:35:15 (Hopper and Osborn 1975, pp.69-71). Some of these questions, and others alluded to below, may be answered by a DES-funded research project on 'mature student participation in education' which is in progress. The fact of the matter for the moment is that the DES tends to look at mature students as absolute numbers rather than proportions of age groups, and the same approach is adopted here. This section looks at the minority of full-time students who are mature and the following section at part-time students, of whom the majority are mature.

The Robbins Committee did not consider it necessary to distinguish between young and mature full-time entrants. It seems that in 1961/62 mature entrants numbered about 10,500, or 14 per cent of all home entrants, and presumably no increase in that proportion was anticipated (HE 1963, App. 1, Table C.3). By 1966/67 the number and proportion had risen to 17,700 and 16.5 per cent; both rose sharply in the next two years to 27,700 and 22.1 per cent; the proportion then remained fairly steady until the later 1970s when it moved up to 24 per cent in 1979-81, representing 35,200 students in 1980/81 (DES, SB12/80; 6/81). The increase in the 60s, until 1968, may be largely attributable to deliberate recruitment of older people into teacher training. Thereafter the increase has been mainly on other courses in the public sector and has more than compensated for the fall in teacher training admissions since 1972. The ratio of men to women has remained fairly constant at around 60:40, but Table 2.3 (p.71) suggests that the women are on average older than the men, the men:women ratios in the three age groups being: 21-24 years 69:31; 25-30 years 63:37; 30+ years 44:56.

The main explanation is presumably to be found in women returning to education after bringing up children, but a recent study in Sheffield has also found that women mature students tended to have drifted from school into dead-end temporary jobs which did not reflect their true ability and suggests that their under-representation in the 21-24 age group is for the same reason as for leaving school, namely insufficient motivation (Roderick 1981). Table 2.3 (p.71) also implies that the older the student is the more likely he is to be taking a vocational (non-degree) course. But the evidence on subjects studied is inconclusive. Students aged 25 and over in polytechnics in 1972/73, relative to students of all ages, were over-represented in the miscellaneous 'professional and vocational subjects', and under-represented in the humanities and art (Whitburn et al. 1976, p.191); but in the universities the mature students are concentrated in the social sciences and humanities (UCCA *Stat. Supp.*, Table B2).

No systematic explanation can be offered of why so many more mature students have embarked on full-time courses. Compared with 10 years ago, mandatory maintenance grants for them are more readily available and have become a little more generous relative to those for young entrants, and, at least until the last few years, local education authorities have used their discretionary power to make awards. But the economic argument that the rate of return on a degree has fallen must apply also to mature students. It may be that there has long been an unsatisfied demand, and that a crucial factor has been a more liberal attitude towards entrance requirements on the part of universities, colleges and the CNAA — an attitude perhaps in part induced by the unexpected stagnation in demand from school-leavers.

PART-TIME STUDENTS
At most there were 17,000 'young' entrants to part-time higher education in 1976/77 (compared with some 95,000 to full-time), giving an Age Participation Rate of about 2.3 per cent (Table 2.3, p.71). Only a small minority are likely to have been admitted on the strength of GCEs passed at school; the majority will have taken a non-advanced FE course (eg ONC or an intermediate professional examination) between leaving school and starting a higher education course. The part-time APR in 1961 was about 3.7 per cent (HE 1963, App. 1, p.39), so it has declined over 15 years by a third, compared with a doubling of the full-time APR (Table 2.4, p.72). The decline is in part because of the expansion in full-time places and in part because entry standards have been raised by professional institutions. For example, if an aspirant to the accountancy profession has to hold two 'A' level passes, he may as well take a full-time degree course in that or a related field as enter a training contract and a part-time professional course; and with the academic qualification for a chartered engineer raised to a degree it is doubtful whether part-time degree courses have expanded to compensate for the loss of the route through HNC.

The proportion of part-time students who are 'mature' has increased and now comprises the great majority : 81 per cent in terms of entrants (31 per cent aged 21-24, 23 per cent aged 25-29, and 27 per cent older), compared with 26 per cent of full-timers. Of part-timers entering universities, perhaps a third are on sub-degree courses in extra-mural departments, a third on degree courses at Birkbeck College London, and a third on degree courses elsewhere (unpublished USR statistics for 1978/79 show one-third to be overseas; this pattern is assumed not to be replicated elsewhere in part-time higher education!). At least a substantial minority on degree courses have higher education qualifications already, as graduates taking specialized degrees or changing their field of study or as qualified teachers seeking graduate status (Hopper & Osborn 1975, p.66; SE 1977, Vol. 6, Table 16). The same is probably true of the 3000 or so AFE part-timers in Table 2.3 (p.71) who were on degree courses, as nearly a third were on education courses (CNAA *Annual Report 1976*, Table G). It should be noted in passing that *in total* there were some 9000 UK residents registered as 'private' study students for external degrees of the University of London, half of them in law — a subject not yet offered by the Open University (Wynne 1979, pp.64, 67). But it is the Open University which now offers the main route to a degree by part-time study. Again, though, a large proportion already have higher education qualifications: of the 1977 entrants, 48 per cent did, mainly (27 per cent) a teacher's certificate or equivalent (OU 1980, Table A4.4). But the university's intake is much more heavily weighted towards the over 30s than that of the rest of part-time study.

Although the proportion of part-time students on first degree courses greatly increased during the 1970s, it was still only about a quarter in 1978/79 (postgraduates excluded; Table 2.2, p.70). The bulk of part-time work therefore remains the directly vocational courses in further education colleges for the HNC, BEC and TEC higher certificates and professional qualifications: indeed of the part-time first-year students in AFE in 1976/77 only 4 per cent were on degree courses (Table 2.3, p.71; *Fifth Report*, p.594). The number of students on such courses increased scarcely at all during the 1960s, but the ratio of day to evening attendance moved from 50:50 to 67:33, representing a substantial increase in student hours and throughput. Evening numbers have remained fairly constant, and the sizeable increase (on all AFE courses from 108,000 in 1972/73 to 156,000 in 1980/81) has been almost wholly in day attendances (Table 2.1, p.69).

There have been striking changes in the distribution of these part-time students between subjects and by sex, almost as striking as the changes among full-timers induced by the cuts in teacher training. These are shown by Table 2.15 (p.83) (which also covers degree and postgraduate students). The proportion of women rose from 8.1 per cent in 1967/68 to 18.3 per cent in 1977/78. Engineering and technology dropped from having 45 per cent of the enrolments to 28 per cent, though the last two years have seen a marked recovery to 33 per cent — representing a numerical increase from 34,000 in 1972/73 to 47,000 in 1980/81. Social, administrative and business studies, on the other hand, moved from 32 per cent in 1967/68 to 50 per cent ten years later, peaked in absolute numbers in 1979/80 and have dropped in 1980/81 to 45 per cent. The swing away from engineering was in part a reflection of women's increased participation but must also have reflected the pattern of recruitment into employment with the rapid growth of the service sector.

WOMEN
This brief section is largely a commentary on figures presented in preceding sections. Some of these figures are summarized in Table 2.16 (p.84), as the

ratio of women to 100 men, and this form of ratio is used below. As the ratios have been calculated from the tables, and as the data for the tables are often in themselves estimates, there may be fairly sizeable cumulative errors, so no significance should be placed on small differences between columns and lines in Table 2.16.

Since 1970 girls have been as likely as boys to leave school with five or more 'O' levels, having been slightly behind in the 1960s. Only in the last couple of years have they stayed at school until age 17 to the same extent as boys, but the narrowing of the gap has been considerable since 1960/61 when the ratio was only 78. The pattern of 17-year-old girls' attendance in non-advanced FE is very different from boys', because day release from employment is much less widely available, and for school and NAFE combined the ratio was 84 in 1976/77. Roughly the same ratio applied in that year to students gaining two or more 'A' levels, but had been as low as 59 in 1960/61. Girls are more likely than boys to get only two 'A' levels: the ratios for those gaining three or more 'A' levels were 75 and 49 in the same two years.

At the point of entry to higher education the picture is more complicated. The ratio was 79 in both 1966/67 (the earliest year for which figures are published) and 1980/81, but was higher and lower in between, because of the expansion and contraction of teacher training. The bulk of entrants to teacher training with less than two 'A' levels were women (3.2 per cent of the age group, compared with 1 per cent for men, around 1970, in terms of Table 2.4 (p.72). If these entrants are excluded, that ratio shows a consistently upward progression, from 62 in 1966/67 to 79 in 1980/81. The rising proportion of sixth-formers who are girls, combined with their historic dearth among 'A' level candidates in the sciences, must be a partial explanation for the shift in the 'A' level leavers away from the sciences — and towards the 'A' level specialization from which progression to higher education is less usual (Table 2.12, p.80). If, in 1976/77, the number of male and female qualified school-leavers had been the same and the progression rates for each specialization had applied to each sex separately, 6 per cent more boys than girls would have entered higher education, giving a ratio of 95. Hence the fall in the Qualified Participation Rate may be partly due to the increased proportion of women among the qualified leavers.

As to the question whether the five 'O' or one 'A' level leaver who in earlier years would have gone into teacher training has found another route into higher education, no firm answer can be given. The marked increase in the APR for women in 1980/81 may indicate a further narrowing of the gap between men and women among qualified leavers, while the growing female participation in NAFE (particularly full-time) may indicate that the less well qualified will come (or are coming) into higher education via an intermediate course.

With regard to women among mature and part-time students in higher education, the ratios are much less favourable. They stood, in 1976/77, at only 64 for full-time entrants aged 21 and over and at a mere 28 for all part-time entrants (Table 2.3, p.71). Nevertheless, there has been a major improvement in part-time enrolments in AFE, from 9 in 1967/68 to 23 ten years later (Table 2.15, p.83).

SOCIAL CLASS

Classifying students by social class usually entails no more than grouping them by their parents' occupation, and does not explain why those from one class should be in a better position to benefit from formal education than those from another. 'Far more important are those attitudes, home environment, parental expectation, membership of anti-school peer groups and subcultures which, whilst themselves highly correlated with social class, are nevertheless present in each and every social grouping, albeit in varying degrees' (Neave 1976, p.77). Nevertheless, social class is a convenient shorthand.

It has been repeatedly shown that, for young people of equal ability, the likelihood of continuing in full-time education after the minimum school-leaving age diminishes the lower the social class of their parents (see Gordon's chapter in this volume for references). A recent study covering men born between 1913 and 1952 shows that since the 1944 Education Act the disparity between classes in staying-on at school has narrowed, though remains wide (Halsey et al. 1980, Tables 8.10, 8.11). In 1975-76 a young person aged between 16 and 19 was four times more likely to be in full-time education if the father was in a professional occupation rather than in unskilled manual work; for someone aged 20-24, the disparity was twelvefold (OPCS 1978, Table 7.3).

Most evidence on the social class composition of higher education is presented in terms of a percentage distribution across the Registrar General's classes:

I	Professional, etc., occupations	
II	Intermediate occupations	hereafter 'middle class'
IIIN	Skilled occupations — non manual	
IIIM	Skilled occupations — manual	
IV	Partly skilled occupations	hereafter 'working class'
V	Unskilled occupations	
N/C	Not classified (incl. armed forces)	

Comparisons over time should (but do not) take account of the changes in the distribution of the whole population (eg of fathers of 18-year-olds), which have been away from the working and towards the middle class, and of changes in the allocation of occupations to classes.

Table 2.17 (p.85) brings together percentage distributions from several soruces of varying reliability, so not too much significance should be placed on small differences, especially in view of the range of proportions 'not classified'. Nevertheless, the following deductions can be made with respect to full-time students. First, the representation of the classes among pupils staying in full-time education after the minimum leaving age to take 'A' levels is already unequal, in part reflecting the fact that middle-class children are twice as likely as working-class to get five or more 'O' levels in the fifth form (Gordon 1980, Table II). Similar distributions are found among full-time 'A' level students in both schools and FE colleges, so the latter are not offering an alternative route particularly for working-class children. Children from classes I and II comprise about 24 per cent of their age group, but take about 60 per cent of the places on 'A' level courses; class IIIN is roughly in balance at 10 and 12 per cent, but in IIIM the balance is clearly the other way, with 38 per cent of the age group having only 18 per cent of the places, and even more so in IV and V, at 23 and 8 per cent. Secondly, the social composition of the university intake has scarcely changed over 25 years, even though by the later years the universities had been augmented by new foundations and by the ex-CATs. Indeed, figures for the last few years suggest that the proportion of entrants from classes I and II is increasing (UCCA *Stat. Supp. 1978-79*, Table E5). Thirdly, the FE and teacher training colleges' profiles in 1961/62 were less weighted than the universities' towards class I and II. Thus for working-class men the proportions were: universities 26; full-time AFE about 38; teacher training 47. But the figures for polytechnic students in 1972/73 suggest a marked shift in AFE towards the middle class. Fourthly, older students in universities are only marginally drawn more from classes IV and V.

Part-time students are drawn much less from classes I and II, generally around 30 per cent against 50 per cent for full-timers, with class IIIM being better represented, at 35-50 per cent against approximately 23 per cent, and IV and V at 16-20 per cent against approximately 9 per cent. But if the *present* occupations of mature part-time students are analysed, these are found to conform more closely to the distribution for full-timers' fathers, even exceeding, at 82 per cent for the Open University, the highest recorded proportion for universities from classes I and II, namely 71 per cent for women entrants in 1955. What this reflects, of course, is the large number of part-time students who are improving qualifications which they have already gained in higher education and are using in employment. Presumably if these students could be extracted, the figures for 'initial entrants' would be more heavily weighted towards the working class.

Age Participation Rates by social class are harder to come by, but Table 2.18 (p.86) gives estimates for c.1961 and c.1977. These suggest that for the middle class the APR rose from 19.5 to 26.9 per cent, and for the working class from 3.2 to 5.0 per cent, and that therefore the 'disparity ratio' narrowed only slightly, from 6.1 to 5.4, during the massive expansion of higher education in the 1960s and 70s.

Two hypotheses about the effect of these wide differentials on the future trend of numbers in higher education need to be considered:

1   That a rising proportion of all children are being born into middle-class families and that, other things being equal, the overall

participation rate will increase.

2   That the depressed participation rates for children of given ability from the lower classes compared with the higher show there to be much untapped talent which, through appropriate educational policies, can be reached by higher education.

The first hypothesis is based on the occupation of the father as reported at the registration of legitimate live births. Between 1970 and 1978, births to classes I and II *rose* by 1.3 per cent and to the other classes *fell* substantially; class IIIN by 28.3 per cent, IIIM by 32.8 per cent, IV and V by 33.5 per cent. Although many caveats should be entered in interpreting these figures, the difference between classes I and II and the rest is so great that in the main it must be due to falling mean family size in classes III-V because of wider diffusion of efficient contraception (OPCS, *Birth statistics 1978* Series FM1, No. 5, Table 11.1). If the APRs by class for c.1977 are applied to the live births in 1970 and 1978, overall rates of 12.0 per cent and 13.8 per cent result, the latter meaning 9400 more entrants from the 1978 birth cohort, due to arrive in higher education in 1996. An increase of this size would not, on its own, compensate for the shortfall in young home entrants from the 1980/81 level caused by the decline in the total size of the age group. Assuming a stable 12 per cent APR, this decline would amount to approximately 36,000 new entrants (DES 1978, Table 5). Furthermore, the reduced proportion of births to working-class parents probably reflects a fall in average family size which, given the well-established link between early leaving and large families, may also increase demand for higher education.

The second hypothesis has found official expression in Model 'E' of the government's discussion paper of 1978, *Higher education into the 1990s*: 'there is also the possibility of taking positive steps as a matter of social policy to encourage participation by children of manual workers to approach more closely the level of participation by children of non-manual workers. . . . It is at least possible that participation by (the former) will by the 1990s be as much affected by the gathering impact of policies in the fields of housing, health and the social services generally as by educational policies' (DES 1978, para. 32).

The hypothesis is given theoretical form by Halsey et al. (1980) in terms of observed trends in boys staying on at school until age 16 or later but can be seen as applicable to later stages of post-compulsory education. They suggest that 'the numbers staying on will start off from a low base, will then increase more or less rapidly before finally levelling off as the "saturation level" is reached. This will give a curve shaped like an elongated "S". If we draw separate curves for each social-class, the service-class curve will reach saturation first and the working class last.' The authors' estimates of what the saturation levels would have been if the school-leaving age had not been raised are acknowledged to 'contain a considerable margin of error, but they do suggest that there would eventually have been a striking narrowing of class differentials. The most conservative estimates suggest that in another twenty or thirty years . . .' the differences between the service (professional/ managerial) and working classes would have narrowed from 47 per cent for the 1943-52 cohort to 20 per cent. These differences would imply that the threshold in terms of measured ability would be approximately the same for both service and working-class boys. Applying the same technique to staying on until 18 or later, they suggest that the three logistic curves are less well advanced, and that the eventual inequality will be greater than at age 16 — and even more so if lines were traced for higher education. Nevertheless, working-class participation in higher education would eventually lift off from the low base at which it still is. Halsey's study ends with boys who were aged 18 in 1970. Edwards and Roberts (1980a, b) take a less optimistic view of the diffusion of demand for higher education down the social scale. They argue that the escalation of enrolments between 1955 and 1970 resulted from the professional and managerial classes putting greater value upon higher education as an avenue for retaining social and economic status. Recruitment increased less rapidly in the 1970s in part because for some groups saturation level may have been reached. But among the rest, ie the majority, of the population no real perception of higher education's nature and possibility has developed, and recruitment, especially from classes IV and V, depends on the child receiving external encouragement and patronage.

There are indeed pieces of evidence and suggestive arguments to indicate how tenuous working-class participation in higher education is. The demise of the grammar schools may have removed a significant channel through which 'patronage' was bestowed (Neave 1976, p.35). The educational plans of the working-class 16-year-old are less likely to be realized. Replies given in 1974 can be converted into APRs comparable on Table 2.17 (p.85). Those who said they intended to go full-time to a university, polytechnic or college of education comprised 33.5 per cent of class I and II, 19.0 per cent of IIIN, 10.4 per cent of IIIM, and 8.0 per cent of IV and V. These compare with estimated actual rates of 29.1, 21.2, 5.6 and 4.1. The actual rates are close to intended rates for middle-class children but half the intended rates for working-class children (Fogelman 1979). Furthermore, it is highly plausible that in a period of rising unemployment the working-class child will be encouraged to leave school and to start earning, possibly to help the family budget.

A final piece of evidence requires rather longer exposition. In Scotland the proportion of university entrants from working-class homes declined by 6 per cent between 1962 and 1972, and by a further 1.3 per cent by 1976. The decline was confined to men and it was middle (non-manual) -class women who increased in proportion. The proportion of qualified leavers increased roughly equally among middle- and working-class pupils, but faster among women than men; and more of the women than men had most of their passes at SCE 'H' grade in non-science subjects. Middle-class pupils tended to pass more subjects at H grade, and at better grades, than working-class.

Furthermore, working-class pupils of each sex were more likely to have most of their passes in non-science subjects, and so to be competing for entry directly with the growing number of qualified women (Hutchison and McPherson 1976; also Neave and Cowper 1979, pp.19-20).

Given this Scottish evidence, the same processes can be inferred as at work throughout the British universities. First, in 1980, among university applicants offering 'A' levels, middle-class students got better scores (UCCA Stat. Supp. 1979/80, Table E7). Secondly, the figures for 1956 and 1980 in Table 2.19 (p.87) are in no precise way comparable, but are suggestive. The proportion of accepted candidates from working-class homes fell from 25 to 19 per cent, but the fall was concentrated among the men (27 to 20 per cent), the figure for women being roughly constant around 19 per cent. Women were 29 per cent of all accepted students at the earlier date and as many as 41 per cent at the later. The decline in working-class men was to the same degree in all faculties except medicine (where there was none), but their representation at both dates was greatest in science and technology, while overall the proportion of arts places rose. In terms of Halsey's model, the logistic curve for middle-class women has come into conflict with, and retarded the progress of, the curve for working-class men — but not necessarily other than temporarily.

REGIONAL VARIATIONS
Up to this point we have treated England and Wales as a single unit, but the pattern of admission to higher education is not uniform throughout. Table 2.20 (p.88) gives indices of Age Participation Rates by region. Three measures are used and a consistent picture emerges. If the regions are ranked by their participation rates, there is a clear break between higher-than-average rates in Wales, Scotland, Southern England, and the North West, and lower rates in the Midlands, East Anglia, the North, and Yorkshire and Humberside. These 'actual' rates may be compared with each region's predicted rate if the only reason for variation is the distribution of their population by social class. Among the English regions, the predicted rates accord fairly well with the actual rates, with two exceptions: the North West has better than expected performance by 10 per cent, while participation in East Anglia seems to be depressed by around 15 per cent. But as the predicted rates for Wales and Scotland are below the average, their actual rates are all the more notable. Wales was about 18 per cent above prediction. The Scottish figure can be directly confirmed: in 1976, the APR for young home entrants was 15.8 per cent, compared with 13.0 per cent for Great Britain as a whole (CUA 1978, p.65). This implies that the APR for England and Wales was 12.6 per cent and that therefore, if England and Wales' rate equalled 100, Scotland's stood at 125. If Table 2.20(E) is weighted for social class (see Table 2.20(F)), 37 per cent more Scots enter university education than would be expected on the basis of what happens in England and Wales. This much higher participation may well be in part

the result of a different educational system (in which transfer from secondary to higher education takes place a year earlier, and which has a broader upper-secondary curriculum). The performance of Wales and the North West is not explicable in such terms, and points, particularly in Wales's case, to the importance of general and political attitudes towards education.

These results are consistent with staying-on rates for 16 to 18-year-olds, in two respects. First, the straightforward percentages of those at school or on GCE or CSE courses full-time in FE colleges, column (B) of Table 2.20, show the same ranking as the higher education indices. Secondly, regression analysis on the proportion of household heads in non-manual occupations can explain 65 per cent of the variation between LEAs' participation rates. Although derived rates using the regression equation have not been published for regions, it seems from the rates for individual LEAs that the same 'over' and 'under' performances as noted above would be found (DES, SB 15/79).

CONCLUSION
This paper does not aspire to offer projections of future student numbers. Nevertheless it is appropriate to conclude by reviewing the last official projections which were guided by the Robbins principle and not premised on a rigid expenditure limit (DES 1978, 1979). For young home entrants these are best considered in terms of the ratios defined on p.46 above and recorded in Table 2.4 (p.72). The QLR was projected in 1978 to move from a base of 14.9 per cent for 1976/77 entrants, to 16.0 per cent for 1980/81 and 17.1 per cent in 1984/85; a year later these figures were revised down to 15.7 per cent and 16.4 per cent. The (provisional) actual rate for 1980/81 was only 15.0 per cent. The QPR, on the central projection in 1978, was to move from 87.9 per cent to 88.7 and 90.0 per cent. The revision of 1979 gives the values for the high, central and low variants in 1981/82 of 84.7 per cent, 82.6 and 79.7 per cent. The value for 1980/81 was 83.3 per cent. The APR, a function of the other two ratios, was given in 1978 for the three variants, as reaching 14.9, 14.0, and 13.3 per cent in 1980/81 — and rising to 21, 18 and 15 per cent in 1994/95. The values in 1979 for 1981/82 were 13.4, 13.1 and 12.6 per cent. Aside from the possible effect on 1981's intake of reductions in funds, the low variant looks the most accurate, as 1980/81's APR was 12.5 per cent.

What are now the prospects for the next few years? There is no sure sign of improvement in the proportion of the age group gaining five or more 'O' levels (Table 2.5(C) and (D), p.73), though possibly the fall in the age group's size, which has just begun to affect the 15/16-year-olds, may remove artificial restraints in access to 'O' level streams. The same applies to the proportions taking full-time 'A' level courses (Table 2.7, p.75), and the proportions gaining two or more 'A' levels; indeed the latter dropped between 1977/78 and 1978/79, particularly in FE colleges. But the reduction in 'O' level/one- 'A' level entrants may be near its end; the QPR excluding 'unqualified' teaching training entrants is the better guide for the future, and that, along with the APR, has recovered slightly in the last two years, especially for women. 'Catching up' of participation by women is of course a growth point, but they are concentrated in the specialisms with lower participation rates. The rising proportion of children born into social classes I and II is not recorded before the early 1970s, and may not have any effect on higher education before the end of the present decade. Many imponderables surround the competing claims of the labour market. The rise in juvenile earnings relative to adult cannot go on indefinitely (though maintenance grants could continue to trail). The number of 17 and 18-year-old school-leavers may soon drop in absolute terms, and their market value may rise if major commercial and public employers still want to recruit from among the better of them. On the other hand, perhaps over a longer period, the presence of graduates who of late years have entered occupations still mainly the preserve of sixth-form leavers will become more visible, as graduates and non-graduates compete for middle-level posts; and the major professions may push on towards an all-graduate entry (Wagner 1976). The progress of the national economy hangs over all these speculations. If a figure must be hazarded, it would be that the APR is unlikely to reach 14 per cent again before, say, 1986 or 1987: that is, not much above the low variant of 1978.

What will happen to mature full-time entrants is even more speculative. Continuation in the next 15 years of the last 15 years' doubling would allow the APR for 18-year-olds to remain at its present level without any reduction in the total size of the intake! A sluggish QPR for the past decade means that the proportion of 'qualified' non-graduates in successive cohorts of 21/22-year-olds has not dropped; but whether many of these people will feel the competition of graduates in their jobs sufficiently to take a full-time course is questionable. Rather the Open University suggests that the demand may be for part-time higher education, of more diverse forms. A great deal of part-time work is what may be called 'second-bite' rather than 'second-chance' higher education, because the entrants already have an advanced qualification. As professions become all graduate (eg engineering and teaching), the demand for topping up to first degree level may drop and be replaced by demand for post-experience professional education — which in its present form (probably) falls outside the statistics used in this paper. Hence a modest rate of increase in mature full-time students and, up to first degree level from the later 1980s, a steady number of part-time students are perhaps plausible projections.

Altogether, within the limits of policy initiatives likely to be taken by either the present government or its successor, there is little prospect of averting a decline in the total size of the higher education system by 1990.

ACKNOWLEDGEMENTS
My main debt is to my fellow members of the CUA Group on Forecasting and University Expansion (CUA 1977, 1978); they will recognize where I

have plundered their ideas. The Department of Education and Science (Statistics Branch), the Open University, the University of Leeds Careers Service, the Universities Statistical Record, and the Universities Central Council for Admissions have kindly provided unpublished data. Discussions with colleagues at the University of Sussex and at Brighton Polytechnic have been most helpful, and my long-suffering secretary, June Brinkley, has transformed my manuscript into legible form.

REFERENCES
Butler, R. (1978) *Employment of the Highly Qualified 1971-1986* Research Paper No. 3 London: Department of Employment
Catto, G., Goodchild, A., and Hughes, P. (1981) *Higher Education and the Employment of Graduates* Research Paper No. 19 London: Department of Employment
Conference of University Administrators (CUA) (1977) Group on Forecasting and University Expansion *Interim Report 1977* Glasgow: CUA
Conference of University Administrators (CUA) (1978) Group on Forecasting and University Expansion *Final Report 1978* Norwich: CUA
Council for National Academic Awards (CNAA) *Annual Report* London: CNAA
Department of Education and Science (DES) (1970) *Student Numbers in Higher Education in England and Wales* Education Planning Paper 2. London: HMSO
Department of Education and Science (DES) and Scottish Education Department (1978) *Higher Education into the 1990s* London: DES
Department of Education and Science (DES) (1979) *Future Trends in Higher Education* London: DES
Department of Education and Science (DES) (1981) *Education for 16-19 year olds* London: DES
Department of Education and Science (DES) (various dates) *Statistical Bulletin* (SB) London: DES
Edwards, E.G. and Roberts, I.J. (1980a) British higher education: long term trends in student enrolment *Higher Education Review* 12 (2) 7-43
Edwards, E.G. and Roberts, I.J. (1980b) Significance and limitations of the Robbins principle. In Billing, D. (Editor) *Indicators of Performance* Guildford: SRHE
Fifth report (1980) House of Commons *Fifth Report from the Education, Science and Arts Committee, session 1979-80. The Funding and Organisation of Courses in Higher Education* HC 787. London: HMSO
Fogelman, K. (1979) Educational and career aspirations of sixteen year-olds *British Journal of Guidance and Counselling* 6 (1) 42-56
Gordon, Alan (1980) Leaving school: a question of money? *Educational Studies* 6 (1) 43-54
Halsey, A.H., Heath, A.F. and Ridge, J.M. (1980) *Origins and Destinations. Family, Class, and Education in Modern Britain* Oxford:

Clarendon Press
HE (1963) Committee on Higher Education (Chairman, Lord Robbins) *Higher Education Report* and *Appendices* Cmnd. 2154. London: HMSO
Hopper, E. and Osborn, M. (1975) *Adult Students. Education, Selection and Social Control* London: Francis Pinter
Hutchison, D. and McPherson, A.F. (1976) Competing inequalities: the sex and social class structure of the first year Scottish university population 1962-1972 *Sociology* 10 (1) 111-116
Kelsall, R.K. (1957) *Report on an Inquiry into Applications for Admission to Universities* London: AUBC
McIntosh, N.E., Calder, J.A. and Swift, B. (1976) *A Degree of Difference. A Study of the First Year's Intake to the Open University of the United Kingdom* Guildford: SRHE
McIntosh, N.E.S., Woodley, A. and Griffiths, M. (1978) Access to higher education in England and Wales. In Pike, R.S., McIntosh, N.E.S. and Dahllof, U. *Innovation in Access to Higher Education* Access to Higher Education no. 5, 147-245. New York: International Council for Educational Development
Neave, G.R. (1975) *How They Fared. The Impact of the Comprehensive School Upon the University* London: Routledge and Kegan Paul
Neave, Guy (1976) *Patterns of Equality. The Influence of New Structures in European Higher Education upon the Equality of Educational Opportunity* Windsor: NFER
Neave, Guy and Cowper, Henry (1979) Higher education in Scotland *European Journal of Education* 14 (1) 7-24
Office of Population Censuses and Surveys (OPCS) (1978) *General Household Survey 1976* London: HMSO
Office of Population Censuses and Surveys (1980) *Population Projections 1978-2018* Series PP2, No. 10 (1980). London: OPCS
Open University (OU) (1980) *Digest of Statistics 1* Milton Keynes: Open University Press
Pissarides, C.A. (1981a) *Staying-on at School in England and Wales* Centre for Labour Economics, London School of Economics, Discussion Paper No. 63 (revised); forthcoming in *Economica*
Pissarides, C.A. (1981b) *From School to University: the Demand for Post-Compulsory Education in Britain* Centre for Labour Economics, London School of Economics, Discussion Paper No. 70 (revised)
Roderick, Gordon (1981) *Analysis of the Demand for University Programmes among Adults and Methods for Market Development* Paper for OECD/IMHE Special Topic Workshop, Paris
SE Department of Education & Science (annually) *Statistics of Education* Volumes 1-6 London: HMSO
Scottish Education Department (SED) *Statistical Bulletin* (SB) Edinburgh, SED

68   ACCESS TO HIGHER EDUCATION

Universities Central Council on Admissions (UCCA) *Annual Report and Statistical Supplement* (annual) Cheltenham: UCCA

Wagner, L. (1976) The Open University and the demand for higher education *Teaching at a Distance* 7, 23-27

Whitburn, J., Mealing, M. and Cox, C. (1976) *People in Polytechnics* Guildford: SRHE

Williams, G. (1974) *Higher Education and the Stable State* Inaugural lecture, University of Lancaster (mimeo)

Williams, G. and Gordon, A. (1975) 16 and 18 year olds: attitudes to education *Higher Education Bulletin* 4 (1) 23-37

Wynne, R. (1979) *The Adult Student and British Higher Education* Amsterdam: Institute of Education of the European Cultural Foundation

TABLE 2.1
Full-time and sandwich home (FT) and part-time (PT) students in higher education 1962/63-1980/81: Great Britain (Thousands)

	Universities				Public sector advanced further education						Open University		TOTALS		
	FT		PT		FT			PT[2]			PT				
	E & W	Scot.	E & W	Scot.	E & W Teacher training	Other	Scot.	E & W Day	Even.	Scot.	E & W	Scot.	FT	PT	FTE[1]
1962/63	87	19	8		47	33	4	50	50	7	–	–	190	115	221
1967/68	155	30	15	3	97	59	16	68	46	10	–	–	357	142	399
1972/73	182	36	20	3	116	86	25	71	37	9	34	3	444	177	501
1974/75	186	37	21	3	108	91	26	80	36	12	48	5	447	205	514
1976/77	200	38	23	3	85	110	26	88	37	13	54	5	460	223	534
1978/79	215	39	24	4	45	128	23	108	40	14	63	6	450	259	536
1980/81	246	40			201 }		156 }						467		

[1] Full-time equivalent, based on: FT and sandwich = 1.0, PT in universities = 0.5, Open University and public sector PT (day) = 0.35, (evenings) = 0.15.

[2] England and Wales figures are course enrolments, so include 2% to 3% double counting.

Source
Based on *Fifth Report*, pp.5-9, except Open University (finally registered u/g, p/g, associate students) from OU 1980. Further detail from HE (1963) App. 1, Tables Z9, Z10 and App.2(A), Tables 28, 53; SE (1977) 6, Tables 3, 13; DES, SB2/81, SB6/81; SED, SB2/H1/1981.

TABLE 2.2
Full-time and sandwich home and part-time students pursuing courses in higher education: by sector, course and mode 1978/79: England and Wales (Thousands)

	Full-time and sandwich[1]	Part-time (day/ heavier loading)	Part-time (evening/ lighter loading)	Total	FTE[2]
1 Universities (UGC list)					
Undergraduate level	185.6	3.1		188.7	187.2
Postgraduate level	27.7	21.4		49.1	38.4
(Total)	(213.3)	(24.5)		(237.8)	(225.6)
2 Advanced Further Education[3]					
First degree	76.9	5.9	2.2	85.0	79.3
Teacher training including BEd	38.5	0.7	0.3	39.5	38.8
HND/C, BEC, TEC	21.3	37.5	4.3	63.1	35.1
Professional qual.	14.1	41.6	20.2	75.9	31.7
Other[4]	11.4	8.5	4.2	24.1	15.0
Postgraduate[5]	10.6	13.7	8.9	33.2	16.7
(Total)	(172.8)	(107.9)	(40.1)	(320.8)	(216.6)
3 Open University					
Undergraduate		54.4		54.4	19.0
Postgraduate	0.1	0.5		0.6	0.3
Associate			7.9	7.9	1.2
TOTAL	386.2	187.3	48.0	621.5	462.7

[1]Generally confined to courses of at least 18 weeks' duration: shorter full-time courses counted as part-time.

[2]FTE conversion factors as in Table 2.1.

[3]Course enrolments. PT numbers therefore include some double counting of students enrolled for more than one course.

[4]May include some postgraduate courses.

[5]Including all in-service teacher training.

Source
1 Estimated from DES, SB 6/81 and SED, SB 2/H1/1981.
2 SE (1978) 3, Tables 11, 16 (pre-publication).
3 OU (1980) Tables A14.1, C3.1, D.2.1.

TABLE 2.3
Home entrants to (first-year students in) higher education: by age (at 31 Dec. 1976), sex, mode of study, and sector 1976/77: England and Wales (Thousands, row percentages in italics)

		Full-time				Part-time				Total
		Univ.	AFE			Univ.	AFE		Open Univ.	
			Teacher quals.	Other degree	Other quals.		day	evening		
20 & under	Male	33.0	2.7	11.4	8.5	–	11.3	2.1	–	68.9
		47.8	*3.9*	*16.5*	*12.3*	*–*	*16.4*	*3.0*	*–*	*100*
	Female	18.6	10.2	6.2	4.3	0.1	3.0	0.5	–	42.9
		43.4	*23.7*	*14.5*	*10.0*	*0.2*	*7.0*	*1.1*	*–*	*100*
21-24	Male	3.3	0.7	3.1	4.3	0.1	16.0	6.3	0.8	34.6
		9.5	*1.9*	*8.8*	*12.5*	*0.3*	*46.3*	*18.2*	*2.4*	*100*
	Female	1.4	0.8	1.0	1.9	0.1	2.9	1.1	0.8	10.0
		13.6	*8.2*	*9.8*	*19.0*	*1.0*	*29.3*	*11.0*	*8.1*	*100*
25-29	Male	1.1	0.4	1.0	2.2	0.2	7.7	6.0	2.2	20.7
		5.3	*1.8*	*4.6*	*10.8*	*0.8*	*37.0*	*29.0*	*10.6*	*100*
	Female	0.6	0.8	0.4	1.0	0.1	1.5	1.0	1.6	7.2
		8.3	*10.4*	*5.9*	*14.1*	*1.9*	*22.4*	*14.3*	*22.8*	*100*
30 & over	Male	0.8	0.4	0.5	2.2	0.2	6.5	6.1	4.6	21.3
		3.8	*1.7*	*2.4*	*10.1*	*1.1*	*30.5*	*28.8*	*21.5*	*100*
	Female	0.8	1.9	0.5	1.7	0.2	2.1	1.3	3.1	11.7
		6.6	*16.6*	*4.5*	*14.9*	*1.9*	*17.8*	*11.2*	*26.6*	*100*
Totals	Male	38.1	4.1	15.9	17.2	0.5	41.5	20.5	7.6	145.6
		26.2	*2.8*	*10.9*	*11.8*	*0.3*	*28.5*	*14.1*	*5.2*	*100*
	Female	21.4	13.7	8.2	9.0	0.5	9.7	3.9	5.6	71.9
		29.7	*19.0*	*11.3*	*12.5*	*0.8*	*13.4*	*5.5*	*7.8*	*100*
	All	59.5	17.8	24.1	26.2	1.1	51.2	24.5	13.2	217.5
		27.4	*8.2*	*11.1*	*12.1*	*0.5*	*23.5*	*11.2*	*6.1*	*100*

Universities: new entrants, excluding transfers between universities
Teacher training: admissions
Other AFE: first year of course (possibly enrolments, cf. *Fifth report*, p.594)
Open University: new undergraduates

Source
CUA (1978) pp.20-21, SE (1976) 4, Table 1, with age distribution from SE (1975) 4, Table 25.

TABLE 2.4
Participation rates for young home entrants to higher education 1960-1980: Great Britain

Academic year of entry	18-year-olds (000s)	Young home entrants (000s)	QLR*	QPR	APR All	APR Male	APR Female	Excluding teacher-training entrants in E & W with less than 2 'A' levels			
								QPR	APR All	APR Male	APR Female
1960/61	700	48	6.1	111.6	6.9						
1962/63	749	54	7.6	95.4	7.2						
1964/65	848	60	8.1	99.6	8.0						
1966/67	834	87.6	10.3	102.5	10.5	11.7	9.2	85.6	8.8	10.8	6.7
1968/69	763	97.4	12.4	103.1	12.8	14.0	11.4	87.1	10.8	12.9	8.3
1970/71	744	102.6	13.8	100.2	13.8	15.0	12.5	85.8	11.8	14.0	9.3
1972/73	752	106.9	14.6	97.3	14.2	15.1	13.2	83.9	12.3	14.1	10.0
1974/75	776	105.5	14.6	93.3	13.6	14.4	12.8	82.7	12.0	13.5	10.1
1976/77	822	107.2	14.9	87.9	13.1	14.4	11.7	82.4	12.3	13.9	10.1
1978/79	859	105.3	15.1	81.8	12.4	14.0	10.6	80.2	12.1	13.7	10.1
1980/81 (prov.)	906	111.7	15.0	83.3	12.5	13.9	11.0	83.3	12.5	13.9	11.0

*In the previous year

Source
DES (1978) App. II; DES, SB 12/80 and 6/81; Fifth Report, 534 (updated with unpublished information from DES).

TABLE 2.5
School-leavers with five or more 'O' level passes or CSE Grade 1

	(A) Left school in the academic year on 1 Jan. of which aged:								(B)		
(A) Age 16 on 1 Jan. (B) year of leaving	Male				Female				Male	Female	All
	15/16	17	18	All	15/16	17	18	All			
1960/61									15.6	14.9	15.3
1962/63									16.5	15.2	15.9
1964/65			6.6				3.8		18.5	17.4	17.9
1966/67		9.3	7.1			9.4	4.6		19.1	18.1	18.7
1968/69	4.2	10.1	7.2	21.6	6.1	10.8	4.9	21.8	21.4	21.0	21.2
1970/71	4.2	10.8	7.3	22.3	6.0	11.3	5.2	22.6	22.0	22.2	22.1
1972/73	4.9	10.6	6.6	22.1	6.5	11.2	4.9	22.6	22.8	23.3	23.0
1974/75	4.8	10.1	7.0	22.0	6.8	10.4	6.5	23.7	21.7	22.8	22.2
1976/77	5.4				7.4				23.6	23.9	23.7

	(C) Left school in the academic year at start of which aged:								(D)		
(C) Age 16 at start of: (D) year of leaving	Male			All	Female			All	Male	Female	All
	15	16	17		15	16	17				
1972/73		16.3				14.8					
1973/74		2.7	15.5			3.1	14.4		22.5	23.1	22.8
1974/75	3.5	2.4	15.6	21.5	5.2	2.9	13.9	22.0	21.4	22.5	21.9
1975/76	3.5	2.6	16.5	22.6	5.2	2.8	14.7	22.7	21.9	22.3	22.2
1976/77	3.7	2.5	16.7	22.9	5.6	3.0	14.9	23.5	23.5	23.7	23.6
1977/78	4.5	2.6	16.1	23.2	6.0	2.8	14.7	23.5	24.0	23.8	23.9
1978/79	4.7	2.6			6.1	2.9			23.3	23.8	23.5
1979/80	4.6				6.2						

(A) By age of leaving, as percentage of the age group, England & Wales
(B) As percentage of relevant age group, England & Wales
(C) By age of leaving, as percentage of the age group, England
(D) As percentage of relevant age group, England

Source
(A) SE (1977) 2, Tables 1 & 6; SE, 1, Table 1.
(B) SE (1977) 2, Table 21.
(C) SE (1979) 2, Table 21 (pre-publication).
(D) As (C).

TABLE 2.6
Percentage (and size in thousands) of 17-year-old age group (at 31 Dec.) in school and non-advanced further education (NAFE): England and Wales

	Men				Women				All					
	School	NAFE			School	NAFE			School	NAFE			Tot.	(Age group)
		FT	PTD	PTE		FT	PTD	PTE		FT	PTD	PTE		
1962/63	14.1	3.0	25.8	8.0	10.9	3.8	6.8	10.2	12.5	3.4	16.5	9.1	41.5	(633)
1964/65	15.3	3.6	25.7	7.2	12.2	4.3	6.8	9.7	13.8	4.0	16.5	8.4	42.7	(831)
1966/67	17.4	4.4	27.6	6.0	14.6	5.3	7.6	7.1	16.0	4.9	17.8	6.5	45.3	(710)
1968/69	19.7	5.6	29.2	5.5	17.5	6.5	7.9	8.0	18.6	6.1	18.8	6.7	50.2	(661)
1970/71	21.0	6.5	28.5	5.0	19.2	7.7	8.2	7.0	20.1	7.1	18.5	6.0	51.8	(668)
1972/73	21.2	7.3	24.4	4.7	20.4	8.8	7.2	7.1	20.8	7.9	16.1	5.9	50.7	(669)
1974/75	20.4	7.6	26.2	4.2	20.1	9.7	7.7	7.0	20.2	8.6	17.2	5.6	51.6	(711)
1976/77	21.6	8.5	21.0	2.8	21.2	12.3	6.4	5.4	21.4	10.4	13.9	4.0	49.7	(740)

FT = full-time. PTD/E = part-time day/evening. Evening institutes are excluded. The figures slightly overstate the position as the numbers of students include small numbers of overseas, advanced and short-course full-time students.

Source
SE 1 and 3.

TABLE 2.7
Percentage of 16-18 year-olds in schools, further education colleges, and universities: England and Wales

	School		NAFE, FT			NAFE, PT		Higher education
	'A' level	Other	'A' level	'O' level	Other	day	evening	
1973/74	14.1	2.8	1.4	1.2	4.7	16.1	6.3	2.4
1974/75	13.9	3.0	1.5	1.2	5.4	16.1	5.8	2.4
1975/76	14.2	3.2	1.7	1.4	6.3	14.8	5.6	2.4
1976/77	14.5	3.5	1.7	1.3	6.6	13.5	4.2	2.4
1977/78	14.3	3.4	1.8	1.4	7.0	13.1	4.7	2.2
1978/79	14.2	3.4	1.8	1.4	7.0	13.8	N/A	2.1
1979/80	14.3	3.5	1.8	10.0		13.8	N/A	2.1

Ages at 1 January. 16-year-olds under minimum leaving age excluded.
Students pursuing both 'A' level and another qualification entered under 'A' level; and both 'O' level and another qualification (but not 'A') under 'O' level.

Source
DES (1981) Table 1 (which is wrongly titled '16-19 year olds').
NAFE, PT evening, estimated from SE, 1 and 3.

TABLE 2.8
Students gaining two or more (three or more) 'A' level passes

	(A)			(B)		
	Male	Female	Total	Male	Female	Total
1960/61	8.7(5.9)	5.1(2.9)	6.9(4.4)	6.5(5.3)	4.5(3.3)	5.8(4.7)
1962/63	9.8(6.9)	5.8(3.3)	8.0(5.1)	8.2(6.8)	5.2(6.4)	7.1(6.6)
1964/65	11.2(7.5)	7.1(4.1)	9.2(5.9)	7.9(6.6)	5.8(4.4)	7.1(5.8)
1966/67	13.1(8.6)	8.6(5.1)	10.9(6.9)	10.6(8.7)	8.2(6.7)	9.6(7.8)
1968/69	14.5(9.6)	10.6(6.0)	12.6(7.8)	12.6(9.4)	9.7(6.1)	11.2(8.0)
1970/71	15.5(10.1)	12.2(7.0)	13.9(8.6)	13.3(10.8)	10.3(7.5)	12.0(9.4)
1972/73	15.3(9.9)	12.8(7.5)	14.0(8.7)	13.6(10.5)	11.6(8.2)	12.8(9.6)
1974/75	15.2(10.2)	12.7(7.5)	13.9(8.8)	13.8(10.1)	14.0(9.8)	14.0(9.9)
1976/77	15.6(10.6)	13.5(8.0)	14.8(9.4)	13.4(9.4)	15.2(9.3)	14.1(9.2)

	(C)			(D)		
	Male	Female	Total	Male	Female	Total
1973/74	14.5(9.8)	12.1(7.1)	13.3(8.5)	8.2(5.7)	9.0(6.4)	8.5(6.1)
1974/75	14.4(9.9)	12.0(7.2)	13.2(8.6)	8.9(6.5)	9.6(6.5)	9.2(6.5)
1975/76	15.1(10.4)	12.4(7.3)	13.8(8.9)	9.0(6.5)	10.2(6.7)	9.5(6.6)
1976/77	15.3(10.5)	12.8(7.8)	14.1(9.2)	9.2(6.4)	10.9(6.8)	9.9(6.7)
1977/78	15.5(10.8)	13.3(8.2)	14.4(9.5)	8.9(6.4)	11.9(7.9)	10.2(7.0)
1978/79	14.8(10.3)	13.1(8.0)	14.0(9.2)	8.6(6.1)	11.8(7.3)	9.8(6.7)

(A)   At schools and FE colleges: England and Wales: as a percentage of the relevant age group
(B)   Percentage of those in (A) at FE colleges
(C)   At schools and, if aged under 20 at 31 August preceding, FE colleges: England: pas percentage of all 17-year-olds on 31 August
(D)   Percentage of those in (C) at FE colleges

Source
(A), (B):   SE (1977) 2, Table 21.
(C), (D):   SE (1979) 2, Table 22 (pre-publication).

TABLE 2.9
Percentage of school leavers with 'A' level passes entering employment:
England and Wales

	With two or more passes		With three or more passes and grade scores of nine or more	
	Permanent	Temporary	Permanent	Temporary
1960/61	19.0			
1962/63	24.1			
1964/65	21.7			
1966/67	17.4	3.8	5.2	3.6
1968/69	16.8	3.6	5.2	4.2
1970/71	18.4	3.8	6.8	3.9
1972/73	22.6	3.6	9.4	4.8
1974/75	22.5	4.9	8.5	6.5
1976/77	24.0	4.8	9.2	6.2
1978/79	23.0	5.5	8.3	7.3

Source
SE (1977) 2, Table 11.

TABLE 2.10
Indices of changes in relative earnings (1965 = 100)

	(A)	(B)	(C)	(D)	(E)	(F)
	Student maintenance grant	Male graduates' starting salaries		Juvenile basic wages	Male adults	
		Arts & Social Studies	Technology		manual	non-manual
1962				88	89	83
1964	94			95	96	92
1966	100	109	105	106	104	105
1968	106	129	116	117	116	117
1970	112	141	132	143	134	141
1972	131	159	147	192	171	170
1974	178	192	189	270	229	213
1976	257	294	289	432	349	320
1978	324	370	370	538	427	391
1980	421	(500)	(495)	750	595	548

Definitions and sources
(A)   Standard term-time maintenance, outside London.
(B), (C)   Median starting salaries of University of Leeds first-degree graduates in arts & social studies/technology entering industry and commerce. Butler (1978) p.18; Catto et al. (1981) p.73. 1980 estimated from data from University of Leeds Careers Serivce.
(D)   Basic weekly rates of wages, men under 21 and women under 18: *British Labour Statistics Yearbook*. 1978-80: average hourly earnings, men under 21: *New Earnings Survey*.
(E)   As (D), for men, aged 21 and over, in manual occupations.
(F)   Actual earnings, men aged 21 and over, in non-manual occupations: *Dept. Employment Gazette* May 1978. 1978-80: average hourly earnings: *New Earnings Survey*.

TABLE 2.11
(A) Home candidates to UK universities admitted through UCCA and accepted on two or more GCE 'A' level passes, percentage distribution by scores
(B) Percentage of GB home entrants admitted to universities

Accepted in y. e. 30 Sept.	(A)							(B)
	Percentage with scores on 3 subjects			Percentage with scores on 2 subjects			'A' level as percentage of total	
	15-13	12-9	8-3	10-8	7-5	4-2		
1968	22.5	40.4	22.5	4.1	5.9	4.7	89.0	
1970	21.4	40.6	23.6	4.0	6.8	3.5	88.7	
1972	22.9	40.0	23.5	3.6	6.1	3.8	89.1	44.8
1974	21.1	37.3	26.0	3.1	8.0	4.5	89.2	47.2
1976	22.1	37.1	25.2	3.3	8.2	4.2	89.1	49.4
1978	23.2	37.3	25.5	2.7	7.3	3.9	89.0	54.2
1980	22.7	39.0	24.4	2.7	7.8	3.6	88.4	52.8

Source
(A) UCCA *Stat. Supp.* Table G.1, and unpublished tables for 1968, 1972 & 1980.
(B) *Fifth Report* pp.10-11.

TABLE 2.12
(A) Percentage of school-leavers with two or more 'A' level passes entering degree courses or teacher training: by specialization at 'A' level: England & Wales
(B) Percentage distribution of school-leavers with two or more 'A' level passes by specialization at 'A' level: England & Wales

		Science + maths[1]	Science[1] only	Other combinations including science	Social sciences	Arts	Social sciences + arts
(A)							
	1968/69	83.2	76.1	56.8	49.5	64.2	62.7
	1972/77	77.0	60.3	56.6	39.7	58.4	57.3
	1976/77	77.4	64.8	56.3	32.7	57.8	54.0
(B)							
Male	1964/65	36.1	13.7	11.0	2.3	17.2	19.7
	1968/69	28.8	16.8	12.8	3.7	18.6	19.2
	1972/73	29.5	14.0	17.0	4.0	15.5	19.9
	1976/77	27.3	13.4	21.2	5.0	12.2	21.0
Female	1964/65	9.6	11.2	12.0	0.6	45.6	20.9
	1968/69	7.6	10.3	13.1	1.4	46.3	21.3
	1972/73	11.3	8.0	16.9	1.6	40.3	22.0
	1976/77	9.3	7.5	19.8	2.2	38.3	22.9

1 The definition of the specialisms differed in 1968, affecting the split between the first two

Source
SE (1977) 2, Table 12.

TABLE 2.13
Percentage of home students with grade scores of 9 or more on three 'A' level passes (%) and the competition factor (C), accepted by UK universities

	All subjects		Medicine, dentistry, health		Engineering & technology		Science		Social Studies		Arts	
	%	C	%	C	%	C	%	C	%	C	%	C
1968	74	1.0	63	0.86	61	0.83	68	0.93	84	1.14	74	1.00
1970	72	1.0	62	0.86	56	0.78	68	0.94	81	1.13	83	1.15
1972	73	1.0	68	0.93	56	0.77	69	0.95	80	1.10	84	1.15
1974	69	1.0	78	1.13	59	0.86	63	0.91	71	1.03	78	1.13
1976	70	1.0	87	1.24	59	0.84	64	0.91	71	1.01	76	1.08
1978	70	1.0	86	1.23	64	0.91	65	0.93	72	1.02	74	1.05
1980	72	1.0	88	1.23	64	0.89	67	0.94	73	1.02	74	1.03

University entrants to Group IV (agriculture, forestry, veterinary science) and Group VII (architecture) are omitted, except in 'all subjects'.

Source
CUA (1978) Table 20; UCCA *Stat. Supp.* Table G1, and unpublished tables for 1968, 1972 and 1980.

TABLE 2.14
Home students accepted by/admitted to UK universities

	1970		1980		
	(A)	(B)	(A)	(B)	(C)
Medicine	76	1.08	98	1.37	33
Dentistry	26	0.36	81	1.14	23
Pharmacy	44	0.60	66	0.92	36
Agriculture, forestry & veterinary science	60	0.83	66	0.92	48
Business management	52	0.72	65	0.91	111
Accountancy					173
Law	88	1.21	98	1.36	53
Architecture					1
T & C planning	60	0.83	73	1.02	145
Other professional & vocational studies					97
All subjects	72	1.0	72	1.0	32

(A) Percentage of students with grade scores of 9 or more on three 'A' level passes
(B) 'Competition factor'
(C) Percentage increase in admissions, 1980 over 1970

Source
(A) & (B) as for Table 2.13.
(C) UCCA *Ann. Report* Table 5.

TABLE 2.15
Part-time enrolments in advanced further education: by sex and subject group: England and Wales (Percentages)

	Full-time 1978/79	1967/68			1977/78			1980/81
		Male	Female	Total	Male	Female	Total	Total
Education	(14.7)	1.6	1.3	2.9	0.5	0.8	1.3	1
Health	(7.3)	2.0	1.8	3.8	3.1	3.7	6.8	6
Agriculture, veterinary science	(1.2)	–	–	–	–	–	–	–
Engineering	(13.5)	44.6	0.1	44.7	28.0	0.4	28.4	33
Science	(16.3)	10.0	1.5	11.5	7.3	2.2	9.5	9
Social/business studies	(23.1)	29.6	2.3	31.9	39.9	9.6	49.5	45
Professional/vocational studies	(4.8)	2.9	0.4	3.3	2.7	0.9	3.6	4
Arts	(19.1)	1.0	0.7	1.7	0.4	6.7	1.1	2
	(100)	91.7	8.1	99.9	81.9	18.3	100.2	100
N(000s)	(320.1)	105.5	9.5	114.0	102.5	23.2	125.7	141

In-service teacher training is excluded

Source
SE (1977) 3, Table 17. DES, SB 2/81. Full-time = univ. undergraduates and all AFE: *Fifth Report* pp.7, 10; SED, SB 2/H1/1981.

TABLE 2.16
Indicators of women's participation in education: female rate or number divided by male rate or number, multiplied by 100

	1960/61 (1962/63)	1970/71	1976/77	1978/79
School-leavers with five or more 'O' levels	96	101	101	102
17-year-olds in school	(77)	91	98	
NAFE, FT	(127)	118	145	
PTD	(26)	29	30	
PTE	(127)	140	192	
School and NAFE	(62)	69	84	
Students gaining two or more 'A' levels	59	79	87	88
Students gaining three or more 'A' levels	49	69	79	78
Higher education				
Young home FT entrants, APR: All		83	81	76
Excluding TT without 2 'A' levels		66	72	74

	FT	PT
age 21-24, number	45	21
25-29, number	60	26
30 and over, number	126	36
All ages, number	69	28

Source
Tables 2.3, 2.4, 2.5 (B) and (D), 2.6 and 2.8 (A) and (C).

TABLE 2.17
Distribution of children (1971) and students in higher education (1956-1979): by social class of father (Percentages)

		Class						
		I	I	IIIN	IIIM	IV	V	N/C
(1)	Children aged 10-14 in 1971, GB	5.0	18.2	9.0	37.3	16.5	6.8	7.3
(2)	'A' level pupils aged 18 in school & FE, FT, 1974, Eng.	20	40	12	18	8		2
(3)	Univ. entrants, FT, 1956, GB							
	Male	21	41	11	22	4	1	–
	Female	26	45	9	16	2	1	–
	All	22	42	11	20	4	1	–
(4)	Univ. students, FT, 1961/62, GB							
	Male	17	40	12	19	6	1	5
	Female	20	43	11	16	6	1	3
	All	18	41	12	18	6	1	4
(5)	Univ. students by age,							
	19 and under	64		11	21	4		–
?Mid-1960s	20-22	71		8	17	4		–
	23 and over	59		10	26	5		–
(6)	Univ. entrants, FT, 1979, UK	19.8	38.0	12.1	14.7	4.5	0.9	9.8
(7)	Teaching training students, FT, 1961/62, GB							
	Male	5	27	16	32	13	2	5
	Female	8	35	14	28	8	2	6
	All	7	33	14	29	9	2	6
(8)	AFE students, FT, 1961/62, GB	12	32	14	28	8	2	4
	PT day	6	20	16	39	12	4	3
	PT evening	5	22	14	39	12	3	4
(9)	Poly. degree students, FT & PT, 1972/73, Eng.							
	Male	46		19		26		10
	Female	51		17		24		9
	All	12	34	18	8	2	16	10
(10)	Poly. non-degree students, FT & PT, 1972/73	11	29	17	10	3	18	14
(11)	Poly. PT students, 1972/73, Eng.	9	23	19	12	4	18	15
	The same, *own* occupation	9	38	29	2	0	15	7
(12)	Open Univ. PT entrants, 1971, UK	8	26	13	34	13	5	–
	The same, *own* occupation	20	62	11	5	1	0	–

Source
(1) *Census 1971. Household composition* Table 26. (2) Williams & Gordon (1975). (3) Kelsall (1957). (4), (7), (8), HE (1963) App. 2 (B), pp.4, 72, 92, 128. (5) Hopper & Osborn (1975) Table 4.8 (6) UCCA *Stat. Supp. 1978-9* Table E5. (9), (10), (11) Whitburn et al. (1976) Tables 4.12, 4.A, 4.B, 6.7, and personal communication; note that the students in (11) are also counted in (9) or (10). (12) McIntosh et al. (1976) p.139.

TABLE 2.18
Age Participation Rates for full-time students by social class: 1961/62 and
c. 1977: Great Britain

Class	c. 1961 (A)	c. 1977 (B)	Percentage distributions assumed in (B)		
			Univ.	AFE	18-year-olds
I	45	42.6	20.9	13.3	5.3
II	19	25.4	41.2	36.7	19.6
III N	10	21.2	14.7	18.9	9.7
Middle	19.5	26.9	76.8	68.9	34.7
III M	4	5.6	16.6	20.0	40.2
IV	} 2	4.7	5.2	8.9	17.8
V		2.8	1.2	2.2	7.3
Working	3.2	5.0	23.0	31.1	65.3
All	7.5	12.7	99.8	100	100
			N=65340	39460	831000

Source
(A)   HE (1963) App. 1, pp.39-40, based on survey of 20/21 year-olds.
(B)   UCCA *Stat. Supp. 1978-9* Table E5 for universities in 1977. AFE
      estimated from Table 2.17 (7), (9), (10) (above). 18-year-olds: *Census
      1971. Household Composition* Table 46, aged 10-14.

TABLE 2.19

(A) Proportion from working-class homes of all home candidates accepted by universities in England and Wales (1956) and in the United Kingdom (1980)

(B) All home accepted candidates by faculty

Faculty	(A)				(B)			
	1956		1980		1956		1980	
	male	female	male	female	male	female	male	female
Medical, dental	16.4	9.5	16.7	15.7	9.4	3.0	4.1	3.4
Technology, etc.	30.1	8.0	21.6	14.5	12.8	0.1	13.4	1.7
Agriculture, Veterinary	11.7	15.3	7.5	19.6	2.6	0.4	1.2	0.7
Science	32.7	21.2	23.3	17.7	18.5	6.1	17.0	8.1
Arts, social studies, education	25.9	20.0	18.2	19.3	27.3	19.6	23.7	26.7
All faculties	26.8	19.1	20.1	18.5	70.6	29.2	59.4	40.6
	24.6		19.4		100		100	

(A) Is based on accepted candidates whose parental occupation was known; and whose application was based on 'A' levels

(B) Is based on all accepted candidates

Source

1956: Kelsall (1957) Table 14, with faculties grouped: 3, 4; 5; 6, 7; 2; 1.

1980: UCCA *Ann. rep. 1979-80* Table 2, and unpublished, with subjects grouped: II; III, VII; IV; V; I, VI, VIII, IX.

TABLE 2.20
Indices of Age Participation Rates: by region (England and Wales = 100)

	(A)	(B)	(C)	(D)	(E)	(F)
England						
North	75	84	86	79	89	
Yorks & Humberside	85	93	92	83	89	
North West	101	104	106	104	94	
East Midlands	89	90	88	82	92	
West Midlands	93	87	90	83	92	
East Anglia	81	87	84	89	100	
Greater London	122	109	107	97	105	
Other South East	111	107	110	128	116	
South West	97	102	97	101	106	
Wales	106	114	110	106	93	
England & Wales	100	100	100	100	100	
(percentage of age group)	(18.4)	(19.1)	(10.9)	(8.5)		
Scotland					126	92

(A) Standard regions (small changes in definition in 1974 have been ignored)
(B) Proportion of 16 to 18-year-olds in school or on full-time GCE/CSE courses in FE colleges, 1977/78
(C) Unweighted mean of proportion of average of 18 and 19-year-olds taking up new LEA awards or entering initial teacher training, 1975/76-1977/78
(D) As (C), but excluding award-holders in FE colleges
(E) Candidates accepted for university entrance, 1979: rates per 1,000 18-year-olds
(F) Predicted Age Participation Rate, on the basis of the distribution of household heads by social class

Source
(B) DES, SB 15/79. (C), (D), SE, 5. (E) UCCA *Stat. Supp. 1978-79* Table F4. SED, SB 2/H1/1981. OPCS *Population estimates 1979. Annual estimates of the population of Scotland 1979.* (F) *Census 1971, Household composition* Table 41 (heads of all households by social class by region; 18-year-olds assumed to be distributed by social class similarly). Age Participation Rates as for c. 1977 in Table 2.18 above.

3

COMPARATIVE PERSPECTIVES ON ACCESS

by Martin Trow

A MODEL OF HIGHER EDUCATION
To consider higher education from the perspective of access is necessarily to
see it from a variety of perspectives. There is the perspective of the politician
and planner, wanting to know what demand for post-secondary education,
and of what kinds, will be felt over the next decades, and what costs and
gains there might be in trying to meet or encourage or deflect or modify that
demand. There is the perspective of those concerned with social stratification
and social equality, both as values to be pursued and as academic subjects to
be investigated. There is the issue of access as it affects academic
achievement — the impact of differing numbers and kinds of students on the
effectiveness of teaching and learning within colleges and universities, on the
nature of the curriculum, the balance of subjects, and the intellectual climate
of colleges and universities. There are hardly any issues in higher education
that cannot be approached through the perspective of access, and in a way
that has the advantage of showing the links and connections among different
elements of higher educational systems.

In the late 1960s and early 1970s I attempted in a series of papers to
understand and explain what was happening to the systems of higher
education in advanced industrial societies. I took as my starting point, as
indeed anyone at the time would have to do, the extraordinary growth of
student populations everywhere in the 1960s and early 1970s.

The 'élite-mass-universal access' model as sketched in a paper written
for OECD in 1973 (Trow 1974) was an effort to bring together within one
framework many problems of higher education which were too often dealt
with in isolation — such problems as student access and selection, the
curriculum, governance, administration, finance, staff recruitment, academic standards, modes of instruction, institutional autonomy, academic
freedom, and the relationships between research and teaching, as well as
between higher education and secondary schooling on the one hand and
adult education on the other. These and other aspects of higher education
were seen in the model as related to one another rather than as discrete or
isolated problems. Such problems and the responses to them could, I suggested, be understood better if seen in the light of a broad historical movement
from 'élite' forms of higher education, through mass higher education,
towards universal access to some kind of post-secondary education. [1]

This broad movement, so the model asserts, can be observed in all
modern industrial societies, but in each country it reflects unique historical,

social, economic, cultural, and political characteristics. Thus, the concepts and ideas surrounding the 'élite-mass-universal access' phases of development were not intended to describe or explain the higher educational system in any specific society at any given moment. Rather, the model was meant to provide a way of raising questions in a comparative context, and of generating problems for closer investigation and research in specific national systems and institutions.

A theory based on a conception of 'phases of development,' as this one was, necessarily focuses attention on the points or periods of transition between one phase and another. I suggested at several places in that paper that national systems experience special strains and tensions at the points of transition from élite to mass higher education, and will do so in the future as they move towards the provision of universal access to some kind of post-secondary education. Some of these tensions and problems arise because of changes required in the way higher education is conceived by the members of the society, in the nature of the student's role, or in the role of the state. Other problems arise at these points of transition because different aspects of higher education change at different times and at different rates: for example, the social characteristics and motivations of entering students may change before the curriculum does, or enrolments may grow more rapidly than financial support.

In addition, the model stressed that a national system of higher education does not shift completely from one phase to another, but rather that institutions created in one phase survive into later phases. Thus, in every modern industrial society, élite institutions survive even as the system as a whole expands to provide mass higher education; and similarly, both élite and mass institutions survive into a period of near universal access. This stress on the *diversity* of modern systems of higher education in any given society — a diversity both between and within institutions — was a central theme in the model and allows us to ask, within its framework, how systems and institutions accomplish the academic division of labour as between mass and élite functions.

UNDERLYING ASSUMPTIONS OF COMMON PATTERNS OF DEVELOPMENT
The underlying assumption behind such an effort to develop a simple conceptual scheme is that there were and are marked similarities in the patterns of development of educational systems across national lines. Now I still think that this was a reasonable assumption, given the experience of the United States and Western Europe between the end of the Second World War and the early 1970s. There were many forces in common behind the very rapid growth of those national systems. All of the Western countries came out of World War II with a broad commitment to a greater democratization of their social structures and their social services. All Western societies, although with some variations in timing and degree, experienced rapid

economic growth in the two decades after 1950. This growth provided resources for the expansion of higher education; it also created demand in the economy for the graduates of universities and higher technical colleges. At least as important, during those decades Western societies all made larger commitments to public social services and to the political management of the economy, which led to very substantial growth in primary and secondary education, health services, social welfare services, town and regional planning, and the like. All of this created continuing demands for the graduates of colleges and universities. Moreover, the growth of the system itself created a very substantial demand for an increase in the numbers of research scholars and scientists for the academic profession itself. This is, on the whole, a familiar story, though aspects of it become clearer as we move away from those decades — for example, I think it is clearer now how very important the growth of the public service was in creating new demand for graduates.

But there was another assumption in the writing of that time, including my own, the assumption that the patterns of growth of Western European systems would resemble the developmental processes that had marked the growth of higher education in the United States. I was not unaware of the marked historical, social, cultural and political differences among the Western European countries and between them and the United States; nevertheless, I tended to believe that the dynamic processes of growth that had been set off in Western Europe during the 1950s and 1960s would have a life of their own, and would exert an autonomous pressure on those societies for a continued expansion of their systems of higher education. I did not assume that all the institutional forms would be the same as in the United States, nor was I prepared to make predictions about how fast or how far growth would go. Nevertheless, I believed that once the European nations expanded their systems to include 15 or 20 per cent of the age grade, and made the institutional changes that such an expansion required, growth could then continue in these now reformed systems toward inclusion of 30, 35, perhaps 40 per cent of the age grade without great difficulty. By 1973, many European countries including West Germany, Belgium, France, the Netherlands, Sweden and the United Kingdom were admitting over 20 per cent of the relevant age grade of high-school leavers to some form of post-compulsory education (Hecquet et al. 1976). Watching this development over a decade and a half, I had come to believe that as European nations expanded their systems, particularly on the non-university side, supply would begin to generate demand. Attitudes toward higher education would begin to change, leading larger sections of society to see college or university as appropriate for them and their children. In addition, I thought, parts of the occupational structure would change in response to the larger supply of educated people, and begin to demand these qualifications, thus permanently increasing the demand for graduates. I also assumed that the efforts being made in most Western European countries to encourage students to stay on in higher secondary schools to gain the qualifications for entry to higher education would bear fruit. I also assumed that the transfer rate of qualified students would continue to rise.

Now, on reflection, I still believe that to be a reasonably accurate account of some of the mechanisms that underlay the growth of mass education in the United States. And what I was saying in that essay was that if European systems were going to grow into systems of mass higher education, they would be driven by some of these same forces. On the whole, I believed that they were going to continue to grow, although I had some reservations. In the same paper, I suggested that growth was dependent on greater diversity, and especially on the creation of a large sector in the higher educational system marked by lower costs and academic standards, and more responsive to market demands than to the autonomous and inner logics of the academic, scientific and scholarly disciplines. And I believed that the relatively greater centralization of control over higher education that occurred in European countries as compared with the United States would work against the growth of diversity.

Thus I was pointing to a dilemma which I was unable to resolve. On one hand I argued that growth would continue to be driven by a variety of forces, mostly located on the demand side: that is, not within governments or the universities themselves but within the larger society. On the other hand I suggested that national government would not be highly committed to indefinite growth, and would not be inclined to create the diverse system of institutions that would be necessary to stimulate and sustain it. I now believe that, on the whole, I was right to suspect that governments would not surrender their control over higher education in the service of larger and more anarchic systems. But I overestimated the strength of the forces for growth stemming from a demand from the general population for places in higher education, or a demand from the economic institutions for graduates.

Three years ago, in 1978 at a conference in Sweden, I had occasion to reflect on the usefulness and validity of that model in light of subsequent developments (Trow 1979).[2] I had then the advantage of seeing a report by Ladislav Cerych and his colleagues (Hecquet et al. 1976) which brought together evidence on the growth of Western European and North American systems in the first half of the 1970s, evidence which seemed to suggest that the patterns of rapid growth that had marked the 1960s had come to a halt, and that these systems were not, as I had anticipated, moving steadily 'toward the development of systems of mass higher education, as in the United States or in Japan.'

As I observed then, 'If we are to increase our understanding of the social forces surrounding the development of higher education . . . it may be useful to review earlier analyses and predictions, and to focus especially on those that seem to have gone wrong, that have not been borne out by subsequent events. On the whole, our understanding has advanced more by confronting negative evidence which contradicts hypotheses and predictions . . . than by adding further illustrations in support of our theories. And I share with Kenneth Boulding the belief that the function of science is to point to our ignorance rather than to our knowledge' (Trow 1979).

It was in that spirit that I thought it useful then, as I do now, to ask why predictions (mine among them) based on an assessment of the forces making for growth during the 1960s were mistaken: that is, why it was that Western European nations did not during the 1970s move toward the development of systems of mass higher education enrolling 40 to 50 per cent of the age grade, as in the United States. A related question which I did not ask at that time was why Japan and the United States also seemed to end their periods of rapid growth, though at higher plateaus of enrolment. It may be useful to note the responses to the first of those two questions that I gave in 1978.

First, the growth of higher education obviously depends on an increase in the number of students who finish their advanced secondary-school education and qualify for entry to colleges and universities. In 1973, drawing upon my American experience, I had assumed that attitudes favourable toward continuing formal education would move gradually from the upper and upper-middle classes more and more deeply into the middle and lower-middle classes, and even, with encouragement from progressive governments, into the working classes. I had seen this happen in the United States until the proportion of school-leavers with a high school certificate reached over 75 per cent. Moreover, while I understood that the academic qualifications for entry into European systems of higher education were on the whole higher than for an American high school diploma, I did not believe that the reserve of ability had been exhausted in the 15 to 25 per cent of the age grade who were then gaining upper secondary school leaving qualifications in most European countries. Moreover, I was impressed by the efforts that various countries were making to ease those qualifications and to extend the opportunity for qualifying to larger sections of the population; the abolition of the matriculation examination in Sweden, and the growth of comprehensive schools, along with the raising of the school leaving age in Britain, were examples of this movement. Nevertheless, on the whole there has not been a steady growth in the numbers and proportions of school-leavers qualified for entry to higher education. Moreover, the transfer rates to higher education of those who are qualified have also not been growing as they were expected to, and in many countries have even shown a decline since 1970. In his essay in the volume which documents this double slow-down Ladislav Cerych observes that 'The finding that many qualified secondary school leavers and/or their transfer coefficient to higher education have decreased in the early 70s, or grown less rapidly than expected, is among the most important and probably the most surprising of the analysis of student flows in . . . this report' (Hecquet et al. 1976).

In trying to explain that phenomenon, several factors come to mind. Cerych himself suggests that the slow-down in the transfer rates may reflect the impact of new policies, in particular those related to the concept of recurrent education. In a sense he is suggesting that the efforts to provide for recurrent education may encourage school-leavers, even those with qualifications, to delay entry into higher education for some years, until after they have gained some work experience. And he points to Sweden as the best evidence for such an explanation. He finds further support for this suggestion in the sudden increase of newly registered students in the past few years in Sweden, which implies 'at least in part, the development of an entirely new clientele in higher education, not only of students who have interrupted for a while their formal educational careers but also of those whom Swedish policy has strongly tried to favor — for example adults without completed secondary education, participants in the 25/5 scheme, students taking single courses, etc.' He suggests that while this trend is clearest in Sweden, which has made the most explicit provision for recurrent education, it may also be present in other countries such as Britain and the United States which have made provision for the education of adults.

But while they may affect transfer ratios, expanded opportunities for recurrent education would not explain the lack of growth in the proportion of the secondary school population which stays on and gains upper secondary qualifications. And in reflecting on why my predictions on that score did not come true, I suggested that I had not given enough weight to the strongly held attitudes of Europeans toward upper secondary schools, and the long historical links of those schools to the learned professions and to élite forms of higher education, particularly the universities. 'If to enter that world was a mark of high academic ability, or more often, of high social class origins, then ordinary people in European countries on the whole have not thought attending university was appropriate for themselves or their children, despite what their progressive governments may have wished' (Trow 1979). The United States, by contrast, had no such long-standing link between its not very élite comprehensive high schools and its élite forms of higher education. 'In the United States, class-linked attitudes toward education are much weaker, and the view of education as an important avenue of mobility, and the more of it the better, is much more widespread even among working-class families and ethnic minorities.' Thus cultural or class values and institutional barriers inhibiting young Americans from staying on in high school until graduation were much weaker, and in some places altogether absent. And a high school diploma, in America, is sufficient to gain entry to some form of post-secondary education.

Involved here are differing concepts of social mobility, and of the role of education in achieving such mobility across generations. It may be that we are seeing one manifestation of the stronger class identifications and structures of European society, which not only have economic and political but also cultural manifestations. And among the latter are these stronger class-linked conceptions of how much and what kind of formal education is appropriate for people in different class positions. This is an old story, but one which may not be changing as much or as rapidly as we thought, or wished. Nor are these attitudes as responsive to public policy as we have imagined.

Thus it may be that the attitudes of secondary school students toward higher education will be a greater constraint on the growth of European systems of higher education than the traditional and structured (but now declining) conservatism of its institutions of higher education. These attitudes may be reinforced by the narrowing of wage rates between youth and adults over the past decade, resulting from trade union and government policies, a narrowing which allows youngsters to contrast a precocious and affluent adult status at age 17 or 18, if they do not go on to post-secondary education, with the dependency and relative poverty of university students, still in statu pupillari at age 21, 22, 23 or older, and with no guarantee of the jobs or careers once thought appropriate for university graduates. But there is clearly a danger of forecasting too little change in popular attitudes, where once we anticipated too much too soon.

Three years ago, using data up to 1975, it was still possible to observe the overall decline in the growth rates of higher education in most industrial societies, and wonder whether that decline 'constituted a very temporary phenomenon only or whether it corresponded to a more permanent trend.' But the data on student flows up through 1979 do not lead to any change in the earlier judgement that Western European nations are not moving steadily toward a diversified system of mass higher education as I and others anticipated (Cerych and Colton 1980). To Cerych and Colton, the overall impression created by the more recent data they have gathered is that 'quantitative developments in higher education over the past few years seem to challenge more than ever any reference to common clear-cut trends (except in the case of the continuous growth in female participation): to a greater extent, perhaps, than at any time in the past, one is confronted with almost annual fluctuations and divergences, both within and between countries. . . . This instability may be explained at least partly by the changing nature of higher education and especially of its students. . . .'

In part, at least, the lack of pattern in the data as compared with earlier periods may reflect the increasing heterogeneity of institutions and of students within the statistical categories. As a result of government policies, we are now lumping quite dissimilar institutions and students into common categories, and the sub-types concealed in those rubrics may be quite differently responsive to different economic and educational forces and events. I suspect that to understand what is happening behind the figures for any given country we will need to disaggregate them, and to look much more closely at finer sub-groups of students, and sub-categories of institutions. For example, we could not understand the Swedish figures after 1976 if we did not know that a substantial part of the growth in their enrolments in higher education has been made up of mature students coming in under the new 25/5 law without needing special academic qualifications or higher secondary school certificates, and for the most part enrolling for one or two

courses, often without the intention of earning a degree — what in the United
States would be called 'Extension students'.

Close attention to the statistics on student flows, the size of age cohorts,
the numbers of qualified school-leavers, transfer rates, the numbers of new
entrants to various forms of higher education, degrees awarded, total
entrolments and all the various rates and trends and disaggregations that
those data make possible, have great value for illuminating the emerging
changes and characteristics of our systems. But they have a tendency in
themselves to shape and finally to limit our understanding of the
development of our systems and our institutions. Because when we try to
explain those rates and trends, we find ourselves turning to various social
psychological explanations — explanations which are rooted in the attitudes
or values or assessments or calculations of some group of actual or potential
college or university students. There is the social psychology of the
economist, and his conception of economic man (or boy). There is the social
psychology of the cultural anthropologist, talking of different class
sub-cultures, and the different attitudes within them towards higher
education. There is the social psychology of the educational psychologist,
interested in the academic abilities and motivations of students, and in the
proportions in an age grade who are 'really able and interested in higher
education'. We can see all these and others in the recent literature on student
flows; their limitations are less apparent.

For example, when we confront the levelling-off, and in some cases the
decline in transfer rates in Western European countries over the past decade,
the 'natural' question that arises, at least for an American, is why should the
desire to continue formal studies not gradually move 'down' and through the
social structure, beyond the social and academic élites which had provided
the students for the old small élite university system? Those systems had
grown greatly in the 1960s — why should they not grow further, and indeed
finally involve nearly the whole population of school-leavers in some form of
post-secondary education, somewhat parallel to the growth of higher
secondary education in the preceding decades?

One explanation, rather favoured by economists, assumed a kind of
rational calculation on the part of potential or prospective students regarding
graduate career prospects. As the proportions gaining degrees increase, the
rate of return on the investment in college education declines. Clark Kerr
suggests that over the two decades between 1960 and 1980, the decades that
he calls 'The Golden Age' of higher education, 'The comparative monetary
value of a college degree (in the United States) fell in relation to a high school
degree with long-run implications for the equalization of earned income. The
rate of return on the investment in college education went down by about
one-third with implications for future attendance rates in college,
particularly for majority males' (Kerr 1980). Roger Geiger, citing the French
economist, Levy-Garboua, points to 'a general correlation between the
economic rewards for university study and the time and effort students are

willing to commit to it. As graduate labour markets have continued to weaken, French students have devoted larger proportions of their time to part-time jobs or leisure activities' (Geiger 1980). It certainly seems plausible that poor job prospects for graduates or a decline in the monetary advantage of a degree should each depress the readiness of school-leavers to make the necessary sacrifices in time, energy, direct costs and foregone income.

But the opposite can be argued, and is, often by the same authors. The very same bulge of college graduates in the labour market which should depress the return on the investment on college attendance creates intense competition among the unfortunate members of this bulge, 'reduced chances for promotion, increased occupational frustration, and, incidentally, a heightened demand for additional higher education' (Kerr 1980). Geiger spells this process out in his concept of 'the penalty effect'.

'The surfeit of college graduates on the labor markets in the 1970s, in the U.S. and elsewhere, has produced the phenomenon of credential inflation. . . .
'Few of the frustrated graduates spend an inordinate period of time in unemployment lines. Rather, they eventually accept less prestigious positions than they had originally hoped for, often ones that had not been considered graduate positions at all. In doing so they effectively displace workers with less education. Thus, the positions in question over time become upgraded to graduate status, and graduates correspondingly become "occupationally downgraded" as they lower their original expectations. As this occurs it might seem graduate status would become less and less enticing, but in fact it is the obverse effect that has the most significant impact. As more workers acquire graduate credentials those with less education are effectively penalized by being pushed farther down the occupational hierarchy. So, at the same time that the pull of superior graduate earnings is weakening, this very penalty effect provides an increasingly powerful push toward college for potential students.' (Geiger 1980)

Geiger argues that 'the penalty effect' drives able students in the United States to try to increase their edge over the competition by staying on in university for a postgraduate or professional degree. In his view, the socially and academically marginal students, with tenuous motivation and conflicting interests, respond to their perception of the uncertainty of the eventual rewards of higher education by 'actually "discounting" the value of an eventual degree by reducing the value of their investment in it.'

'This discounting assumes two forms. First, the cost is kept low either by attending inexpensive community colleges or by mixing schooling with part or full-time work. Secondly, the investment is made incrementally, course by course, semester by semester. Schooling can be interrupted or discontinued any time that circumstances would seem to warrant. And, apparently it often is: the actual enrolment patterns of individual Marginals are notoriously irregular, reflecting their tenuous motivation and the interference of non-academic activities. This makes these patterns sensitive to immediate labor market conditions. Work and education in many cases would seem to be strongly inter-related, so that the more satisfactory working opportunities become the less they desire additional education, and vice-versa. For example, in 1975, as the economy was just beginning to emerge from a severe recession, community college enrollments mushroomed by 25%, but in 1978, when employment was at record levels, total enrollments were down by some 3% with a decided shift from full-time to part-time status.' (Geiger 1980)

This explanation of the behaviour of 'marginals', focusing on rather subtle interpretations of their attitudes towards study, their ambition, and their assessments of the cash value of academic credentials, all presuppose an institutional system which allows marginal students to creep along, semester by semester, accumulating credits toward degrees, working part-time without penalty or opprobrium. That is a good deal easier to do in the United States than in most Western European countries. In the United States that pattern swells enrolment rates, and provides genuine access to higher education and its credentials and degrees. A comparable kind of calculation in France, by Geiger's testimony, leads marginal university students to spend less time in class, and to drop out when they make no academic progress. What is needed, evidently, is a closer examination of the quite different educational outcomes of similar student attitudes and behaviours in different systems, or the different attitudes and behaviours of similar students generated by different institutional structures and arrangements. To put it differently, we need a social psychology of 'student flows', appropriately disaggregated, and rooted in the varying organizational forms and processes that characterize our different national systems of higher education.

I am not suggesting that this kind of analysis is not now done. It is precisely what characterizes the best work in our area of interest. But it should be done more systematically and continuously, at once the object of our efforts and our criticism. For we must go beyond the invaluable demographies to empirical research on the attitudes and behaviours of the actors in our institutions, and this means ethnography as well as survey research. At the same time we need to have a sophisticated sense of our colleges and universities as organizations and systems — how and why they are what they are and behave as they do. And this, I think, means historical and comparative perspectives on our systems, as well as the more familiar organizational studies of them.

These strictures apply to my own work with as much force as to others'.

In my speculations above, and in the paper I wrote in 1978, on why my earlier predictions of steady growth in transfer rates had been in error, I suggested that I might have underestimated the strength of class-based attitudes toward higher education, the fact that ordinary people in European countries, especially those of lower-middle and working-class origins, 'on the whole have not thought attending university was appropriate for themselves or their children, despite what their progressive governments may have wished.' By contrast, 'in the United States, class-linked attitudes toward education are much weaker and the view of education as an important avenue of mobility, and the more of it the better, is much more widespread even among working-class families and ethnic minorities.'

That assertion needs to be studied critically and empirically. In 1978 14 per cent of the students in American colleges and universities came from families in the bottom 20 per cent of the national income distribution. That is, I think, a higher proportion than is found in other advanced industrial societies. But it is an open question whether that relatively high proportion is a result of the class values and attitudes toward education that I spoke of, or of the existence of cheap and convenient public community and four-year colleges which are counted as part of our system of higher education, but in Great Britain are relegated to the residual category of 'further education'. We know, for example, that in the United States the establishment of a community college will almost immediately increase the proportion of working-class students in that community who continue into post-secondary education.

I raise these critical questions not for their own sake but because they have implications for policy. Sweeping interpretations of the data on student flows at the level of the social psychology of groups or of substantial values may distract our attention from the possibilities of influencing behaviour, even in the framework of those attitudes and values. It is when we examine such assertions critically and comparatively, and especially across different systems of education, that we are reminded of the potential effects of public policy on the forms and structures of education, and through them on behaviours and outcomes that concern us.

But if we are to be interventionists and activists, then we must be sensitive to the potential costs of our interventions, to the trade-offs involved, and to the almost certain unintended effects of changes in institutional arrangements. This reflection embraces again the issue I touched on earlier of the relation between access and educational achievement, at least as that relation shows itself currently in Britain and the United States.

Despite all the disillusion in Western Europe with the United States as idea and as nation over the past two decades, American higher education still exists for Europeans as a model or exemplar of what a system of mass higher education with broad access might look like. For example, Shirley Williams, in a critical comment on British education, observes that 'the institutions of higher education in Britain do not see themselves as resource centres for their own cities or counties in the way that American universities do. But there need be no tension between this role and the role of being internationally recognized centres of academic excellence. The University of California at Berkeley, for instance, manages both without damaging its reputation' (Williams 1981).

While the United States may no longer be an exemplar toward which other nations move, as I once anticipated, or, in other words, if it is no longer a central part of a predictive model of development, it may still be useful as a point of comparative analysis, and as a source and empirical test of policies and programmes elsewhere. It can serve this function not only in the somewhat platitudinous sense that we can all learn from one another, but in the more specific sense that the United States may have developed institutional forms and arrangements that Britain and others can adapt to their benefit.

The feasibility of the transfer of social technology across national and cultural borders is a large and problematic issue. We all know that we cannot simply import social arrangements from other countries and insert them in our own systems; like many organ transplants, they 'don't take' and are rejected by the host country. But we also know, and see all round us, institutional ideas and arrangements which have been borrowed from other countries and with appropriate adaptations and modifications are now part of our institutional systems. Half the nations in the world adopted the British parliamentary idea, with a range in variations in outcome as wide as the range of adopting countries. But while it may be possible for some American patterns and arrangements to be imported by Britain — one thinks, for example, of the easy transfer of academic credits, open enrolment institutions that permit full-time work for degrees, student loans — it is I think important to understand the historical and institutional context which gave rise to those patterns, and the quite different ones to which it is proposed to adapt them. Such close comparative scrutiny[3] may allow us to anticipate the probabilities of success or failure, and to anticipate the inevitable strains that alien forms set up in institutions, as well as the kinds of modifications (or deformations) that they inevitably undergo. We may also learn something about the unintended consequences that those imports are likely to engender, along with or in place of their intended effects.

GREAT BRITAIN: HIGH STANDARDS AND CONSTRAINED ACCESS
When we reflect on the differences between the British and the American systems of higher education, we are forced to confront the relationship of access to academic standards. My sense is that in Britain since World War II there have been two broadly different views on higher education. The conservatives have held that only a rather small proportion of young men and women have the talent and ambition to do really advanced intellectual work, and that by sequential selection and preparation through the schools those few could be identified and prepared to pass the examinations necessary for entry into the universities or university-like institutions. The progressives

have believed that the 'pool of ability' was potentially much larger than the existing arrangements allowed to emerge. They believed that growing up in a class society itself created sharp differences in academic motivations and achievement among children differently located in that society, and moreover that the secondary school system that emerged from the 1944 Act itself was one of the institutional restraints on the emergence of larger numbers able to qualify for higher education. Their first prescription for reform was the comprehensive secondary school with a higher school-leaving age, designed to bring larger numbers, and especially larger numbers of lower- and working-class children, nearer to the point of university entry and much nearer to the entry to sixth form in which continued attendance was a prerequisite for university entry. The reformers' second prescription called for expansion of the university system, partly in response to the anticipated growth of demand for places, partly out of a sense that an increased supply stimulates demand. Third, the reform movement called for the creation of alternative forms of higher education, as rigorous and demanding in their way as university studies, but linked more directly to the needs of 'new students' from more modest social origins, with a presumed stronger vocational interest. Fourth, the same people, on the whole, were the force behind the Open University, an alternative route to degrees and certificates for mature students already out of school and at work, an institutionalized way to bridge the generation as well as the class gap, and make modest amends to those who had come of age before the comprehensive schools and wider opportunities for university entry had been created.[4]

I do not mean to minimize the significance of the differences between academic conservatives and progressives in Britain. But from a trans-Atlantic perspective what these two broad strands in British opinion have in common outweighs the issues on which they differ. What their views share are at least these elements:

1   Entry to higher education, whether university or non-university, shall be through evidence of academic qualification: passing national exams toward the end of secondary schooling, plus in a few institutions additional tests and interviews also aimed at assessing academic achievement and potential.

2   The academic standards of institutions which award degrees shall be high, and, so far as possible, similar throughout the country, with appropriate variations for different courses and subjects.

3   Standards shall be kept high by arranging that the strongest institutions, departments, scholars and scientists are held up as the appropriate models for all of higher education. While it is recognized that not every scientist can be a Nobel Prize winner, it is taken as a norm that work of world class can be expected at every university, and that the differences in this respect among the universities are differences in degree and not in kind. And while there is a certain ambivalence and uncertainty in this respect with

regard to the polytechnics, there has been since their creation the assertion both from government and from the polytechnics themselves that they would and should create their own forms of excellence.

The uniformity of high standards across the whole system is achieved in a number of ways. First, there is the character of the student intake, all meeting at least the common minimum requirements for entry, and the great majority of them, at least in the university, young and attending full time. In addition, there are other mechanisms to achieve and sustain a national standard of excellence. There are the assumed high common standards of the university Honours degree; the visiting examiners to apply those common standards throughout the system; the common salary schedule for academic staff; the roughly common workload among the various institutions; the application (at least until very recently) of common criteria by the UGC and other funding agencies to the grant requests of the various institutions; the role of the CNAA, with, in its early days, its largely university staff membership, certifying courses in the public sector.

Both the high and the uniform character of academic standards are reinforced by the pattern of student stipends, which however inadequate they may seem to British academics and their students, are generous by the standards of many countries, and certainly, in the aggregate, expensive. The provision of such stipends can only be justified, in Britain or elsewhere, for the support of highly qualified students in institutions of high quality, the combination ensuring an intense and effective education that promises substantial returns, economic, social, cultural and political to the society which provides that support.

But the high and common standards which mark British universities and polytechnics alike ultimately rest on the provision of other educational resources: the rich staff/student ratios, for so many years tenaciously and indeed successfully defended at or near 1:8 through decades of economic hardship, and now, perhaps under the greatest pressure, moving to 1:10 on average.[5] Moreover, and in support of this staff/student ratio, there is a relatively high provision of other educational resources: buildings, offices, libraries, laboratories, staff support and the like, on a high and common standard throughout the system.

What I have been describing is an élite system of higher education, or at least the public life of that system, its economic base and organizational structure. Its private life reveals itself in two major ways: what actually happens to students during their exposure to it — the shaping of mind and sensibility, the development of intellectual skills and capacities, and so on — and the scientific and scholarly research at international standards that is produced by the academic staff, sometimes with the help of students. The high rate of retention until graduation is also a mark of such a system, and of a kind that allows the defenders of British universities to claim a particularly favourable cost/benefit ratio. Those effects on students and scholarship are accomplished by an élite system of higher education, rather than, as in the United States, by the élite parts of a mass system. It is significant that in the British system of higher education both of these effects — resulting from intense teaching and a high level of research — are found throughout the system, the best internal evidence that Britain is indeed running an élite system rather than a mass system with some élite institutions.

The best evidence that this system I have described is still alive, and not the hollow bulk of former institutions, like other survivors of earlier times, is that the people who are employed by the system still work so hard to make it work as it has. It is always impressive to an American to see the heavy loads of teaching in British universities, the readiness of the staff to serve on the committees which bring academic values and standards to bear on the operation of the institution (the only real alternative to bureaucratic management by non-academics); and the readiness of university lecturers and professors to read scripts and to serve as external examiners.

I have been pointing to a network of structures, organizations, norms, patterns of behaviour which are tightly interlocking and mutually supportive, holding together finally not only by custom and habit, but by the continuing conviction that this is what a university is and how it should work. At the heart of the web are the universities, quantitatively dominant as well as normatively pre-eminent. The polytechnics and other institutions of higher education in the public sector share many of the central characteristics of the universities, including roughly comparable staff/student ratios, a similar salary schedule, comparable requirements for entry, and student stipends, at least for those taking full-time or sandwich work. Even the Open University, created precisely to reach a segment of the population that did not continue on to higher education directly from school, and which waives the university and polytechnic entry requirements, is staffed and paid at university standards, and teaches and awards degrees within those standards. This system of élite higher education includes the sixth form and sixth form colleges, which prepare students for entry into higher education.

The parts and shape of a web such as this are, as the clinicians say, over-determined. For example, the commitment of this élite system to high (and consequently expensive) standards throughout British higher education is surprising to Americans, accustomed to wider diversity, greater variation both of standards and costs, and the resulting hierarchy of institutions that characterizes the American system. In Britain, I believe, the commitment to the formal equality of degree-granting institutions is related to the widespread belief after World War II that more working-class youth — long excluded from universities in any significant numbers — should be given better access both to universities and to other forms of higher education.

But this belief, as much a moral conviction as an estimate of the untapped 'pool of ability', was accompanied by a resolve that if working-class youth did, against all handicaps, gain the necessary qualifications, then they deserved 'nothing but the best' by way of higher education. No second-class institutions, no higher education 'on the cheap', for those who had been, at least educationally, for too long second-class citizens. If there were institutions especially attractive to working-class students, then they should be as good in their way as the universities — if not immediately in academic terms, then at least in cost. This feeling lay behind the transformation of the colleges of advanced technology into universities, as well as the ongoing level of support for the polytechnics.

While an American observer may find no strictly academic necessity for such a firm principle of equality — both of cost and of nominal academic standard — across the whole range of British higher education, it is perhaps required by Britain's particular social and political history, and especially by its class relations. By contrast, the United States, as a society, does not feel especially guilty towards the working class or its children (as it does towards black and some other minorities). So where Britain says 'nothing but the best', with all the implications for a constraint on access which that slogan has, Americans are likely to feel that 'something is better than nothing', and take it as a matter of course that students from less affluent families will, on average, go to less expensive institutions, many (though not all) of lower academic standard.

So British political values, as well as its institutions of higher education, place great constraints on access. One can try to increase the total numbers in the system, more or less successfully as Britain did during the 1960s. One can try to modify the social composition of entrants to higher education, increasing the numbers of under-represented groups, either of class or of ethnic group origin. One can try to modify the age distribution in universities and bring more mature students into the system. And one can try to bring more part-time working students into the system. But as long as one is meeting high standards both for entry and for successful completion of work toward the degree, the network of institutional and normative forces sketched above will make it very difficult to bring about any substantial change in the number or kind of students admitted.

THE UNITED STATES: EASY ACCESS AND PROBLEMATIC ACHIEVEMENT

In Great Britain, at least in the modern era, society has made a commitment to high uniform standards in its requirements both for entering into the system of higher education, as well as for the work required to earn a degree. Efforts to expand access or to make it more equitable have been constrained within the limits of those standards. In the United States, by contrast, and almost uniquely in the world, society has almost from its beginning taken ease and breadth of access to some form of post-secondary education as desirable, and its colleges and universities have for the most part struggled to achieve such standards of performance in teaching and scholarship as are compatible with ease of access. Looking at the system as a whole (though of course this would not be true for any specific institution) society has not let standards of achievement stand in the way of growth either at entry, or for the earned degree. To take one important example, in 1965 there were about 275,000 black students enrolled in all American colleges and universities. By 1977 that figure had grown to 1.1 million, and currently has levelled off at about one million — roughly 10 per cent of the whole population in colleges and universities. (Incidentally, the proportion of blacks attending college or university full-time in the United States is currently about 72 per cent, a little higher than the 70 per cent of white students enrolled for full-time study.) If we take students of black, Asian and Native American origins together, they constituted 6.6 per cent of the undergraduate enrolments overall in 1960, and almost exactly twice that, or 13 per cent, in 1978 (Kerr 1980).[6]

A substantial growth of the minority student population was a major national commitment in the United States during the decade of the 70s. The minorities wanted it, the federal governments under both Republican and Democratic administrations supported it, and the institutions of higher education themselves, almost without exception, were totally committed to it. The reasons for this national commitment take us quickly to the issue of the role and functions of higher education in American society. In the fifties and sixties society began the broad effort to transform a racial group defined by its physical characteristics and history of subordination into an ethnic group, alongside the many others that make up American society. In order for this to occur, it is necessary to create a large and educated black middle class so that blacks are differentiated by class and occupational interests just as are other groups. But that almost certainly could not have happened if our colleges and universities, like those in Britain, had been committed to a high and common standard of achievement throughout.[7]

American colleges and universities are beginning to perform the same function for recent immigrants of Hispanic origin — both Puerto Ricans and Mexicans. As completion of secondary education has become nearly universal in the United States, and as its standards and the value of its credentials have declined both relatively and, recently, absolutely, higher education has become a central vehicle for social mobility as well as social integration. It has thus inherited some of the functions performed traditionally (at least after the middle of the nineteenth century) by our comprehensive high schools. Colleges and universities will perform those functions differently — they are voluntary institutions, whereas high school attendance was mostly involuntary, and they are linked to the national scene, and to the national and international academic disciplines, while the high schools were very closely tied to their local communities. But as with the high schools, taking on a broad commitment to social mobility and social integration places strains on the integrity of universities and colleges as academic institutions and on their standards of achievement.

APPROACHES TO THE AMERICAN SYSTEM

A systematic approach to the issue of America's peculiar commitment to ease of access over uniform high academic standards would involve answers to at least these questions:

1   What were the origins of that commitment? Has it been that way from the beginning — and given our roots in English and Scottish culture and institutions, how and when could it have diverged so sharply? The answer to that question is a footnote, though a fascinating one, to the emergence of the American nation during our colonial period.

2   Whatever its origins, what were the institutional arrangements and the social, political and economic structures, that developed to permit and sustain a system of openness and diversity? This is in part a story of the weakness both of central government and of the academic guilds, and of the extraordinary strength of market forces from earliest days in American higher education.

3   How did the system that developed in the nineteenth century, and especially after the Civil War, respond to the enormous pressures for growth and further diversification that followed World War II? More abstractly, what functions has mass and universal higher education played in the social, political and economic life of the country over the past hundred years, and how does it continue to perform those functions? The GI Bill and the role of the veterans of World War II in the colleges and universities are part of that story; the role of the system in the racial revolution is another part; and the substantial changes that have taken place in the role of women in society, particularly in their opportunities for leadership in business, industry and the professions, is yet another.[8]

4   A narrower but no less crucial question is: How does a system seemingly so dominated by its broad social functions and market forces deal with the issue of competence, performance and achievement?

It is of course not possible to answer such questions systematically in this essay. But by way of illustration, I shall discuss the relative power of the market in American higher education, and try to show how the influence of market forces, almost uniquely in the world, affects every aspect of our system in ways that must influence their transferability to other societies. We are speaking, as in the case of British higher education, of a system, a web of interwoven elements, mutually supportive, receptive to some kinds of change and resistent to others, with its own strengths and weakness, and generating its own characteristic set of problems. For Britain, in a word, the problems of higher education have been how to increase its links to the larger society, how to strengthen its popular functions, broaden and make more equitable the access to it, and increase its contributions not only to industry and the economy but also to the local and national communities, and to applied knowledge of all kinds. In the United States the problems for higher education are how to maintain the integrity of the institutions, their commitment to their own standards and values, to their 'autonomous' functions, in the face of powerful social and market forces at work on and in them.

In approaching a system, one can start almost anywhere, and eventually implicate almost everything in it. One place to start is with the peculiar American commitment to a generalized, non-specialized education for undergraduates. Almost everywhere American colleges award degrees on the successful accumulation of a certain number of credits, earned there or in some other 'accredited' institution, of which a substantial proportion, usually 40 to 60 per cent of all units earned, are taken outside the student's field of specialization. Indeed in most four-year colleges and universities, the first two years are largely given over to meeting these 'breadth' requirements outside the major field, and a substantial part of the last two years is also taken in work outside the major. In many colleges and universities a student may not even necessarily 'declare' a major field of concentration until the third year, and even then the major itself may be a broad and self-designed interdisciplinary major. The actual courses taken to fulfil these breadth requirements are chosen by the student, sometimes with the help of a counsellor, from the very wide array of undergraduate courses offered by most colleges and universities. This great freedom of choice immediately points to the vulnerability to market forces both of the curriculum and of the institution at large.

But we can also quickly see the implications of that set of arrangements for access to higher education. It means, among other things, that a student need not have done specialized studies in the last years of secondary school, thus allowing not only a delay in deciding upon a field of specialization, but also a delay until the very last moment in deciding whether to continue on to post-secondary education. Indeed, it allows that decision to be made some years after leaving secondary school without further handicap.

But the pattern of general education has broader social and historical sources. If we enter the American web by moving along this strand of general, non-specialized studies, we begin by observing that general education is thought to be in the service of an American conception of 'liberal' education, which is rooted, in the United States as nowhere else, in the curriculum, and is vulnerable as nowhere else to the market.

A concern for general education is a peculiarly American problem for two reasons. First, in most European industrial societies (let us set aside Japan) university education is, as it has been almost from medieval times, very closely linked to a preparation for a career — in one of the old professions of law or medicine or the clergy, or in the civil service, or in teaching in a university or an élite, selective secondary school. In the nineteenth and twentieth centuries the range of professions that students prepared for in European universities broadened to include engineering, business management, social administration, and other non-élite forms of primary and secondary school teaching. But on the whole, what we think of as a liberal education — the cultivation of certain qualities of mind, the capacity to reflect on experience and to bring to it an historical perspective, certain critical and analytical capacities, the capacity for making independent judgements, the cultivation of aesthetic sensibilities — all of these and more are, or were until very recently in European societies, to a very large degree the task of the élite secondary school — the gymnasium, lycée, or grammar school. By the time young men (and the exclusion of the other gender is not accidental) reached university, a year or two older on average than in the United States, they were ready to begin their serious professional education. And on the whole what they studied in university was closely keyed to their subsequent professional careers, even where, as in Great Britain, the study of classical civilization was thought to be an appropriate preparation for entry into the civil service. This is not to say that their liberal education was not furthered in the university, but only that it occurred, when it occurred, as a by-product of a professional education — through reading outside formal study, through membership of literary and drama societies, through hearing and playing music, and travel, and above all through conversation. Unlike Americans, Europeans did not believe that students only learn what they are taught, and they placed the burden of much of what we call liberal education on the influence — informal, unscheduled, and unsupervised — of the university environment: that is to say, on the cultural and intellectual resources of the university, of the student culture, and of the city or town in which it was located and to which it was linked in many ways. This conception of liberal education works, when it works, in élite universities, with students who already have a broad and often superb advanced secondary education, and who often come from privileged and educated homes where liberal education was already implicit in the culture of the family, its books and dinner conversation. And the whole of the life of the student in the traditional British university — long vacations, freedom from the American student's relentless round of classes and examinations, and from the necessity to hold other kinds of paid jobs during university years — made it possible for his liberal education to be a function of the student's life and status rather than of the curriculum.

In America, things are otherwise, and have been for a long time. We can find certain similarities and parallels to European universities on the American scene — the importance of extra-curricular literary societies in the old pre-Civil War college, and even the meetings, lectures, theatre and dance and musical performances that mark the calendar of every modern American college and university. Nevertheless, liberal education in America is embedded in the curriculum rather than in the culture: it is, as we say, institutionalized in the liberal arts departments of the university, and when it is threatened, the threats are more visible because they are felt directly by its institutions.

Why liberal education is in this country a matter of the university curriculum rather than of the culture sheds light on the enormous difference between our systems of higher education and those of Western European countries. It was a mark of the élite university systems throughout Western Europe as recently as fifteen or twenty years ago that enrolments came to no more than four to six per cent of the age grade. Students were drawn very largely from well-to-do and educated homes, and had gone through the élite preparatory secondary school systems that subjected them to an education of a depth and intensity — in history, literature, science and mathematics — that we find almost unimaginable for late adolescents in our own country.

So it was social selectivity, the character of European secondary education, and the style and culture of university life that allowed liberal education to be carried on outside the curriculum in Europe. In America, throughout our history, but increasingly over the past century, the democratization of access to higher education, the relative weakness of our comprehensive high schools as compared with the élite preparatory schools of Europe, and the social and cultural isolation of our institutions have forced us to provide consciously and purposely what elsewhere could happen spontaneously and as the natural outcome of a set of social arrangements.

Liberal education in the United States is thus both stronger and more vulnerable than in Europe. It is stronger in that it can be made a required part of the student's experience of college life, through the coercive mechanisms of general education, breadth requirements and the like. Many European academics admire the forms of American general education, and decry the early, and in their view premature, specialization of a professionally oriented system — especially as the informal liberal education that went on in and around European universities breaks down with the expansion and democratization of access and the decline of the élite university culture in Europe.

But if liberal education in America is stronger for being institutionalized, it is also more vulnerable to market forces, and especially to the ebb and flow — recently more ebb than flow — of recruitment and enrolment and of the volatility of student subject preferences. Here I think it may be helpful to reflect on the central role of the market in American higher education, again by contrast with European countries.

THE MARKET AND HIGHER EDUCATION

The concept of markets in higher education is a way of talking about the many actors in a system of higher education who make decisions, and about the aggregate effects of the decisions made by these actors — students, faculty members, and administrators — located in a large number of colleges and universities. In markets we see operating a pattern of social choice, the relatively independent actions of self-interested parties, whose behaviour is not formally directed or co-ordinated, the outcomes of which no one has planned, but which is a 'resultant' rather than a 'solution' (Banfield 1961). The significance of markets in higher education is that as compared with other forms of social action the outcomes are not the result of planning or centralized purposive decision; moreover when the sellers (producers) are relatively numerous, their behaviours are marked by competition among them for the custom of the buyers. And that strengthens the influence of the buyers in the market over the character and quality of the product, indeed, over the very character of the producer.

We can see this when student age cohorts decline, and when colleges and universities compete for their enrolment. We can see it also when the sellers are graduates competing for relatively few job openings, for example in academic positions. Similarly, when research groups compete for scarce funds, funding agencies gain power over the character, direction and quality of the research they buy — in some areas of social science this may include influence over the nature of the research findings.

Between roughly 1955 and 1970 in the United States the student demand for places outstripped the supply, and many suppliers, that is colleges and universities, could raise the conditions for entry. The influence of a few top medical schools on the behaviour of pre-medical students (and on their undergraduate institutions) is still a case in point. Indeed in a number of élite colleges, universities, and professional schools, applications still far outrun available places, and the producer retains its power in the market even when enrolments nationally are stable or declining. But apart from the quite unusual period of rapid growth in demand between roughly 1955 and 1970, the supply of places has on the whole outstripped demand; and buyers or potential buyers at both ends, students and the employers of graduates, have had a powerful influence on the behaviour of most colleges. This influence is likely to be even greater in a period of declining demand and declining enrolments.

We can see the emergence of the strength of market forces in the early history of American higher education. We can see those forces in the very structure and workings of our institutions. And we can see the American market at work by comparison with the systems of other societies. Let us look at it in each of these ways: historically, comparatively, structurally.

A multiplicity of forces and motives lay behind the establishment of colleges and universities throughout American history. There were, among others, a variety of religious motives; a fear of relapse into barbarism at the frontier; a need for various kinds of professionals; local boosterism, philanthropy, and speculation in land; and these in all combinations. But the number and diversity of institutions competing with one another for students, resources and teachers and bringing market considerations and market mechanisms right into the heart of this ancient cultural institution required the absence of any central force or authority that could limit or control its proliferation. Especially important has been the absence of a federal ministry of education with the power to charter new institutions, or of a single pre-eminent university that could influence them in other ways.

The closest we have come as a nation to establishing such a central force was the attempt first by George Washington, and then by the next five presidents, to found a University of the United States. Washington saw the possibility of creating one really first-class university by concentrating money and other resources in it. As he noted in his last message to Congress: 'Our country, much to its honor, contains many seminaries of learning highly respectable and useful; but the funds upon which they rest are too narrow to command the ablest professors in the different departments of liberal knowledge for the institution contemplated, though they would be excellent auxiliaries.' Here indeed, Washington was right in his diagnosis. The many institutions that sprang up between the Revolution and the Civil War all competed for very scarce resources and all suffered to some degree from malnutrition. Indeed, malnutrition at the margin is still a characteristic of the American system.

Defeat of the national university (by a Congress which essentially feared federal institutions and was committed to states' rights) meant that American higher education would develop, to this day, without a single capstone institution. Had we concentrated resources in a university of world standard early in our national life, it might have been the equal of the great and ancient universities of Europe or of the distinguished new universities then being established in Germany and elsewhere. As it was, whatever the titles of our institutions of higher learning, the nation did not have a single genuine university until after the Civil War. But the other side of the coin is that our hundreds of state and private colleges might never have been born if there had been a great federal university in Washington to establish and monitor academic standards. If those colleges had been created (for many of the forces behind them would still have existed) they would have been relegated to a separate second class of institutions, offering post-secondary training in vocational subjects for young men and women of modest social origins, but not the same curriculum, credits, or degrees offered by the small number of colleges and universities able to meet the standards established by the national university. Such a two-class system exists today in many European countries.

The University of the United States failed: and the ironic result is that without any central model, or governmental agency able to create one or more national systems, all of our 3000 institutions, public and private, modest and pre-eminent, religious and secular, are in some way part of a common system in higher education.

The failure of the University of the United States, and the success of Dartmouth College in 1819 in its appeal to the Supreme Court against being taken over by the State of New Hampshire, were both victories for local initiative and for private entrepreneurship. The first set limits on the role of the federal government; the second set even sharper limits on the power of the state over private colleges. Together, these two events constituted a charter for unrestrained initiative in the creation of colleges of all sizes, shapes and creeds. Almost any motive or combination of motives and interests could bring a college into being in the United States between the Revolution and the Civil War; its survival depended largely on its being able to secure support from a church, from wealthy benefactors, from student fees and even perhaps from the state. The colleges thus created were estabished relatively easily, but without guarantees of survival. As a result their behaviour resembled that of living organisms in an ecological system — competitive for resources, highly sensitive to the demands of their environment, and inclined, through the ruthless processes of natural selection, to be adaptive to those aspects of their environment that permitted their survival. So we see in this frog pond a set of mechanisms that we usually associate with the behaviour of small entrepreneurs in a market: the anxious concern for what the market wishes, the readiness to adapt to its apparent preferences, the effort to find a special place in that market through the marginal differentiation of the product, a readiness to enter into symbiotic or parasitic relationships with other producers for a portion of that market. All of this obviously bears on the tension throughout our history between liberal education and vocational/professional studies. We are employing a language that Europeans tend to find strange and often distasteful when used in connection with institutions of higher learning. But distasteful or not, an American must insist on this central and distinguishing characteristic of American higher education, that it is a network of institutions which resembles in its behavour the myriad of small capitalistic enterprises that were springing up everywhere at the same time and in the same places, and often in response to the same forces.

The market has been involved with American higher education since the beginning in the most blatant ways. For example, some of the motives that led to the establishment of colleges were simply those of the land speculator. In America, as Louis Hartz has noted, the market preceded society, a central and powerful fact whose ramifications can be seen in all of our institutions and throughout our national life. We are, to put it crudely, not embarrassed by the market. We still believe it is a perfectly sensible mechanism for the ordering of our affairs — and not just economic affairs, but cultural and intellectual life as well. We did not inherit the corporatism of medieval life, or the statism of absolute monarchy. We were from our origins a liberal society, and our arguments have been the arguments of various branches of liberalism. But Europeans, even those who rather like the market in economic affairs, find its presence oddly embarrassing in the realm of culture, or religion, or statecraft, or scholarship.

The reference to Europeans prompts us to ask in what other ways societies organize and manage systems of higher education. Broadly speaking, there are three (Clark 1979):

1   Through political decisions — as the outcome of the play of power and interests in political arenas.

2   Through bureaucratic regulation: essentially, through management by a ministry and its civil service.

3   Through the power of organized professional guilds, applying

academic norms and values in the service of the university as defined by the professors.

Every system organizes itself and makes its decisions through some combination of all of these ways. But the relative weight and importance of one or another — market mechanisms, professional norms, bureaucratic regulations, and political decision — varies greatly between national systems.

One the whole, academic guilds are highly conservative regarding access and standards in universities, but in the United States the academic profession has been traditionally weak, and still is so in all but the small number of élite colleges and research universities. Governments too, on the whole, want to control access, both within their conceptions of 'national needs' and also within the severe constraints of scarce resources and competitive demands, especially when almost the whole of the costs of higher education are borne by the public treasury. But here again, in the United States these powerful constraints on growth and ease of access are weak. And so market forces are relatively strong: and the market in the United States not only engenders demand for places, but forces the lowering both of academic, cultural and institutional barriers to entry, and with some help from politicians, even of economic barriers.

If we contrast American and British attitudes, Americans are on the whole ambivalent, seeing in markets virtues as well as threats and dangers to education. By contrast, Europeans tend to dislike market mechanisms in education, and do everything they can to reduce their influence. This difference arises out of our profoundly differing feelings about culture.

For Europeans, the consumers of higher education are by definition incompetent, or at least less competent than their teachers and academic administrators, who together produce instruction. Markets threaten the 'integrity' of cultural institutions by increasing the power of consumers as against producers: that is, the people who are presumably most competent to supply some given kind of cultural entity, whether it be the performance of music or higher studies in philosophy or physics. Europeans try very hard to reduce the influence of the incompetent mass on high cultural matters, and to preserve a realm of élite determination of cultural form and content. In higher education most importantly, they try to insulate the financing of institutions from student fees. They may do this by direct state funding of institutions and also by controlling enrolments. But even if they allow enrolments some degree of autonomous growth, they try to prevent them from governing levels of financial support. In the United States, enrolment-driven budgets in all but a few institutions, both public and private, ensure that most institutions are extremely sensitive to student preferences, especially when the numbers of students are declining. We can see very clearly that as a result the power of the consumer — whether student or employer — will strengthen the standing of vocational and professional studies, while the often weak academic guilds stand opposed to the market in their defence of liberal education.

114 ACCESS TO HIGHER EDUCATION

We can see other examples of the comparative hospitality of American institutions to market forces. One of them, for example, can be seen in the way in which Congress decided to provide major public funding for colleges and universities. After sharp debate in the early seventies, the federal government chose to fund colleges and universities chiefly by providing grants and loans to students, rather than through direct support to the institutions themselves. Thus the decision was to subsidize higher education through the consumers rather than directly to the producers. The result was to strengthen substantially the relative power of consumers over producers, especially in a period of declining demand.

Other countries, on the whole, do not want to strengthen the power of students as consumers, for fear of the effect on the character, quality and standards of their institutions and national system. The maintenance of a national system of universities with high common standards requires that the system be managed by state agencies in collaboration with the academic guilds. The question of how to make those systems responsive to national needs is decided by political agencies, advised by civil servants and academic committees. Sometimes, for example as in Sweden, representatives of the great economic interests, corporations and trade unions, are placed on the boards that shape higher educational policy. (This has resulted in a powerful tilt toward vocational and professional studies in Swedish universities.) In addition, a strongly egalitarian series of governments have, through political means, increased access for mature students with work experience, reducing the academic criteria for entry. But almost everywhere outside the United States, the combination of political, bureaucratic and professional structures operates to insulate higher education from competitive market forces, and controls and ultimately constrains access.

One can see the differences between market systems and those dominated by other principles of organization and political decision making in broad patterns of organization and finance. But we can also see the influence of market mechanisms in the private life of higher education, in the very processes of teaching and learning. One such example is our peculiar system of earned and transferable 'credits', a kind of academic currency that we all take for granted in American institutions. The unit credit system is almost wholly absent from other systems where degrees are earned by passing examinations or writing dissertations. But our credits, units that can be accumulated, banked, transferred, and within limits automatically accepted as legal academic tender toward an earned degree throughout the system, make possible the extraordinary mobility of our students in three distinct dimensions: between field of study, between institutions, and over time.

Our credit system, together with our system of courses, each examined and graded separately, is related to the American conception of a liberal education, a broad unspecialized undergraduate curriculum, not keyed to any specific occupation or profession, but emphasizing a certain familiarity with all the major areas of learning. Our conception of a liberal education, especially its emphasis on the elective principle, requires the credit system — or, looked at differently, the credit system is made possible by an undergraduate curriculum which is based on the aggregate of specific units of instruction rather than the accumulation of knowledge in a specialized area that can be examined at the end of three or four or five years, or that produces a dissertation as evidence of competence achieved.

An inventory of unique qualities must include a reference to the multiplicity of subjects taught in our colleges and universities, a product of the extraordinary hospitality of our institutions to almost any subject that might have a claim to be useful, or to be rooted in a body of skill and knowledge that can be studied and taught. But this range of studies, often the subject of somewhat derisive comment by Europeans, would not be possible if we had a central agency maintaining high standards and scrutinizing new subjects for their appropriateness as judged by traditional university criteria. Our openness to new subjects is linked to the absence of a central administrative body that certifies institutions and subjects, as well as to our consequent reliance on market forces to sustain our many weak and impoverished institutions.

By way of illustration, a recent report notes that in the past year alone,

'The number of courses offered by (American) colleges and univer- sities. . . increased by an estimated 15 per cent. . . . Among the largest increases were course offerings in nursing and allied health fields, up 22 per cent, and engineering, up 20 per cent. . . . The increase in course offerings came at a time when many colleges and universities had been forced to trim their budgets, and in some cases reduce the number of courses they offered. The proliferation of courses may, in part, have been the result of the efforts of some institutions to attract more students by offering a wider choice of courses. New courses also have been designed to appeal to a particular group of students, such as refresher courses for older women re-entering the job market.' (*Chronicle of Higher Education* 1981)

Market forces are a prime source of the American system's unique qualities — its size, diversity, flexibility, openness and responsiveness. But while the market is a source of great strengths, it is also the source of profound problems and corruptions. Take, for example, the elaborate, indeed sometimes desperate, efforts of many, especially weaker, institutions to recruit students, whether for their tuition fees or for the enrolment-driven formulas by which most public institutions are funded. Most institutions do not confront the question of whether the strenuous recruitment of some of these students serves the interests of the students as well as those of the institution. Sometimes the justification for these activities draws on the widespread American belief (only now beginning to be questioned) that on the whole people ought to get as much formal education as you can persuade them to sit still for; sometimes this is combined with the market's classic disclaimer of moral responsibility — caveat emptor. But whether the market is for warm bodies to meet budgets, or for black or brown bodies to meet affirmative action targets, it is clear that there is not a perfect correspondence between the interests of the recruiting college or university, and the recruited student. Important moral issues arise in this area. One can question the institution's responsibility in recruitment for what might be called 'consumer protection,' or, after students have been admitted, for providing counselling and other support services. The 'revolving door' has moral dimensions, as well as academic and financial implications for colleges and universities. Grade inflation and the lowering of demands and standards to attract students are among the other pathologies of colleges and departments that are acutely threatened by the decline of enrolments and the fear of administrative action or budget cuts. There are similar dangers on the research side.

I have been trying to suggest that the market principle is the ultimate source of the great diversity and responsiveness of American higher education to the needs of the larger society around it, and also the source of grave problems and pressures toward academic corruption and pathologies. Moreover, these pressures are likely to be greater in the coming decades of financial constraint and enrolment decline. The market, it is said, knows neither love nor hate. But also, the market and those governed by it know the cost of everything and the value of nothing.

The growth of remedial work in colleges and universities is a specific example of how market forces and political pressures together can threaten liberal education, by creating yet another competition for its time and resources. Over the past two decades there has been a substantial and measurable decline in the academic achievement performance levels of students entering American colleges. Between 1968 and 1980 mean Scholastic Aptitude Test Verbal scores declined nationally from 466 to 424; SAT math scores went from 492 to 466 in the same period (University of California 1981). There have been many explanations for this trend: changes in family structure, geographical mobility, the increase in television watching and a waning respect for parental and other forms of authority are all cited. But what is taught and learned in the primary and secondary schools under increasing social, political and economic pressures and distractions, is a key element.

Overall, the response of American colleges and universities to the threat to their standards takes a characteristic form. Market, as well as academic considerations, make it impossible simply to ignore the general decline in achievement. But on the other hand, the institutions of higher education have little direct influence on the school system, since there are no political agencies through which that influence could be exercised. Instead, almost all of them, private and public, large and small, increasingly try to remedy in college academic deficiencies accumulated during the primary and secondary years. In this past year, without any central direction or co-ordination, the number of remedial courses taught in colleges and universities across the country rose by 22 per cent: 25 per cent in private institutions and 19 per cent in public. 'Even the more selective private liberal arts colleges . . . offered twice as many remedial courses in the fall of 1980 as in the fall of 1979' (*Chronicle of Higher Education* 1981).

The problems of the schools in America are now also the problems of its colleges and universities. This has perhaps always been true — the weakness of our schools has been in part a function of their commitment to open access and the postponement of final decisions about career determination. But now more than ever, some of what we do in higher education is dictated by what others do not do in the schools. One might also say that we can afford our wretched high schools because of the extraordinary openness and effectiveness of our community colleges and four-year colleges in remedying the defects of the school system.

Everyone is in favour of providing remedial work in college — at least until we begin to assess the costs. The decline in the ability and preparation of our entering students poses painful dilemmas for the faculty. A University of California report puts the issue very clearly:

'The effects of underpreparation are felt not only by students, but also by faculty. Those we interviewed told us, unequivocally, that teaching has gotten harder, that a professor can no longer assume a common level of knowledge or skill in a class because preparation is so varied, but more importantly, that faculty are now being asked to handle problems, especially in writing, that they were never trained to handle.
'The faculty we talked to who are affected most by composition problems seem to see two choices. They can either spend a great deal of time on an individual basis helping students and reconsidering their own teaching methods, or they can ignore it, keep going as they are, leave the problems to learning specialists trained to handle them and invest their time elsewhere where they feel more comfortable and productive. One English professor said, "I have a choice in my Shakespeare class: fake it and teach the course anyway, giving the students C's or B's; or adjourn Shakespeare and teach writing."
'On top of this frustration, many faculty are also worried about class standards. If faculty members choose to spend their time working with students on writing, they have to assign less reading because students have a finite amount of time to spend on any course. If, on the other hand, the faculty chooses to ignore the problem, there is a fear they may assign easier reading, require less writing, and give more multiple choice exams, in order not to face problems in composition. And not assigning writing means less practice for students who need more, exacerbating the problem.

'This squeeze between a rock and a hard place is felt by mathematics faculty, too. They usually expressed it to us as "a need to protect the integrity of our calculus courses." For them, the problem can be solved by requiring prerequisites they control, even though they would prefer that students take those courses in high school instead. But there is an outcome, felt especially in mathematics, that service courses are beginning to overwhelm the real mission of the University departments. As one professor put it,

"Everyone agrees that we should help students who need it, but what concerns us is that there are *so many* students who need it. Offering pre-calculus classes has decreased the availability of the upper division courses that should be taught by anything calling itself a University math department. There is now a little resentment about what the increase in service courses is doing to our department and alarm about what will happen if it gets worse." ' (University of California 1981)

The costs of remedial work are felt in faculty morale, and in resources that are unavailable for regular course work. In the academic year 1979-80, the University of California spent over $5 million on basic skills courses and programmes for underprepared students. Some of them are not offered for credit, and are not specially supported by state funds, but must be supported by stretching the general instructional support funds. And this does not include the considerable amount of faculty time that goes into such preparatory courses.

CONCLUSION

What does all this have to do with access to British higher education? I do not want to impose a simplistic summary on what is in fact a complicated set of issues, both within and across national boundaries. But perhaps a few inferences can be drawn.

1   The 'élite-mass-universal access' model linked the phases closely to size, and made movement from one phase to another a function of growth. We might now consider the possibility that an élite system can acquire some institutions and characteristics of mass higher education without growth much beyond present levels. Increasing awareness of that possibility helps to explain the persistent interest of British progressives in the issues of access to their system of higher education.

2   The forms of access to higher education characteristic of the United States are best understood in the light of its history, its organization and structures, and the functions American higher education performs and has performed in American life. That web of elements includes patterns and arrangements, such as trans- ferable credits, which are especially attractive to progressive

Europeans, as well as problems and difficulties, such as the growing need for remedial teaching, which are painfully apparent to Americans.

3   It may well be that some of what is admired in American higher education can be borrowed and adapted to different circumstances, without having to import all of the problems and difficulties which are associated with a given structure or arrangement in the United States. But such efforts would profit from careful analyses, both of the proposal, and of the rather different meanings and consequences it would carry in the two quite different systems. In the course of this kind of analysis, it may be profitable to focus closely on certain key differences between our institutions — as, for example, the ability of big American universities to teach students of very different qualification and ability within the same institution, while in Britain the tendency is for sharper 'streaming' between its universities and other forms of higher and further education.

It may seem characteristically bland for an academic to end an essay with a call for more research and closer study before taking action. But we might specify what we should be looking at so closely. The next step, I suggest, is to take one or more concrete proposals — let us say, for an open-door full-time degree-granting British university. Can we do the kind of analysis of such a proposal — its costs, academic forms and structures, political feasibility, etc. — that would improve the chances for successful social action? It may well be (indeed I suspect it is) the case that such a proposal, just now, would involve too great a deformation of the web of British higher education, its values and institutions, to be a practical idea. But a close study of such an idea might reveal which of its elements are least acceptable, and which potentially adaptable, to the existing academic and political structures. And those insights might guide the slower work of incremental reform. After the pleasures of reflection, even academics might find it rewarding to be efficacious.

NOTES

1   Those 'forms' of higher education are discussed in detail in my OECD paper (Trow 1974). Very briefly, élite education systems prepare up to 15 to 20 per cent of an age grade for a traditional set of careers in teaching (university and university-preparatory), the higher civil service, and the established professions; mass higher education systems prepare up to 50 per cent of the age grade for a wide range of white-collar occupations; universal access systems prepare even larger numbers for life in advanced industrial societies, severing the link between post-secondary education and occupations.

2   Parts of this section are drawn from or responsive to that paper.

3   The work of Burton Clark is an important contribution to the

comparative perspectives needed (see, for example, Clark 1979).

4   This is similar to the motives that led to the 25/5 provisions in the Swedish reforms of higher education.

5   This compares with the staff-student ratio of 1:17.5 at Berkeley. But that is not a fair comparison. Berkeley, like other big state universities, is essentially a comprehensive university, combining in the same institution élite and mass forms of higher education, kinds of work that in Britain are divided among universities, polytechnics and colleges both of higher and of further education. Leading private research universities in the United States, like Stanford and Yale, as well as the best four-year liberal arts colleges, like Swarthmore and Oberlin, have staff-student ratios very close to those in British universities.

6   Sources: United States Census of Population (1960) *Subject Reports*; for school enrolment, *Final Report PC (2)-5A*; National Center for Educational Statistics (1968) *Digest of Educational Statistics* Washington, DC: US Government Printing Office, Table 100.

7   This raises an interesting problem for the United Kingdom, which is just beginning to see the problem of the integration of a racial minority into its more homogeneous society. I have no doubt that the 'normal processes' of acculturation, over three or four generations, will produce significant numbers of students of West Indian origins who are qualified in the normal way for entry into British colleges and universities. Can British society, or the West Indians, wait that long; and if not, how can the process be speeded up?

8   In 1960 women constituted 38 per cent of the total undergraduate enrolments in American colleges and universities. In 1979 the proportion was over 50 per cent. Whereas in 1960 they made up 29 per cent of all graduate students, by 1979 they constituted 47 per cent of the graduate student population (Kerr 1980).

REFERENCES
Banfield, E. (1961) *Political Influence* New York: The Free Press
Cerych, L. and Colton, S. (1980) Summarising student flows *European Journal of Education* 15 (1)
Chronicle of Higher Education (1981) 22 (18) pp.1, 8
Clark, B.R. (1979) The many pathways of academic coordination *Higher Education* 8
Geiger, R.L. (1980) *The Limits of Higher Education: A Comparative Analysis of Factors Affecting Enrolment Levels in Belgium, France, Japan and The United States* Working Paper of the Higher Education Research Group, Yale University
Hecquet, I., Verniers, C. and Cerych, L. (1976) *Recent Student Flows in Higher Education* Paris: OECD
Kerr, Clark (1980) *Higher Education: What We Have Learned From the Golden Age and Lessons for the Age of Survival* Walker-Ames Lecture,

University of Washington (unpublished)
Trow, Martin, (1974) Problems in the transition from elite to mass higher education. In OECD *Policies for Higher Education* Paris: OECD
Trow, Martin (1979) Elite and mass higher education: American models and European realities. In *Research into Higher Education: Processes and Structures* Stockholm: NBUC
University of California (1981) *Report to the Policy Committee on the University of California's Activities to Assist Underprepared Students* University of California
Williams, Shirley (1981) *Politics is for People* Penguin Books

4

THE EDUCATIONAL CHOICES OF YOUNG PEOPLE

by Alan Gordon

This chapter examines the range of factors influencing the educational choices of young people between the ages of fifteen and eighteen. Their age range covers two critical transition points: the minimum school-leaving age when young people first have an opportunity to participate voluntarily in full-time education; and the age of eighteen, where typically those who continued their studies two years previously, and who followed GCE 'A' level courses, have the chance of applying for a place in higher education. While a large part of the chapter is devoted to young people's decision to try for a higher education place, any summary review of this kind must also give proper attention to the probably more important decision to stay on in full-time education beyond the minimum school-leaving age. The large majority of young people are effectively excluded from consideration for higher education because of their prior decision to leave school at sixteen.

The main factors reviewed here have been grouped under three headings. First, the influence of such social factors as home background, sex, parental education and attitudes, and so on; second, the influence of school-related factors; and third, the effects of such economic variables as the material circumstances of the home, educational maintenance allowances, and young people's perceptions of the benefits and costs associated with continued education.

SOCIAL FACTORS

Since 1944 a large number of research reports, some government-sponsored, have drawn attention to the under-representation of young people from working-class home backgrounds in post-compulsory education. Parental occupation, education and attitudes have all been shown to be closely associated with a young person's progress (or lack of progress) through to the highest levels of the education system. This part of the chapter reviews some of the major evidence on the influence of the home environment on educational achievement beyond the minimum school-leaving age.

Parental Occupation

As far as access to higher education is concerned it is difficult to agree with Joseph and Sumption's (1979) general comment that 'class distinctions have faded to the point where they are no more significant than the shape of a man's hat and the intervals at which he is paid'. Research evidence over a period of some thirty years indicates the scale of class differences in post-compulsory education and the ways in which very little has changed by the 1980s (see, for example, CACE 1954, 1959; HMSO 1963; Douglas et al. 1968; Schools Council 1968; Fulton and Gordon 1979; Halsey et al. 1980). There are numerous well-researched commentaries that document:

> '(the) well-known fact that working-class children (and particularly the children of unskilled manual workers) are under-represented in selective secondary and higher education; and that even at the same levels of ability they are far more likely than middle-class children to deteriorate in performance and to leave school at the earliest permitted age.' (Craft 1970)

This situation is not, of course, peculiar to this country. Similar inequalities in participation in higher education are found in most other developed countries too (OECD 1970; Bockstael and Feinstein 1970; King et al. 1974; Neave 1976).

One of the Robbins Committee's most important findings was that the proportion of children from non-manual home backgrounds who obtained places in higher education was some six times as great as the children of people in manual occupations (HMSO 1963). Indeed, the difference between professionals and those from unskilled manual families was of the order of twenty to one. Figures for social class participation are given by Farrant in Chapter 2 (Table 2.17, and 2.18, pp.85 and 86), and discussed on pages 59-63. As he shows, these differentials have scarcely narrowed even though the absolute age participation rates for all social classes have risen. Indeed, the university differentials are almost unchanged from the levels prevailing some fifty years ago — and are somewhat wider than those of the early and mid-1970s.

These statistics can only ever inform us of the end result of education and socialization processes that, from an early age, militate to the cumulative advantage of some groups of young people and against others. As Table 4.1 clearly shows, while pupils from different types of home background are reasonably evenly (but not equitably — compare the whole population) distributed at the GCE Ordinary Level examinations, thereafter the dominance of the 'Service Class' shows itself.

The failure of working-class young people to carry on their full-time education beyond the age of sixteen and into higher education might well cause less concern if it could be shown that ability, however measured, varied greatly between different social class groups, so that the education system was meritocratically keeping the most able within its care and attention. Much research and argument has taken place over the past two decades on the question of the extent to which equal opportunities[1] in education have been achieved for young people of similar abilities and attributes (eg Westergaard and Little 1964). Halsey et al. (1980) suggest that, in fact, the ability threshold for working-class young people to enter university is markedly higher than for other young people with fathers in either service or intermediate occupations. Their research showed that, on average in the years 1950-1970, a would-be student from a working-class background had to be some 6.6 IQ points brighter than a similar higher education aspirant from a service family background (Table 4.2).

TABLE 4.1
The class composition of successive stages of education selection (%)

Fathers' social class*	Whole sample	'O' levels	'A' levels	University
Service class	13.7	35.5	49.1	52.4
Intermediate class	31.4	34.2	29.4	27.9
Working class	54.9	30.2	21.5	19.7
All	100	99.9	100	100

*This differs from the Registrar-General's social class definition used in Chapter 2. See Halsey et al. (1980)

Source
Halsey et al. (1980) Tables 2.1 and 10.6

TABLE 4.2
IQ thresholds for university entry

Fathers' social class*	IQ
Service class	120.8
Intermediate class	125.6
Working class	127.4
Service class/working class IQ handicap	6.6

*See Table 4.1

Source
Halsey et al. (1980) Table 10.7

Halsey et al. (1980) are particularly concerned that 'past selection processes, especially to the highest education in the universities, cannot satisfy either meritocrats, or still less egalitarians'. Some twenty years ago, too, Floud (1961) concluded that differences in class chances could not be 'easily attributed to differences in measured ability'. But if we ask whether selection for university is more or less meritocratic than earlier selection processes, even very recent figures produced for upper-secondary and further education (eg Dean et al. 1979) indicate that young people with fathers in higher occupations are similarly over-represented in full-time education after sixteen. It seems in fact that it is at the minimum school-leaving age that the greatest amount of differentiation between the social classes occurs (see, for example, Gordon and Williams 1977; Fulton and Gordon 1979; Halsey et al. 1980). The latter conclude that 'the school-leaving age would therefore seem to be the crucial stage for public policies aimed at reducing class inequalities of educational opportunity'.

To focus on application and participation rates in higher education, then, might well lead to a failure to appreciate the important policy issues of demand for, and access to, full-time post-compulsory education. If working-class young people survive in the education system until the age of eighteen their chances of going on to higher education are not so very different from their middle-class classmates. Halsey et al. (1980) found that while seventy per cent of boys from service class backgrounds who continued their full-time studies until the age of eighteen went on to university, the figure for boys from intermediate and working-class families who did so was only a little lower at sixty per cent. The expansion in non-university higher education, which occurred too late for most of Halsey's sample, may have moved these figures even closer together.

While it is, of course, necessary to review the scale of the influence of social class on young people's progress in the education system, this does not tell the reasons for class inequalities. As Neave (1976) points out, social class may be a good predictor of academic survival, but it does not explain. For that we must go beyond the statistics of differential demand and participation.

The Pool of Ability
In the early 1960s there was a belief in some quarters that the number of young people with the capacity to benefit from higher education was rigidly limited, and that any expansion in the number of places provided by institutions of higher education could only be filled by dredging the depths of this fixed pool of ability. Because of these fears, support for the maxim that 'more means worse', publicly propounded by Kingsley Amis, was reasonably widespread, and included support from some of those teaching in the universities. The Robbins Committee marshalled a great deal of evidence to demonstrate that the notion of a rigid pool of talent limited by biology and inherited abilities was misguided. The committee went to to say:

'In short we think there is no risk that within the next twenty years the growth in the proportion of young people with qualifications and aptitudes suitable for entry to higher education will be restrained by shortage of potential ability. The numbers who are capable of benefiting from higher education are a function not only of heredity but also a host of other influences varying with standards of education provision, family incomes and attitudes and the education received by previous generations. If there is to be talk of a pool of ability, it must be a pool which surpasses the widow's cruse in the Old Testament, in that when more is taken for higher education in one generation more tend to be available in the next.' (HMSO 1963)

More recent research, too, has stressed that fears of a limited 'pool of ability' are unjustified (Halsey et al. 1980). Indeed, a more common anxiety is the converse — that there still exist high levels of untapped ability amongst young people from manual home backgrounds and among girls. It is still true that 'many manual working class pupils who have the ability to benefit from a sixth year at school or college are failing to do so' (Douglas et al. 1968). In theory at least, the wastage of talent would be substantially reduced if the advantages 'conveyed by the chance of birth, as a male, into a professional family' (Fulton and Gordon 1979) could be made available to all young people.

Parental Attitudes
Roberts (1980) is one of many to comment on the reasons for class-related disadvantage in the education system. Reviewing research on the benefits of those born into middle-class homes, he suggests that one advantage is 'having articulate and confident parents who recognise the relevance of education for life chances . . . .'

Morover, Roberts (1980) has few doubts about the strength of middle class parental expectations for their children:

'Middle class parents do not treat success as a prize reserved for the intellectually brilliant, but act on the assumption that it lies within the grasp of any industrious child of their own.'

This assessment does not differ greatly from those of other researchers over more than twenty years. Floud (1961) wrote of '. . . fundamental differences as between the social classes in ways of life, values, attitudes and aspirations, as well as in material circumstances.' She concluded that, in the short run at least, parental attitudes towards education are very much class-typed. Similarly, Gordon and Williams (1976) say that social class differences

'can be accounted for in terms of parental interest and encouragement, the influence of lifestyle and transmitted aspirations and the familiarity pupils and parents have with both the demands of post-compulsory education and with the types of jobs available after continued study.'

And Thomas and Wetherell (1971) comment that class groupings are usually associated with material circumstances and the standard of living enjoyed. This theme is returned to below.

Neave (1971) observed that external examinations, particularly CSE and GCE 'O' levels, perform very different functions for middle-class and working-class parents. For middle-class parents the success of their children in examinations serves to justify further support and encouragement, while failure leads not to acceptance but to calls for additional work and effort. They are in fact more likely to offer support and encouragement throughout their child's schooling. Working-class parents, on the other hand, (and those who were early-leavers themselves) generally only seem to offer the same kind of encouragement once good examination results are available as evidence of their child's academic potential. Morris (1969) suggests that parental encouragement is important at two stages. First, in supporting children's provisional intentions and second, in reinforcing a student's determination to carry on with a course of action already started.

Parental Education

Parents' experiences of post-compulsory education certainly influence their attitudes towards whether their children should continue their studies after the age of sixteen or eighteen (eg CACE 1959; HMSO 1963). In sixth forms, further education and higher education, students whose parents had themselves continued in full-time education are over-represented (Williams and Gordon 1975; Dean et al. 1980). A large number of studies (eg Thomas and Wetherell 1974; Rauta and Hunt 1975) have pointed out the high correlation between the age at which parents and their children left school. In addition, Neave (1975) found that the amount of influence parents have over their child's decision to stay on in or leave full-time education was strongly associated with the amount of education they themselves had received. Parents who had left school before their fifteenth birthday were much less influential. Both middle-class and more highly educated parents generally take more interest in their children's schooling[2] (see, for example, Douglas 1964; Douglas et al. 1968).

Peers

A possible influence on leavers is '. . . anti-school peer groups and subcultures . . .' (Neave 1976). It is evident that among some groups of working-class pupils there is a deep-rooted cultural hostility towards the main objectives of secondary and continued education (Willis 1977). But it seems that, for the decision to go on to university at least, the importance of the influence of peers depends on children's social background. The peer group is more important the less support is received from home, and peers are least influential for those young people whose parents have some experience of post-compulsory education themselves. In addition, for those hoping and planning to go on to higher education, 'the peer group appears to be influential for precisely those who already derive their main support from the school' (Neave 1975).

TABLE 4.3
Students' rating of school influence as related to peers' influence on the decision to try for university (%)

Peer Group	School Influences		
	Low	High	n = 100%
Not influential	64	36	462
Influential	44	56	375
Highly influential	36	64	132

Source
Neave (1975) Table 6.8

As far as a counter-school culture is concerned, however, some working-class pupils in compulsory education do derive great support from their peers: it can hardly be said that the secondary school regime supports their lack of interest or their disruption, but it acts as a common focus for disenchantment (Willis 1977).

Sex
One of the anxieties expressed by the Robbins Committee was over the wastage of female talent. On grounds of economic efficiency, rather than equity, they felt that much better use had to be made of academically able women who represented 'what must be the greatest source of unused talent.' To some extent these ambitions have been realized, as Chapter 2 shows (see especially Table 2.16 (p.84) and pages 57-59). Women's participation in all types of full-time higher education now stands at forty-three per cent of students (provisional figures: DES 1981). In addition, it does appear that girls' educational ambitions in recent years have converged with those of boys (Fulton and Gordon 1979). If these ambitions materialized this would represent a further improvement in relative chances. In spite of these trends it seems still to be the case that the general environmental and educational disadvantages of working-class young people are compounded in the case of girls. Many working-class parents still attach more importance to their son's education than to their daughter's. 'The resources — cultural, economic, psychological — necessary for a working-class child to overcome the obstacles on the way to a university place are very rarely expended on behalf

of a girl' (Westergaard and Little 1964).

Similar criticism has also been levelled at schools' attitudes towards girls' education. Blackstone and Weinreich-Haste (1980) have recently commented on the ways in which girls have been 'taught' to under-achieve. Sharp (1976) blames this under-achievement and the low career aspirations of many girls on teachers and careers counsellors. A combination then of home and school environment prevents many girls from fulfilling their educational potential. The most important issue now, however, is probably not the general aspirations of girls, but their often limited choice of subjects.

General
Throughout the 1960s and 1970s there was a general expectation among both educationalists and policy makers that the expansion of British higher education, together with the reorganization of secondary education along comprehensive lines, would lead to an opening up of higher education to those of lower social origins. The evidence above is unequivocal on this point: in spite of these developments the proportion of students who come from working-class backgrounds is virtually the same as half a century ago. This is the 'sad statistic' to which Jackson and Marsden (1966) drew our attention some fifteen years ago. It is clear that:

'the expansion of educational provision has not involved a major redistribution of opportunities between children of different classes . . . .
'. . . as in the past the growth of student places in higher education from the early 1960s met a demand which, in effect, came mainly from professional, managerial and other non-manual homes. The scales remain heavily weighted against young people of manual working-class origin, though probably not quite so much as before.' (Westergaard and Resler 1975)

In view of the persistence of the social class inequalities in access to upper-secondary and higher education reviewed above, one has to ask whether Bernstein (1970) might have been correct in his assessment that 'education cannot compensate for society'. Westergaard and Little (1964) took a similarly pessimistic view of the extent to which education can provide equal opportunities, bearing in mind the inequalities that exist outside the classroom. 'The persistent class differentials in educational opportunity in the final analysis are anchored in the equally persistent divisions of the society at large.' Others, however, are more hopeful about the possibilities of specific educational change in improving young people's opportunities and life chances.

THE INFLUENCE OF SCHOOL
The Robbins Committee clearly recognized that both the quality of primary and secondary education and the organization of schooling would affect the

proportion of young people with the abilities and attitudes appropriate to higher education (HMSO 1963). What the committee did not foresee was the growth in the number of pupils attending non-selective schools over the past two decades. This structural change in the organization of schooling has been called 'a gigantic experiment with the life chances of millions of children; and the results will not be known for years' (Ford 1969).

Official pronouncements have, at least until recently, claimed that comprehensive[3] reorganization has already enhanced young people's chances of continuing their studies in higher education. A Department of Education and Science discussion paper on future trends in higher education commented that:

> '. . . in the education field itself, comprehensive reorganization is already transforming secondary schooling; when this process is complete no children will be educated in institutions which, by their status, nature and organization, are apt to cut off their pupils from higher education opportunities.'

Moreover,

> 'in the climate which re-organization will have created higher education may be made a more attractive prospect for young people from poorer home backgrounds.' (DES 1978)

The hope that equalizing opportunities in secondary education will have a spill-over effect on participation in higher education has, of course, been a major spur to comprehensive reform. Intuitively, at least, one might expect that the reorganization of secondary education will affect not only the number of young people staying on in sixth forms, colleges and institutions of higher education, but also the social class mix of those staying on. This is, however, an area that has remained relatively unresearched, and the research evidence that does exist is somewhat contradictory.

Many studies have shown that remaining in full-time education after the age of sixteen is closely connected to the type of school attended (eg Rauta and Hunt 1975). A Schools Council survey of sixth-form pupils (Schools Council 1970) found clear differences between different types of school in the participation rates of manual workers' children. Just over half of the sixth-formers in comprehensive schools came from manual working-class home backgrounds, compared with a third of those attending maintained grammar schools and a fifth of those in independent and direct-grant school sixth forms. A more recent study undertaken in 1975 revealed a broadly similar pattern (Gordon and Williams 1977): among those students studying for GCE 'A' levels, thirty-six per cent of pupils in comprehensive school sixth forms came from manual working-class backgrounds, compared with twenty-two per cent of those attending other forms of upper-secondary education. More recently still, however, when an even higher proportion of pupils were studying in comprehensive schools a survey of just under 4500 16-19 year-olds in sixth forms and colleges found that different institutional types contained an approximately equal proportion of students from any one social class group (Dean et al. 1979). As a result, students from manual home backgrounds were similarly under-represented in all forms of 16-19 year-old education, whether comprehensive schools, grammar schools, sixth-form colleges, tertiary colleges or further education institutions. This finding is rather different from earlier ones and appears to belie the claim by Benn and Simon (1972) that 'the higher proportion of working-class students in sixth forms [is] also reflected in university entrants from comprehensive schools.'

However, one study undertaken (much earlier than Dean et al.) to inquire specifically into the social origins of pupils from comprehensive schools who go on to higher education did seem to show that '. . . a significantly higher proportion are of working class origin than is the case for students as a whole' (Benn and Simon 1972). In a study of students who had attended comprehensive schools Neave (1975) found that thirty-eight per cent of university entrants came from manual social class families, compared with twenty-eight per cent of university entrants nationally. He felt that the delayed selection implied by a comprehensive system would allow universities and other higher education institutions '. . . to draw upon a far wider social reservoir than has hitherto been the case.' Neave remained convinced that comprehensive reform would mean '. . . a change in university clientele' and that it would have '. . . profound repercussions . . . on the type of student entering university'. His conclusions (based on students who entered university as long ago as 1968) have, however, been criticized on a number of counts. In particular, it has been argued that any adequate assessment of the impact of reorganization has to grapple with the question of what the outcome would have been had comprehensive reform not taken place. As Bellaby (1977) points out, this question cannot be answered by surveying only the comprehensive population.

In addition, as noted earlier on, the number of students from manual working-class backgrounds as a proportion of all students in universities has remained virtually unchanged for the last fifty years, in spite of a three-fold expansion in the number of places since 1960 and the introduction of widespread maintenance grants. Comprehensivization, then, has not in the short run conspicuously improved the relative rates of participation in higher education by traditionally under-represented groups — unless, as Fulton and Gordon (1979a) point out, in a drawn battle with other factors that would otherwise be worsening the situation.

The influence of the school goes beyond that of structural change however. The pedagogic experiences of pupils must also be important; and Lawton (1977) has suggested that one reason for the education system's failure to achieve what he calls social justice is the lack of attention that has been paid to curriculum issues. It is certainly the case that questions on the effects of the content of education and of teaching methods have been relatively neglected. One exception, however, was the 1970s debate on examination reform for upper-secondary students and the possible replacement of GCE 'A' levels by a two-level five-subject curriculum and examination structure. This debate focused on the curricular and examination needs of sixth-formers, aiming both to provide a suitably rigorous academic preparation for those going on to higher education, and to have some currency for those students planning to leave full-time education for work at the age of eighteen (Schools Council 1973). A two-level curriculum that involved the study of three subjects to N (Normal) and two to F (Further) level for those planning to go on to higher education attracted some support, with the possibility remaining for upper-secondary students to study all five subjects at N level. As with comprehensive restructuring, the aim was, by providing a curriculum open to a wider range of abilities and interests, to postpone selection and streaming. In spite of Schools Council support this particular proposal for reform foundered, partly because of doubts about the effects of widening the knowledge base of higher education entrants, and partly because of the possible resource implications.

More recently, a British research team argued on the basis of somewhat limited evidence that 'secondary schools do have an important influence on their pupils' behaviour and attainments' (Rutter et al. 1979), and that schools could be a force for the good, even in deprived areas. Their work was acclaimed as contradicting the arguments of Jencks and his associates (1972) in the United States that educational change on its own is ineffective when set against the influence of wider society. Rutter's argument was that the effects of apparently similar educational institutions on young people's ambitions, attitudes and achievements do in fact differ widely, and that weak and strong educational practices can be found in any type of structural arrangement. A series of factors that can be described as the 'ethos' of the school are, if so, much more influential than the formal criteria by which a school selects or receives pupils and organizes them for teaching purposes: what may first appear to be a uniformly structured secondary education system will, on closer inspection, turn out to be a quite heterogeneous system with a wide range of practices, attributes and institutional structures. For the future, then, the policy issue may be to identify and try to promote good practice, rather than indulge in further structural reform.

To some extent therefore, the debate has shifted from organizational issues to concern about curricula, method, assessment and standards. This is perhaps not surprising since nearly nine in ten lower-secondary pupils in the state sector now attend nominally comprehensive schools (DES 1980). However, the structural arrangements for post-compulsory education are still a contentious issue. This particular debate encompasses such issues as the size of school sixth forms (including concern about falling group sizes), and the advantages or disadvantages of tertiary colleges, sixth-form colleges, school sixth forms, and institutions of further education as centres of learning for 16-19 year-olds (Dean et al. 1979; King et al. 1975). Whatever the evidence that can be harnessed to show the impact of school type or of pupils' educational experiences on the demand for and access to higher education, it is clear that for many secondary school pupils higher education is at best an irrelevance. A large number of young people effectively cut themselves off from opportunities in higher education by their decision to leave school at the age of sixteen. And for many it is their experience in compulsory education that has led them to quit as soon as it is legally possible. It has to be recognized that for many young people 'school . . . is merely a dull though prolonged preamble to a working life that is itself to prove desultory and unchallenging' (Carter 1966). Young people who have enjoyed and had success in their primary and lower-secondary education are much more likely to want 'to continue on paths they have a liking for or excel in' (Barnard and McCreath 1970). On the other hand, of course, for other pupils where '. . . school life produces not passing fits of revolt but a real and continuous sense of frustration, the right thing is to leave' (CACE 1954).

A survey of fifth-formers undertaken in 1975 found disenchantment with school or with teachers to be a major reason given for the decision to leave at sixteen. Thirty-eight per cent of the boy-leavers questioned and forty-five per cent of the girls said that they had decided to leave because they were 'fed up' with school (Gordon and Williams 1977).

ECONOMIC FACTORS
There is also a range of economic factors that may influence some fifth- and sixth-formers. Alienation from school and the desire for money of their own are frequently given by young people as the two most important reasons in the decision to leave school.

> 'These two factors can be viewed in push and pull terms. The alienation from school will tend to push fifth-formers out of secondary education as soon as they are legally able to do so; this disaffection with education compelling potential leavers to search for alternatives at the earliest possible opportunity. The attractions of work, or rather the attractions of the money that will be gained from working, will tend to pull the fifth-former out of full-time education and into employment.' (Gordon 1976)

However, while money may well be a powerful influence on young people's decisions, it is only one of many economic factors that need to be taken into account when presenting an overall picture of influences on the demand for upper-secondary and higher education.

There are in fact several ways in which economic considerations might affect demand. The material circumstances of the home is one. A second is the direct and indirect costs of staying on at school or college, the impact of which on any individual is obviously affected by his or her material circumstances. A third is the prospective student's perceptions of the personal economic benefits to be derived from continued education. In addition, there may be more general economic, social and cultural benefits, perhaps related to labour market opportunities.

The Material Circumstances of the Home

The desire for money of their own is one of the most common reasons given by fifth-form leavers for their decision to leave. A third of the girl-leavers and over a quarter of the boys in a 1975 survey of fifth-formers said that this played a major part in their decision (Gordon and Williams 1977). Ryrie et al. (1979) also reported that the opportunity to earn money was the most frequently expressed reason for leaving school. Another study (Dean et al. 1979) also found a strong emphasis on concern over lack of income, with thirty-eight per cent of the young people surveyed saying they were 'very much' influenced to leave because if they had continued their studies they 'would not be earning any money'. Even those who did stay on described shortage of money as the main disadvantage of post-sixteen education.

Earning one's own money, though, is only part of the problem. For some fifth-formers the option of remaining in full-time education after the minimum school-leaving age has never been realistic because of financial constraints at home. In one study forty per cent of the fifth-formers questioned (both intending stayers and leavers) thought that they ought to leave school for work to start helping their families financially; but very few sixth-formers who had stayed on felt the same obligation (Gordon 1976). Twelve per cent of the National Child Development Study's sample of sixteen-year-old school-leavers felt that their parents needed them to go out to work to bring additional money into the household (Fogelman 1976). This need for extra income is especially likely to be a problem for the children of one-parent families, of low wage earners, of benefit recipients and, as the Robbins Committee pointed out, of large families.

> 'Clearly the economic circumstances of the home are very influential: even in families of the same occupational level, the proportion of children reaching full-time higher education is four times as high for children from families with one or two children as from those where five or more children have claims on the family's resources.' (HMSO 1963)

Educational Maintenance Allowances

Twenty years ago Floud (1961) made the point that in low-income households 'fees cannot be paid nor can adolescent earnings be foregone by the family'. She went on to recommend that educational maintenance allowances be introduced for full-time pupils staying on past the minimum leaving age, but expressed the anxiety that even this would fail to prevent all wastage of talent from the 'able children of impoverished families'. Such a call for financial support to 16-19 year-olds is one that has been taken up again relatively recently.

'It is evident that it is at the end of compulsory education that the full effects of social class and the financial position of pupils' parents are felt. If we wish to remedy the waste of human resources of those who leave full-time education prematurely, then one way of doing so is to make grants for sixteen year-olds widely available at a level that will both provide an incentive to stay on for the pupil, and relieve the financial burden from the shoulders of parents.' (Gordon 1976)

Given the apparent importance of monetary influences, it is likely that the widespread introduction of educational maintenance allowances would have a positive effect on staying-on rates at the age of sixteen, and would probably have a subsequent spill-over effect on the number of entrants to higher education. A survey of 3000 fifth-formers undertaken in 1977 suggested that a uniformly available grant of £8 a week would, in the year of the study, have increased the number of boys staying on after sixteen by 4.8 per cent, and the number of girls by 5.6 per cent (Fulton and Gordon 1979). 'It is clear from these findings that a grant to the pupil of £8 a week or thereabouts, together with continued access to child benefit for the parent, could have a significant impact on staying-on rates' (Fulton and Gordon 1979). Maintenance grants could be particularly effective in helping young people from low-income families.

Since the mid-1970s an additional disincentive has been the different kinds of income support schemes for young people who leave school. These have been usefully surveyed by Maclure (1979). However, the discussion in 1981 has taken on a new dimension. From 1981 school-leavers are able to claim Supplementary Benefit from Easter, if they leave school then; if they stay on at school even for part of the summer term, for example to take external CSE or GCE examinations, they cannot claim benefit until September. Under the earlier rules, Supplementary Benefit could be claimed towards the end of May by examination candidates who were leaving school in the summer. In effect, summer leavers are now losing the equivalent of three months' benefit. The change was introduced as a cost-saving innovation to prevent young people claiming Supplementary Benefit through the summer months and then returning to school or college in September. Early indications are that the new rules are acting as an incentive for some fifth-formers to leave school at Easter and forego their chance of gaining CSE or GCE qualifications (Berliner 1981). The difficulties which school-leavers are experiencing in finding jobs [4] seem to be acting as an additional incentive for them to leave school at the earliest opportunity. If they cannot find a job, then at least they have not lost their early entitlement to Supplementary Benefit. It has been reported, however, that some government officials are concerned about the problem and the effects of the new rules are being monitored (Stevens 1981). One particular cause for concern is that once the rules' implications are more widely recognized the number leaving at Easter in 1982 and subsequent years may increase substantially (Berliner 1981).

The previous Labour government's means-tested educational maintenance allowance scheme was estimated to cost £110 million a year to cover
England and Wales (Maclure 1979). Although agreement to proceed with a
pilot scheme had been reached before the fall of that government in 1979, it
was clear that the cost implications of the full scheme were causing concern.
However, 'The present government is now spending around £200 million on
supporting unemployed young people — on the condition that they leave
school' (Stevens 1981).

Student Grants
In attempting to explain shifts in the demand for higher education Williams
(1974) adopted an economic framework that suggested that there are three
types of reason why demand may change: 'first, the costs may change;
second, the benefits may change; third, people's perception or evaluation of
the costs and benefits may change' (Williams 1974).

    In Chapter 2 Farrant presents data (Table 2.10, p.78) on the trends in
costs and benefits (in earnings differentials and the value of the student
grant) and reviews the research of Pissarides which suggests that earnings
and employment prospects are more significant in affecting demand than is
the cost of the student maintenance grant. However, one unexpected aspect
of the student grant system is worth attention. A 1975 study found that while
eighty-four per cent of the undergraduate population surveyed had the
maximum maintenance grant reduced by a 'parental contribution', nearly
three-quarters of these students in fact received less than the assessed
contribution from their parents. For twenty-nine per cent of these students
the shortfall was over £100. In all, therefore, some two-thirds of all
undergraduates are maintaining themselves on less than the amount thought
to be necessary (DES 1975).

    Policies designed to replace the existing student support scheme in
Britain by a system of student loans had an airing in 1980 and early 1981.
But this particular reform appears to have been shelved, at least for the time
being. It is argued by opponents of loan schemes that any such increase in
the costs of becoming a graduate would have a detrimental effect on the
demand for places in higher education, and that loans would act as a
particular disincentive for students from working-class backgrounds who
would be especially unwilling to take on a long-term debt. The Robbins
Committee also claimed that loans would deter women from seeking places
in higher education. '. . . British parents would be strengthened in their
age-long disinclination to consider their daughters to be as deserving of
higher education as their sons . . .' (HMSO 1963).

The Formal Economic Benefits of Higher Education
It has been suggested that one factor in accounting for the stagnation in
staying-on rates 'could be the reduction in the leavers' perceived value of
spending extra years obtaining qualifications, in terms either of getting a job

or of current or long-term salary prospects' (DE 1976). Although there are, of course, 'many intangible benefits of higher education not susceptible to sordid economic analysis' (Williams 1974) such tangible benefits as jobs and salaries do lend themselves to an economic approach.

Williams (1974) found new graduates taking longer to find suitable employment than previously. In addition, increasing numbers were entering occupations of lower status (ie non-traditional graduate jobs): during the 1970s this appears to have been particularly the case for business studies and arts graduates (DE 1981). The prospects for all new labour market entrants have deteriorated substantially since the mid-1970s. However, even in the absence of severe economic recession, the longer-term employment prospects of graduates in the 1980s appear generally less good than those of graduates who entered the labour force in the 1960s and early 1970s (DE 1974; 1978), although prospects for different subjects vary (DE 1981).

There is, too, evidence that over the last twelve years or so the earnings of non-graduates have risen somewhat faster than those of graduates (DE 1981; see also Chapter 2, Table 2.10, p.78). However, the average lifetime earnings of graduates are still higher than those of other workers. Figure 4.1 shows the actual age-earnings profiles of men and women with degrees, GCE 'A' levels and no qualifications in 1975/76 (the actual profiles are marked A). This kind of information has been used in the past to compute private rates of return to staying on at school or going on to higher education, taking into account wherever possible the different abilities and social class backgrounds of the people concerned (eg Blaug 1965; Blaug et al. 1967; Ziderman 1973; Psacharopoulos 1973; Psacharopoulos and Layard 1979; Wilson 1980; DES 1980c). The aim has been to provide some answers to Ziderman's question, 'Does it pay to take a degree?' It appears that over the 1970s there have been some fluctuations in the private rate of return to higher education, but on a generally downward trend (DE 1981). Wilson found a significant decline of about one third in the private rate of return to becoming a qualified engineer or scientist in the decade to 1976-77, although it appears that most of this drop occurred before 1973-74. He found private rates of return in 1976-77 varying from 8 per cent to 10 per cent depending on the discipline studied. But one of the most recently published calculations of marginal private rates of return to boys' education found a return of 19 per cent for a first degree over 'A' levels in 1978 (DES 1980c).

Recently it has been demonstrated that it is possible not only to compare the actual private costs and benefits of post-compulsory education but also to find out what kind of return young people *think* there is from studying for GCE 'A' levels or a degree. Figure 4.1 also shows the earnings expected by fifth-formers in 1977; they are grouped according to whether they planned to go on to higher education, to leave full-time education at eighteen, or to leave at sixteen (see Williams and Gordon 1981). This information has been used as a starting point to calculate ex ante (ie perceived) private rates of return to continued education. Taking into account the different family backgrounds,

FIGURE 4.1
Actual* and expected relative age-earnings profiles (Median)

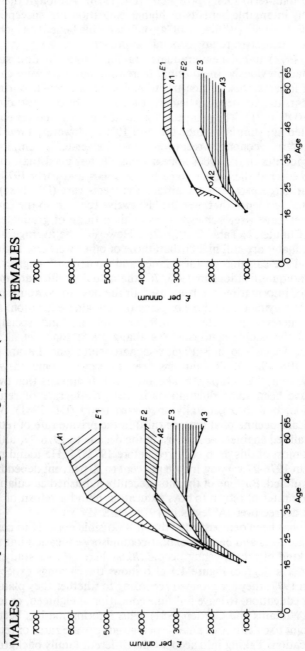

A - Actual, 1 - Degree, 2 - GCE 'A' levels, 3 - No qualifications   E - Expected, 1 - Higher education, 2 - Upper-secondary, 3 - Work
* 'Actual' profiles for males derived from OPCS(1978) Table 7.9.
'Actual' profiles for females derived from SED 4A GHS 1975/76. Kindly made available by OPCS.
Only one observation of actual earnings, A2, is available for women with 'A' levels.

Source Williams and Gordon (1981)

abilities and other relevant characteristics of those who do and do not plan to stay on after the minimum school-leaving age, the conclusion was reached,

'. . . that in 1977 16 year-old boys perceived the private rate of return from staying on to age 18 as 17 per cent, with a further 10 per cent from continuing further to take a degree. For girls the expected returns were lower: 9 per cent for upper secondary and 8 per cent for higher education.' (Williams and Gordon 1981)

It appears that at the end of compulsory schooling young people in general do have fairly accurate perceptions of the labour market opportunities with which they are confronted and the ways in which these opportunities are related to educational qualifications.

'The implications of these findings for an understanding of changes in the demand for higher education during the 1960s and 1970s are considerable. They lend support to claims that one of the prime motives for the rapid expansion of the 1960s and much slower growth of the 1970s was economic. . . . As far as policy is concerned, these results aid in the prediction of the demand for higher education in that they help to demonstrate that the demand is not autonomous but influenced by changes in the private economic costs and benefits of a degree level qualification.' (Williams and Gordon 1981)

The General Economic Benefits of Higher Education
The analysis of perceived rates of return imputes motives to potential students, but whenever potential or actual students in higher education have been questioned about their motives directly, the benefits in terms of job prospects, wider job choice, enhanced promotion prospects, higher salaries, and so on have featured strongly in their answers.

Morris (1969) found that applicants to higher education saw it very much in terms of useful vocational preparation and as necessary for their future careers. According to Neave (1975), the most important reasons for going to university were to gain useful qualifications, and to study for a career that the student already had in mind. Another study, of second-year university undergraduates, found that ninety per cent mentioned factors related in one way or another to their future occupations as one important consideration (Startup 1972). In particular, they thought that a degree would give access to more interesting work (seventy-two per cent); a better-paid job (fifty-one per cent); a wider choice of occupations (forty-seven per cent); and more secure employment (twenty-four per cent). Two-thirds of the undergraduates questioned in another small study of second-year university students said that going to university would give them better career prospects (University of Reading 1973). Other benefits included better chances of employment, the prospect of a more stable career, and higher earnings.

Cohen (1970), in a study of sixth-formers, found the vocational purposes of a university education strongly emphasized by his sample, and that 'Expectations were strong that learning at university and college should above all else be "applicable".' The aim of gaining qualifications for a chosen career, or to enter higher education, or to improve career prospects generally all featured strongly in a survey of upper-secondary and further education students (Dean et al. 1979). Other such studies have come up with similar conclusions (eg Schools Council 1970; King et al. 1974). In selecting specific courses in higher education too, the usefulness of the chosen course for a particular job has been found to be more important than any other factor (Gordon and Williams 1977). In the United States, as well as in Britain, labour market opportunities have been found to be extremely influential (eg Dole 1970).

It is clear from this brief review that while there is obviously a wide variety of reasons for staying on into the sixth form or going on to university, economic factors are extremely important.

'The motives that impel sixth formers to seek higher education are many, varied and seldom clear-cut. A minority wish to continue for its own sake the study in depth of a specialised subject to the top of their bent. . . . Some students have a specific career in mind. A larger number are anxious to develop over a wider field what the Robbins Committee called the general powers of the mind. . . . Some ask for no more than a stimulating opportunity to come to terms with themselves, and to discover where their real interests and abilities lie. Others have no better reason than involuntarily to fall in with the advice of their teachers and the example of their contemporaries. But not far from the surface of most candidates' minds is the tacit belief that higher education will go far to guarantee them a better job.' (HMSO 1972)

A decade earlier the Robbins Committee was more forthright: 'We deceive ourselves if we claim that more than a small fraction of students in institutions of higher education would be where they are if there were no significance for their future careers in what they hear and read . . .' (HMSO 1963).

POLICY ISSUES AND CONCLUSIONS
At the 1978 North of England Education Conference Shirley Williams, at that time Secretary of State for Education, reflected on the achievements of the British education system:

'We have transformed our school system, raised the school leaving age, massively expanded our higher education, instituted reasonably generous awards for post-eighteen year-olds, and here, between sixteen and eighteen, thousands of our eager, able and energetic youngsters trickle away. Of course, I would welcome their going into the world of employment if they were getting effective training in skills and effective opportunities to continue their education on a part-time basis; but most of them are not.'

In spite of all of these changes in educational policy, the traditional under-representation of young people from working-class backgrounds persists in upper-secondary and higher education. It is clear from this research review that it is at the school-leaving age that most working-class drop-out occurs. It is therefore in the period leading to and including the minimum school-leaving age that at least some public policies must be directed that are aimed at reducing social class inequalities. Educationalists and policy makers cannot console themselves with the thought that participation in the higher levels of the education system is equally open to the equally talented: it would seem that notions of meritocracy have little to do with who does and who does not continue their education at key transition points.

However 'hard (it may be) to say to what extent the selectivity of higher education represents a denial of equal opportunity, and to what extent it results from variation in people's appetite for education' (Jencks 1972), there is little doubt that education policies can be formulated that will whet the appetites of young people for continued study. Access can be improved; demand can be stimulated; and participation in upper-secondary and higher education by under-represented groups can be increased. A combination of educational, social and economic policies might well do all of these things, and tap the presently untapped pool of ability and remedy the waste of one of Britain's most valuable resources — human capital.

The development of educational practices in the latter years of compulsory education, designed to bring out the specific talents of poorly provided-for groups, and to encourage continuation, could pay dividends in this respect. But while specifically educational policies and practices may somewhat improve access to and participation in upper-secondary and higher education, they do have to be supported by other policies. Class inequalities are associated with, and perhaps exacerbated by, the inabilities of families to afford the cost of post-compulsory education. While financial support, albeit subject to parental means-test, is widely available for the over-eighteens in higher education, there is little monetary help for young people (and their families) when they first choose to stay on beyond the minimum school-leaving age. Research evidence indicates that the introduction of educational maintenance allowances on a national basis would help to raise demand for post-compulsory education. Any government concerned with equalizing educational opportunities, and with the provision of highly skilled personnel for the future development of the economy, would do well to place the introduction of educational maintenance allowances very high indeed on an agenda of educational reforms.

In December 1980 a government report titled *Education for 16-19 Year*

Olds stated that 'We need more and better education and training for this age group.' However, this bland report did not even seriously consider the benefits to be derived from educational maintenance allowances (benefits possibly increased at a time of high and increasing juvenile unemployment), side-stepping this particular issue with the now-familiar reference to the need to reduce public spending, commenting that 'as long as the need for expenditure restraint continues there is no prospect of introducing any reasonably generous 16-19 awards system.'

It is clear that the government of 1981 and the Department of Education and Science have virtually no *educational* policies for sixteen-nineteen education or for higher education, other than the general *economic* policy drastically to reduce public expenditure on both, regardless of the educational implications. Such a policy further reduces general opportunities in post-compulsory education and exacerbates existing class inequalities: it also denies the need for educated labour in the future.

NOTES

1   Much depends, of course, on what is meant by equality of opportunity. A variety of interpretations are usefully discussed by Warnock (1975) and Bowman (1975).
2   Other analysts see class differences as primarily economic or political rather than educational or cultural in origin. There is in fact little research evidence that working-class parents have lower general educational ambitions for their children, except to the extent that they are unaware of opportunities available, or are unable to conceive that their own children are capable of competing on equal terms with other children. For both working-class parents and their children the possibility of upward mobility through education 'seems so remote as to be meaningless' (Willis 1977). It is certainly correct that working-class parents command fewer resources and have less power over educational institutions.
3   Comprehensive reorganization can take a number of different forms. There are still large numbers of secondary schools that carry the label 'comprehensive' but which are selective, or from which able pupils have been 'creamed off' (see Bellaby 1977).
4   The number of young people aged eighteen or under who are registered as unemployed increased by eighty per cent during 1980.

ACKNOWLEDGEMENTS
I am grateful to those who found time to read and comment on earlier drafts of this chapter: Miki David and Roy Parker at the University of Bristol, and Oliver Fulton and Gareth Williams at the University of Lancaster. The sins of omission and commission that remain are, of course, my own. Special thanks are also due to Carol Emmett, who cheerfully and patiently typed a number of versions of the chapter.

REFERENCES
Barnard, G.A. and McCreath, M.D. (1970) Subject commitments and the demand for higher education *Journal of the Royal Statistical Society Series A (General)* 132 (3) pp.358-408
Bellaby, P. (1977) *The Sociology of Comprehensive Schooling* London: Methuen
Benn, C. and Simon, B. (1972) *Half Way There* Harmondsworth: Penguin
Berliner, W. (1981) Children abandon exams to claim instant benefits *The Guardian* 30.3.81
Bernstein, B. (1970) Education cannot compensate for society *New Society* No. 387, pp.344-347
Blackstone, T. and Weinreich-Haste, H. (1980) Why are there so few women scientists and engineers? *New Society* No. 907
Blaug, M. (1965) The money rate of return on education in the UK *Manchester School* 33 (3) pp.205-251
Blaug, M. (1970) *Introduction to the Economics of Education* Harmondsworth: Penguin
Blaug, M., Peston, M. and Ziderman, A. (1967) *The Utilization of Educated Manpower in Industry* Edinburgh: Oliver and Boyd
Bockstael, E. and Feinstein, O. (1970) *Higher Education in the European Community* New York: Heath Lexington
Bowman, M.J. (1975) Education and opportunity: Some economic perspectives *Oxford Review of Education* 1 (1) pp.73-84
Carter, M. (1966) *Into Work* Harmondsworth: Penguin
Central Advisory Council for Education (CACE) (1954) *Early Leaving* London: HMSO
Central Advisory Council for Education (CACE) (1959) *15 to 18* (Crowther Report) London: HMSO
Cohen, L. (1970) Sixth form pupils and their views of higher education *Journal of Curriculum Studies* 2 (1) pp.67-72
Craft, M. (Editor) (1970) *Family, Class and Education: A Reader* London: Longman
David, M. (1980) *The State, The Family and Education* London: Routledge and Kegan Paul
Dean, J., Bradley, K., Choppin, B. and Vincent, D. (1979) *The Sixth Form and its Alternatives* Slough: NFER Publishing Company
Department of Education and Science (DES) (1977) *Ten Good Schools: a Secondary School Enquiry* London: DES
Department of Education and Science (DES) (1978) *Higher Education into the 1990s: A Discussion Document* London: DES
Department of Education and Science (DES) (1980) Provisional statistics of schools — January 1980 *Statistical Bulletin 16/80* December 1980. London: DES
Department of Education and Science (DES) (1980a) University statistics *Statistical Bulletin 13/80* October 1980. London: DES

Department of Education and Science (DES) (1980b) Trends in entry to full-time higher education *Statistical Bulletin 12/80* September 1980. London: DES

Department of Education and Science (DES) (1980c) *The Rate of Return to Post-Compulsory Education during the 1970s: an Empirical Study for Great Britain* London: DES

Department of Education and Science (DES) (1981) Higher education in Great Britain: early estimates for 1980-81 *Statistical Bulletin 6/81* April 1981. London: DES

Department of Employment (DE) (1974) *Employment Prospects for the Highly Qualified* London: Department of Employment

Department of Employment (DE) (1976) Young people leaving school *Department of Employment Gazette* 84 (5) pp.455-460

Department of Employment (DE) (1978) *Employment Prospects for the Highly Qualified* Manpower Paper No. 8. London: Department of Employment

Department of Employment (DE) (1981) *Higher Education and the Employment of Graduates* Research Paper No. 19. London: Department of Employment

Devlin, T. and Warnock, M. (1977) *What Must We Teach?* London: Temple Smith

Dole, A.A. (1970) Stability of reasons for going to college *Journal of Educational Research* 63 (8) pp.373-378

Douglas, J.W.B. (1964) *The Home and the School* London: MacGibbon and Kee

Douglas, J.W.B., Ross, J.M. and Simpson, W.R. (1968) *All Our Future* London: Peter Davies

Floud, J. (1961) Social class factors in educational achievement. In Halsey, A.H. (Editor) *Ability and Educational Opportunity* Paris: OECD

Fogelman, K. (1976) *Britain's Sixteen Year Olds* London: National Children's Bureau

Ford, J. (1969) *Social Class and the Comprehensive School* London: Routledge and Kegan Paul

Fulton, O. and Gordon, A. (1979) The British pool of ability: how deep, and will cash reduce it? *Educational Studies* 5 (2) pp.157-169

Fulton, O. and Gordon, A. (1979a) *Admission Policies in Post-Secondary Education: The Impact of Structural Change on the Demand for Upper Secondary and Higher Education* SME/ET/79.25. Paris: OECD

Furneaux, W.D. (1961) *The Chosen Few* Oxford: Oxford University Press

Gordon, A. (1976) *Education or Employment? A Dilemma for Fifth Formers* A Paper presented to the Annual Meeting of the British Association for the Advancement of Science at the University of Lancaster

Gordon, A. (1980) Leaving school: a question of money? *Educational Studies* 6 (1) pp.43-54

Gordon, A. and Williams, G. (1976) *Individual Demand for Education. Case Study: United Kingdom* SME/ET/76.21. Paris: OECD
Gordon, A. and Williams, G. (1977) *Attitudes of Fifth and Sixth Formers to School, Work and Higher Education* University of Lancaster: IPCE (mimeo)
Halsey, A.H., Heath, A.F. and Ridge, J.M. (1980) *Origins and Destinations: Family, Class and Education in Modern Britain* Oxford: Clarendon Press
HMSO (1963) *Higher Education* (Robbins Report) Cmnd. 2154. London: HMSO
HMSO (1972) *Education: A Framework for Expansion* Cmnd. 5174. London: HMSO
HMSO (1977) *Education in Schools: a Consultative Document* Cmnd. 6869. London: HMSO
Hopkins, A. (1978) *The School Debate* Harmondsworth: Penguin
Jackson, B. and Marsden, D. (1966) *Education and the Working Class* Harmondsworth: Pelican
Jencks, C. (1972) *Inequality: A Reassessment of the Effect of Family and Schooling in America* New York: Basic Books Inc
Joseph, K. and Sumption, J. (1979) *Equality* London: John Murray
King, E.J., Moor, C.H. and Mundy, J.A. (1974) *Post-Compulsory Education: A New Analysis in Western Europe* London: Sage
King, E.J., Moor, C.H. and Mundy, J.A. (1975) *Post-Compulsory Education 2: The Way Ahead* London: Sage
Lawton, D. (1977) *Education and Social Justice* London: Sage
Maclure, S. (1979) Financial support for the 16-18s *Education Policy Bulletin* 7 (1) pp.99-124
Morris, R.N. (1969) *Sixth Form and College Entrance* London: Routledge and Kegan Paul
Neave, G. (1975) *How They Fared: The Impact of the Comprehensive School upon the University* London: Routledge and Kegan Paul
Neave, G. (1976) *Patterns of Equality* Slough: NFER Publishing Company
OECD (1970) *Group Disparities in Educational Participation and Achievement* Paris: OECD
Office of Population Censuses and Surveys (OPCS) (1978) *The General Household Survey 1976* London: HMSO
Psacharopoulos, G. (1973) *Returns to Education: An International Comparison* Amsterdam: Elsevier
Psacharopoulos, G. and Layard, R. (1979) Human capital and earnings: British evidence and a critique *Review of Economic Studies* XLVI, pp. 485-503
Rauta, I. and Hunt, A. (1975) *Fifth Form Girls: Their Hopes for the Future* London: HMSO

Roberts, K. (1980) Schools, parents and social class. In Craft, M., Raynor, J. and Cohen, L. (Editors) *Linking Home and School* (Third Edition) London: Harper and Row

Rutter, M., Maughan, B., Mortimore, P. and Ouston, J. (1979) *Fifteen Thousand Hours: Secondary Schools and Their Effects on Children* London: Open Books

Ryrie, A.C., Furst, A. and Lauder, M. (1979) *Choices and Chances* London: Hodder and Stoughton

Schools Council (1968) *Young School Leavers* London: HMSO

Schools Council (1970) *Sixth Form Pupils and Teachers* London: Books for Schools

Schools Council (1973) *Preparation for Degree Courses* Schools Council Working Paper 47. London: Evans/Methuen Educational

Sharpe, S. (1976) *Just Like a Girl: How Girls Learn to be Women* Harmondsworth: Penguin

Startup, R. (1972) Why go to the University? *Universities Quarterly* 26 (3) pp.317-332

Stevens, A. (1981) Pupils may get dole to stay at school *The Observer* 5.4.81

Thomas, R. and Wetherell, D. (1974) *Looking Forward to Work* London: HMSO

Turner, R.H. (1960) Modes of ascent through education: sponsored and contest mobility. In A.H. Halsey, J. Floud and C. Arnold Anderson (Editors) *Education, Economy and Society* New York: Free Press

Universities Central Council on Admissions (UCCA) (1980) *Statistical Supplement to the Seventeenth UCCA Report 1978-79* Cheltenham: UCCA

Universities Central Council on Admissions (UCCA) (1980a) *Seventeenth UCCA Report 1978-79* Cheltenham: UCCA

University of Reading (1973) *Student Motivation* Reading: University of Reading (mimeo)

Warnock, M. (1975) The concept of equality in education *Oxford Review of Education* 1 (1) pp.3-8

Westergaard, J.H. and Little, A.N. (1964) Educational opportunity and social selection in England and Wales: trends and policy implications *British Journal of Sociology* 15 (4)

Westergaard, J.H. and Resler, H. (1975) *Class in a Capitalist Society* London: Heinemann

Williams, G.L. (1974) The events of 1973-74 in a long term planning perspective *Higher Education Bulletin* 3 (1) pp.17-44

Williams, G.L. and Gordon, A.G. (1975) 16 and 18 year olds: attitudes to education *Higher Education Bulletin* 4 (1) pp.23-37

Williams, G. and Gordon, A. (1981) Perceived earnings functions and ex ante rates of return to post compulsory education in England *Higher Education* 10 (2) pp.199-227

Willis, P. (1977) *Learning to Labour* Farnborough: Saxon House

Wilson, R.A. (1980) The rate of return to becoming a qualified scientist and engineer in Great Britain, 1966-76 *Scottish Journal of Political Economy* 27 (1) pp.41-62

Woodhall, M. (1970) *Student Loans, a Review of Experience in Scandinavia and Elsewhere* London: Harrap

Ziderman, A. (1973) Does it pay to take a degree? The profitability of private investment in university education in Britain *Oxford Economic Papers* XXV, pp.262-274

5

MATURE ENTRY

by Geoffrey Squires

INTRODUCTION

Adults and Adulthood

During the last decade, there has been a marked increase in research into adulthood and ageing. This increase is noticeable in not one, but several disciplines — biology, physiology, psychology and sociology. Much of this research is gerontology, concerned with the very old, in whom the problems of ageing are most visible and acute. However, a more general shift of interest towards adulthood, and away from childhood, is discernible, and with it a growing realization that what had previously been thought of as a simple plateau or a straightforward, linear decline is a much more complex and interesting phenomenon.

Concurrently, public interest has grown. The word 'ageism' has been coined; there are now organizations, such as Age Concern, which attempt to look after the interests of the very old; pre-retirement courses are now quite common; and there are increasing references to 'mid-life' and 'mid-career' problems. For women, the middle years are increasingly being seen as a time of opportunity rather than stagnation, though whether those opportunities can always be realized is another matter. Our attitudes towards adulthood seem, therefore, to be undergoing a shift. The fact that this shift is diffuse and imprecise does not make it any the less important; it can issue in a thousand more tangible changes. It cannot be fully explained; but it cannot be wholly ignored.

The change in the age structure of the population — both here and in the United States — must have something to do with it. This is not a simple redistribution in favour of the old, but rather a series of wave and trough movements overlaying what appears to be a longer-term trend towards an older population. One such trough is already affecting the schools, and will soon affect higher education. Between now and 1996 the number of people aged between thirty and forty-four will increase by about 1.6 million, the number over forty-four by about 0.3 million, and the number aged between sixteen and twenty-nine will decrease by about 0.6 million. Any conceptual re-orientation towards adulthood is thus underpinned by a palpable social change, and the redistribution of resources which that implies.

Another general factor which may affect our perception of adulthood is employment. Here again it is not easy to distinguish the wave and trough movements of cyclic unemployment from longer-term structural unemployment. Unemployment disturbs our sense of adulthood. Being at school is another of the things that distinguishes the child from the adult. Does the unemployed adult then perceive education as a sensible alternative to employment, or as further confirmation of his loss of adult status? Just as the growth of contraception has altered the child-rearing and therefore life-pattern of many women, opening up problems and possibilities that simply did not exist before, the rise of unemployment may cause many men (in particular) to reconsider their traditional life-pattern as a continuous wage-earner.

Adults in Higher Education
So far, we have mentioned some general factors which bear on our perception of adults and adulthood. However, there are more precise and immediate reasons for examining the place of adults in higher education. There have, of course, been adult or 'mature' students in higher education for a very long time. In the late nineteenth century the growing 'civic' universities such as Birmingham, Manchester and Leeds did a good deal of their teaching in the evening and attracted a substantial proportion of students who were already in employment. The adult, extra-mural provision of the universities developed strongly from the 1920s onwards, although it was marginal to the mainstream of higher education. Adults have studied at Birkbeck College London, or for London external degrees, for many years. There has always been a smattering of older students at other universities, and some of the new universities, such as Sussex, made a deliberate attempt to attract mature entrants. However, three things have happened in the last decade which have thrown mature students into particular prominence.

First, the designation of the polytechnics in the late 1960s and early 1970s. The age structure in further education has always been more mixed and less narrowly identified with eighteen-to-twenty-one year-olds than in higher education, mainly because of the prevalence of part-time study. The polytechnics are gradually being detached from the rest of further education, first under the heading of 'advanced further education' (AFE) and now as 'public sector higher education' (PSHE), and the colleges and institutes of higher education are included in this change. The result is that a substantial portion of the higher education system in the UK now has a tradition of mixed age intake. Some trends, such as the increase in full-time degree work, may tend to modify this tradition, but others, such as the growth in modular credit schemes, should help to sustain it.

Secondly, the opening of the Open University in 1971 was significant for several reasons. It immediately increased the number of adult students in higher education by nearly 20,000; it demonstrated publicly that adults could study successfully for a degree; and it showed, moreover, that adults without the conventional 'A' level requirements could achieve pass rates not very far below those with qualifications. In one sense, the OU was merely confirming what some people had known or suspected all along; but the great difference lay in its visibility. As the most public of the universities, its image is almost as important as its reality. Press stories of dockers, fishmongers, and grandmothers who received their degrees are, of course, unrepresentative of the main body of OU graduates, but that is not the point: they are symbols of what can be done, often against great odds. They consititue a counter-myth against the traditional myth that old dogs cannot learn new tricks, the belief that higher education is for the young only. The consequent change in adults' self-concepts affects not only potential OU applicants, but all potential adult students in higher education.

Thirdly, mature entry to higher education was spotlighted by the DES discussion document *Higher Education into the 1990s*. Against the background of an impending fall in the eighteen-year-old intake, this document discussed, inter alia, the

'. . . possibility . . . that the demand, which is already beginning to make itself felt, to devote more educational resources to those already in employment might result in more systematic opportunities for recurrent education for mature students. Priority might be given at first to those who had missed higher education opportunities at normal entry age. But this might not preclude more radical developments, such as a systematic scheme for continuing education at an advanced level, or indeed at a non-advanced level.' (DES 1978)

'Model E', of which this was an element, excited a good deal of interest, not to say self-interest, in the higher education world, for it promised a way of avoiding the impending fall in student numbers for the best of reasons: expansion and equalization of educational opportunity. With the subsequent change of government, Model E disappeared from public view, although a Model E Reconnaissance Group within the DES continued work on the subject. (The report of this group is not available, though the *Times Higher Education Supplement* printed a summary of its main conclusions.)

Although the climate of higher education has changed drastically since 1978, and Model E is no longer a formal policy option, the effect has been to make many academics and institutions much more aware of the potential of mature student entry than they were previously. This awareness has been sustained by more recent statements by both the UGC and the DES (DES 1980).

It thus seems an appropriate time to examine the whole question of mature entry to higher education more carefully. Not only is there the general ground swell of interest in adulthood, but there are specific reasons why mature students should be of concern to those involved in higher education. Such an examination is not, however, easy. To begin with, mature students cannot be discussed as a relatively homogeneous group. Consider the following cases:

— A young man leaves school with three 'O' levels and works as a clerk in an insurance company for several years. He gets bored with the job and its lack of prospects, and studies at the local FE college to get some

'A' levels. He is subsequently admitted to study psychology at a university as a full-time student. His girl-friend, later wife, who has a job with British Gas, helps to support him while he is working.

— A woman leaves school with two 'O' levels, works as a typist for several years, then marries and has two children. Both of these are at school by the time she is twenty-nine, and she decides to enrol as an Open University degree student, partly because one of her friends has, and partly to prove to herself that she can do better than she did at school.

— A man in his late thirties is suddenly made redundant by the manufacturing company for which he has worked in a managerial capacity for fifteen years. He finds great difficulty in getting a similar job anywhere else, and decides to look for an intensive full-time one-year vocational course which will re-equip him for a new career.

— A woman in her early forties, whose children are now teenagers, decides she wants a job again, but a reasonably interesting one. (Before her marriage she worked as a secretary.) She is interested in the social work field, especially relating to children, but is not quite sure what level of qualification she would need to get a satisfying job in, say, the adoption service.

— A retired teacher, mentally active, wants to deepen her late-developing interest in history. She goes to an extra-mural class for one year, which she finds interesting but not very demanding; on the other hand, she does not really feel like committing herself to a full degree.

These five cases by no means cover the wide spectrum of potential mature students and their needs, but they at least show how misleading it can be to think of mature students as a single group. Not only are there differences of age, sex, and family circumstances, but there are important differences in what such students need and expect from higher education. In some cases they will want a full degree, in other cases something less; in some cases a vocationally-orientated course, in others a general one; in some cases full-time study, in others part-time. In some cases, further education or adult education rather than higher education will provide the appropriate opportunities. We shall try, therefore, in this chapter to retain a sense of the *plurality* of mature students and their needs. This is not always easy, since the statistics of mature students, and a good deal of the writing about them, tend to lump them together as a group which contrasts with an equally undifferentiated group of eighteen-year-olds.

We shall define mature students, for these present purposes, as students aged twenty-one or over at entry to higher education. There are several reasons for choosing twenty-one, rather than twenty-five, the age at which mature student grants begin to apply. First, twenty-one is still connected with adulthood in many people's mind. Secondly, anyone who enters higher education at twenty-one is likely to have been in employment for at least three years: a significant aspect of adulthood. Thirdly, the Open University uses twenty-one as the threshold for (most of) its entry. Fourthly, the UCCA figures show that twenty-one-plus entry is of a quite different magnitude to the main, eighteen and nineteen-year-old entry, and cannot be confused with it (although university definitions of 'mature' vary from seventeen to twenty-five).

Higher education will be defined as comprising studies of, or leading up to, first degree level. There is an intended ambiguity in the phrase 'leading up to'. One of the major curricular changes in higher education in the last decade has been the gradual disaggregation of what used to be an indivisible, holistic degree pattern, of which the increased role of advanced further education is a symptom if not a cause. Formerly, one studied consecutively for three years; now studies can be interrupted. Formerly one studied in one place (and preferably in residence) whereas now one can transfer somewhat more easily. Formerly, finals counted for everything; now one can accumulate the degree by instalments of credit (Squires 1979). The two patterns exist side-by-side today, but the net effect is to make higher education much less easily definable than it used to be. How do we classify a student who has gained some credits towards a degree, and then, apparently, drops out? As a failed degree student or as a successful post-secondary student? This ambiguity is particularly important in relation to mature students; and the previously clear demarcation between higher and continuing education is by now decidedly blurred.

This chapter divides into three main sections. First, it reviews trends in the enrolment of mature students in higher education over the last ten years. Secondly, it attempts to analyse the factors which have influenced these trends and seem likely to influence them over the next ten years. Finally, it comments on higher education policies as they affect mature students.

In doing so, three main questions are addressed. First, are there likely to be more or fewer mature students in the future? Model E has raised hopes in some minds that mature students will save higher education from decline in the next decade. Secondly, what kinds of higher education are mature students likely to need? Clearly, we have to examine not only degree-level, but sub-degree level studies as well. (Postgraduate studies constitute a further topic dealt with by Rudd in Chapter 6.) And thirdly, what can be done either to stimulate or depress the demand from mature applicants? What are the main policy 'levers' in this area?

All of the above questions imply an element of prediction. Forecasting the demand from eighteen-year-olds is difficult enough, as various abandoned projections over the years have shown us; forecasting demand from a group as multifarious as mature students is many times more difficult, and all we can hope to do here is to make a reasoned guess. In any case, it is more accurate to view future demand not as something that is going to happen, but something that can be made to happen, or at least be stimulated or depressed. At the same time we must not fall into the opposite trap of believing that a deft touch on the policy controls will always produce the exact, desired result. Higher education policy has more in common with sailing a boat than driving a car.

Although there is now a considerable literature on mature entry to higher education, most of it specific to one institution, it is more appropriate here to draw on it in passing, rather than to make a formal review. In any case, there are still many questions on which little or no empirical evidence exists. Of necessity, we shall be dealing with many unknowns.

A REVIEW OF TRENDS
In this section, we shall review trends in the enrolment of mature students (aged twenty-one or over at entry) in higher education, as a preliminary to analysing in more detail in the next section the factors affecting such trends. The figures will relate to the universities, the Open University, and advanced further education, and will usually be for the most recent available decade. The purpose of this review is not to attempt quantitative extrapolations into the next decade, but to give an overall picture of numbers and trends.

Two general points should be made. First, the statistics currently available on mature entry do not always allow us to disaggregate totals in the ways that we would wish. Thus, while we can get a general picture of trends, it is sometimes impossible to distinguish between full-time and part-time, men and women, or different adult age groups within those trends. Secondly, overseas students have been excluded from the figures. They tend to be significantly older than UK students on entry to higher education, and thus inflate the figures for mature entry as a whole. For example, in 1979/80, of the 7000 overseas new entrants to universities in the UK, almost half (3,495) were aged twenty-one or over (UGC, private communication). Our interest in this chapter is in mature entry by UK students. Postgraduates have also been excluded. (These figures are for the whole United Kingdom and are therefore not comparable with those of Chapter 2, Table 2.3, p.71.)

Universities
Have the number and proportion of mature students entering the universities increased or decreased in the last decade? Table 5.1 gives figures for full-time/sandwich undergraduate new entrants for the whole of the United Kingdom. It can be seen from this that the number of mature students has increased slowly but fairly steadily from 8500 in 1971/72 to 10,200 in 1979/80. This growth is accounted for by an increase in the number of women, and of men aged twenty-five and over (the age at which mature student grants begin to apply). The proportion of mature students has, however, fallen marginally from 13.3 per cent of the total intake in 1971/72, to 13.0 per cent in 1979/80, although this statement conceals a sharp rise in the proportion of women, and a fall in the proportion of men, sharp in the case of those aged 21-24. Obviously, if the eighteen-year-old intake fell significantly, the proportion of mature students would rise, but the numbers involved are not large.

TABLE 5.1
Full-time/sandwich home undergraduate new entrants to universities: by sex and age: United Kingdom (Thousands: column percentages in brackets)

		1971/72	1973/74	1975/76	1977/78	1979/80
20 & under	M	36.2 (57.0)	35.3 (55.3)	38.0 (54.5)	40.6 (54.1)	41.2 (52.3)
	F	18.9 (29.7)	20.1 (31.5)	22.3 (32.0)	24.7 (32.9)	27.4 (34.8)
21-24	M	4.4 (7.0)	3.7 (5.8)	4.0 (5.8)	3.9 (5.2)	3.8 (4.8)
	F	1.1 (1.8)	1.4 (2.2)	1.5 (2.2)	1.7 (2.3)	1.9 (2.5)
25 & over	M	2.0 (3.2)	2.1 (3.2)	2.3 (3.3)	2.4 (3.2)	2.4 (3.0)
	F	0.9 (1.3)	1.3 (2.0)	1.5 (2.2)	1.7 (2.2)	2.1 (2.7)
Total		63.6 (100.0)	63.9 (100.0)	69.8 (100.0)	75.1 (99.9)	78.9 (100.1)
Total 21 and over		8.5 (13.3)	8.4 (13.2)	9.4 (13.5)	9.7 (12.9)	10.2 (13.0)

Source
UGC, private communication.

As to part-time undergraduates, most of whom are mature by our definition (see Table 5.2), UK universities (excluding the Open University) enrol a much smaller proportion of part-time students than do universities in many other countries. The figures involved are therefore very small compared with the total intake. Table 5.2 (which is unavoidably incomplete) shows that the *total* part-time undergraduate population has risen from 3145 in 1971/72 to 3703, in 1979/80. Of this 3703, 85.9 per cent were aged twenty-one or over. The time series is scarcely long enough for us to comment meaningfully on trends. Again, however, women, at least those over twenty-five, are a rising proportion. It will also be noticed that, as the figure for 1973/74 suggests, the part-time total fell (for three years) after the opening of the Open University in 1971. With the very recent growth of part-time degrees offered by other universities, one might now expect to see a continued upward trend. But even in 1979/80, Birkbeck College London alone accounted for 30 per cent of the home part-time undergraduates.

TABLE 5.2
Part-time home undergraduates in universities (other than the Open University): by sex and age: United Kingdom (Numbers: column percentages in brackets)

		1971/72	1973/74	1975/76	1977/78	1979/80
20 & under	M	not available		198 (6.2)	171 (4.8)	188 (5.1)
	F	not available		374 (11.7)	361 (10.2)	333 (9.0)
21-24	M	not available		425 (13.3)	388 (10.9)	453 (12.2)
	F	not available		287 (9.0)	306 (8.6)	307 (8.3)
25 & over	M	not available		1110 (34.6)	1297 (36.5)	1320 (35.6)
	F	not available		810 (25.3)	1027 (28.9)	1102 (29.8)
All ages	M	2061 (65.5)	1662 (60.5)	1733 (54.1)	1856 (52.3)	1961 (53.0)
	F	1084 (34.5)	1084 (39.5)	1471 (45.9)	1694 (47.7)	1742 (47.0)
Total		3145 (100.0)	2746 (100.0)	3204 (100.1)	3550 (99.9)	3703 (100.0)
Total 21 & over		n.a.	n.a.	2632 (82.2)	3018 (85.0)	3182 (85.9)

Source
UGC, private communication

The Open University
The Open University does not admit students under twenty-one at all (except for a very small experimental group); hence it is entirely devoted to mature entry in our terms. Table 5.3 gives the figures for OU entrants over the last decade, in the form of an admissions cycle, whereby initial applicants eventually become registered students. The figures for the first year of entry

TABLE 5.3
Applications and admissions to the Open University (undergraduates only)

	1971	1972	1973	1974	1975	1976	1977	1978	1979	1980	1981
Applications	43,444	35,182	32,046	35,011	52,537	52,916	49,956	45,293	42,754	45,311	43,004
Places available	25,000	20,500	17,000	15,000	20,000	17,000	20,000	21,000	21,000	20,000	21,000
Provisionally registered students (Jan 1)	24,191	20,498	17,004	14,475	20,045	16,311	19,886	20,882	20,709	19,439	Not available
Finally registered students	19,033	15,564	12,405	10,856	14,830	12,230	14,971	15,669	16,729	14,150	Not available

Source
Analysis of Applications for Undergraduate Study with the Open University in 1981 Open University information services, November 1980.

are a unique case, and can be excluded from our analysis. After 1971, the numbers of finally registered students fluctuate around a mean of about 14,000 ranging from 10,856 in 1974 to 16,729 in 1979; most of the fluctuation reflects the variable number of places available. Applications, likewise, fluctuate rather than show any discernible trend, and seem to have levelled off in the 40-45,000 range. Two points may be noted: first, that the number of finally registered students is often around a third of the number of applicants; and secondly that the rate of initial inquiries to applications in 1980 was itself 2.44:1 (84,051 inquiries). In other words, between initial inquiries and final registration, some 70,000 adults (or five times the number who finally registered) decided that the Open University was not for them, or were selected out. This suggests a considerable potential demand for some form of post-school education, and we shall return to this later in the chapter.

These statistics do not include associate students, for whom Table 5.4 gives figures. These are students who register to take individual courses, not the degree programme. The number of such students has risen fairly steadily from 2042 in 1973 (when the programme began) to 8917 in 1979. (This figure does not include students on short courses, of whom there were about 14,000 in 1980.)

TABLE 5.4
Open University Associate Students (excluding short courses): applications and final registrations

	1973	1974	1975	1976	1977	1978	1979
Applications	3,356	2,211	6,591	7,462	10,648	11,384	14,181
Registrations	2,042	1,336	4,359	4,486	5,974	7,209	8,917

Source
Open University Information Services

Advanced Further Education
Turning to public sector higher education, which comprises the polytechnics, colleges/institutes of higher education, and 'advanced' courses in other further education institutions, Table 5.5 gives us figures for full-time initial home entrants. These are broken down into 'Initial Teacher-training', where the *total* intake has been reduced in the last seven years to a quarter of its previous size, and 'Other Public Sector', where the total intake has almost doubled. In initial teacher training, the proportion of mature entrants rose with some fluctuations from about 26 per cent in 1969/70 to 31 per cent in 1979/80. However, in the other public sector category, the increase is much more marked: from 31 per cent in 1969/70 to nearly 38 per cent in 1979/80. Mature entrants now account for 37 per cent of *all* public sector full-time

entrants. (The highest proportion of full-time mature students is found on advanced but non-first degree courses: 51 per cent as against 27 per cent on first-degree, non-teacher-training courses in the public sector in 1976/77 (CUA 1978).) Mature students are represented in even higher numbers on *part-time* advanced courses in the public sector, on which the vast majority (95 per cent) of students are enrolled in courses other than for first degrees (see Chapter 2, Table 2.2, p.70). Seventy-two per cent of home entrants to part-time, day, advanced courses in 1976/77 were aged twenty-one or over, and no less than 90 per cent of those to part-time evening courses (CUA 1978). These proportions and the trends are striking, and demand explanation. Unfortunately, we do not have figures which allow us to do it adequately.

TABLE 5.5
Full-time/sandwich home initial entrants to Advanced Further Education: by age: England and Wales (Thousands: column percentages in brackets)

		1969/70	1971/72	1973/74	1975/76	1977/78	1979/80
(a)	*Initial teacher training*						
	20 & under	27.4	27.8	25.2	19.5	8.1	5.8
	21 & over	9.8 (26.3)	10.3 (27.0)	9.6 (27.6)	8.1 (29.3)	2.7 (25.0)	2.6 (31.0)
	Total	37.2	38.1	34.8	27.6	10.8	8.4
(b)	*Other public sector*						
	20 & under	18.4	20.8	20.9	24.3	28.9	31.4
	21 & over	8.1 (30.6)	9.4 (31.1)	10.4 (33.2)	12.5 (34.0)	16.7 (36.7	19.0 (37.6)
	Total	26.5	30.2	31.3	36.8	45.5	50.5

Source
DES (Statistics Branch), private communication.

We have now seen the overall figures for mature entrants to the whole of the higher education sector. However, figures relating to adult education are also relevant, in so far as adult education students form a pool of potential HE applicants. Most LEA adult education is not closely related to higher education either in terms of content, or level, and we need not therefore consider it here. However, the courses provided by the 'Responsible Bodies'

— eg university extra-mural departments and the WEA — are closer to higher education in the type of subject studied, and on the whole in their academic level. Most students see these courses as an end in themselves, and do not want to take on more systematic, assessed courses; but some use them as a stepping-stone to more sustained study. Table 5.6 shows that the pool is very large indeed — nearly 300,000 students — and that there is a slightly wobbly, upward trend. (Adult education courses are price-sensitive, and recent fee increases may well cut into these totals.) Even if only a tenth of such students were interested in some form of higher education, this would still mean a pool of nearly 30,000 potential applicants; which, together with OU 'non-registering' students (assuming no overlap) makes a total of 100,000 per year.

TABLE 5.6
Students taking courses of adult education provided by responsible bodies

	Male	Female	Total
1969/70	105,093	144,043	249,136
1970/71	106,658	148,072	254,730
1971/72	115,378	155,767	271,145
1972/73	112,181	155,118	267,299
1973/74	112,434	156,940	269,374
1974/75	115,613	159,441	275,054
1975/76	118,230	167,672	285,902
1976/77	121,380	165,795	287,175
1977/78	n.a.	n.a.	272,973
1978/79	n.a.	n.a.	280,154

Source
Statistics of Education, Vol. 3 and DES (Statistics Branch), private communication.

The figures available to us here can do no more than suggest general proportions and trends. Three general features emerge. First, in the majority of categories, the trend is either stable or upward, both in terms of numbers and proportions. Secondly, the very marked increases in the polytechnics and colleges (PSHE) contrast with the very slight increases in the universities. Thirdly, there are indications of a fairly substantial pool of demand, or, perhaps more accurately, of demands. This leads us to the necessity of disaggregating the whole concept of a 'mature student' into finer categories; first a more detailed analysis of the factors affecting demand is necessary.

FACTORS AFFECTING MATURE DEMAND

The previous section reviewed trends in mature entry to higher education over the last decade. Are these likely to continue over the next ten years? So many different factors can affect the trends that we cannot know for certain. The natural attitude is to act as if the future will be an extrapolation of the recent past. Some analysis is therefore in order, if only to test this implicit 'continuation model'.

There are three main problems with such an analysis. First, one has to arrive at a satisfactory classification of the relevant factors. Useful examples are given by Harnqvist (1978) and by Williams and Gordon (1976). But secondly, even if one arrives at a satisfactory model of classification of the factors affecting demand for education, one still faces the problem of *weighting* such factors. How far does an increase in fees outweigh a reduction in entry requirements? Will a more positive self-concept among adult students outweigh the prospect of worse graduate unemployment?

Thirdly, there is the problem of assumed rationality. Explanatory models tend to display what Carley has called 'analytic rationality' (Carley 1980) yet there is no guarantee that individual students do in fact consider all the relevant factors, weigh them carefully, and then make a decision. They may not know all the relevant factors; they may be influenced by unconscious factors (eg the desire to get out of a marriage) or they may consider different factors at different stages in the decision process. Nevertheless, the point of such models is to account not for the unique decisions of individuals, but the aggregate effect of large numbers of such decisions.

In short, the problems of forecasting demand for education are much greater than those of a manufacturer forecasting the demand for even a new and untried market product. Where the market product has a definite price, education is an aggregate of a lot of different costs, which are often difficult to estimate individually (eg fees, travel, books and materials, loss of income, loss of overtime; possibly offset by grants or loans). And where the market product may often have a fairly precise benefit some of the benefits of post-school education are notoriously difficult to quantify. It is little wonder that analyses of educational demand tend, after due acknowledgment of subjective factors, to concentrate only on those things which are most concrete and observable; pricing policy, admissions requirements, and employment statistics. This is an approach that we shall try to avoid, believing it to be imbalanced. (It should be added, however, that among these 'concrete' factors can be found many of the policies which are susceptible of relatively easy change.)

We have already suggested that the implicit assumption about the future is that it will constitute, roughly, a continuation of the recent past. We will therefore confine our analysis to attempts to foresee any major challenges to that assumption; in other words, to predict major changes in the climate, rather than try to forecast the weather from day to day. Five broad headings, ranging from the personal to the institutional, will be used.

Personal Factors
Although the term 'self-concept' is a relatively new one, common sense has always told us that what a person thinks of himself or herself is an important influence on behaviour. In compulsory education, the self-concept has a major bearing on learning achievement (Burns 1979). However, in post-compulsory education, it affects demand as well. An adult may consider that he or she is not capable of, or not suited to studying for a degree, for a variety of reasons: too old, too busy, too lazy, not intelligent enough, not disciplined enough, not likely to get on with a crowd of eighteen-year-olds. Adults on 'return to study' courses typically express doubts about themselves, on many counts; they complain about their concentration, their memory, their mental block about writing essays, not to mention sitting exams.* They tend to be surprised and relieved to find that other adults have similar doubts and uncertainties, and one value of return to study courses, quite apart from teaching 'study skills' is to allow adults to share these problems with each other.

At the same time, such self-doubts are now counteracted by the belief that it can be done: a belief that appears to be spreading. Adults have studied for years in night classes in FE, or in adult education. However, the widening belief that adults can study successfully for a degree or something near it is probably due mainly to the Open University and its visibility. And the more adults who do get degrees, or Diplomas in Higher Education, the greater the chance that an aspiring mature student will know someone, or someone who knows someone, who has done it. That chance will still be much greater among middle-class students than working-class, but it is as if a small but significant ripple were spreading throughout the adult population. The analogy here must be with the women's movement: diffuse, generalized, uneven in its impact, yet impossible to ignore in any analysis of late twentieth-century attitudes towards work, family life, child-rearing, or, indeed, education.

Secondly, adult roles have been becoming gradually less well defined over a number of years. Male/female roles within marriage have been challenged in a number of ways. The maternal role has been altered by efficient contraception. The male wage-earning role is affected by unemployment. Roles within jobs have also changed: there is less deference, more questioning of authority. Teacher/pupil roles at school have also changed. Old people have, to some extent, had their role taken away. The notion of 'participation' has affected political roles. and so on. The resulting

---

*These comments are based on a number of *Return to Study* courses which the author has run, as well as on literature on the subject.

adult roles are more complex, and more fluid than they were, say, in the immediate postwar years.

How might this change affect mature entry to higher education? Often it may not provide a positive incentive but simply remove an obstacle. One aspect of role fluidity is experimentation with new or different roles, and education in some circumstances provides the context, and the legitimation, for that. Such students would be entering higher education not so much to study a subject, as to develop their lives.

We have discussed the adult's self-concept and roles, but what of his or her interests? Enrolment on a course can also grow out of a self-developed interest, hobby, or intellectual need, which may have developed late in life, or been held in abeyance for some years, while other activities took priority. Tough has shown that small-scale, self-directed adult learning (which he labels 'learning projects') is ubiquitous in the adult population, and does not mirror the sadly familiar, social maldistribution of formal education activities (Tough 1979). A 'learning project' might be defined as up to ten hours spent over the previous six months trying to master any cognitive, affective or psycho-motor problem: anything from handling a relative's estate, to putting in double-glazing, or developing an interest in fossils. The implications of Tough's work are mainly for adult education, which he suggests should be largely directed towards backing up and developing these pre-existing learning initiatives. Many, perhaps most, learning projects are remote from higher education both in terms of content and level. However, some may develop to the point where a short degree-level course (as distinct from a full degree) would be the appropriate next step. Some existing adult education courses and some OU associate students courses may fall into this category.

There are other trends which may affect the personal aspects of mature student demand. Changes in the age at which people get married and have their first child; the number of one-parent families; changes in housing conditions; the provision of nurseries and pre-school education; all of these may bear on the decision to enrol. However, it is difficult even to speculate on the effects of such factors, the more so since those effects may differ with different forms of higher education. For example, a tendency to delay having a first child might increase the possibility of doing a full-time course in one's early twenties; but it might make little or no difference to part-time enrolments.

I have suggested that a subtle but significant shift in self-concepts and role perceptions may make adults more likely to enrol in some form of post-school education (not necessarily higher). Such generalizations obviously need to be qualified in terms of social class and other factors; for example, the shifts I have described are more obvious in the middle class than the working class. However, the general conclusion must be that such changes as occur are more likely to increase than to decrease demand.

Occupational Factors

By occupational factors, we mean factors related to an adult's paid employment which may either encourage or hinder his or her enrolment in higher education. We must first distinguish between attitudes towards higher education, and arrangements for facilitating it. Even if no formal arrangements for job-release or paid educational leave (PEL) exist, the attitude of an employer (and colleagues, workmates) towards enrolment in higher education can be important. Will he allow time off to do examinations? Will he be supportive or hostile? There are many small ways in which the mature student's life can be made easier or more difficult by an employer or the people he works with. Some mature students keep quiet about their studies because they feel that their workmates will laugh at them, or regard them as an odd-ball. However, if a general shift in attitudes is indeed taking place, it will affect the workplace as well as the family.

Beyond this, formal arrangements for job-release and paid educational leave are involved. A recent NIAE study estimated that some three to four million people in England and Wales were in receipt of PEL in 1976/77 (Killeen and Bird 1981). In terms of students, two-thirds of this was 'in-house', ie provided by the employer. But in terms of student days, some 40 per cent of all provision was made by higher and further education institutions, which typically run much longer courses. Some idea of the relative distribution of PEL courses between institutions can be gained from Table 5.7 based on the study's sample representing 23.8 per cent of England and Wales.

It is not possible to make a precise distinction between further or non-advanced and advanced or higher education from this table, but a rough estimate would be that higher education courses account for about one-third of the total sample.

There thus appears to be a substantial element of PEL-related courses in higher education already. It would be interesting to know, first, if the provision is increasing or decreasing and, secondly, whether the distribution between the universities and PSHE is changing. It would also be interesting to know how much of the provision consists of short courses, and how much of longer courses leading to a qualification. (Note that degree courses are excluded from the figures.)

While there is a ground swell of support for (or at least interest in) PEL, not only in the UK but in other countries, notably France, Germany and Sweden, both the present economic stringencies and the attitudes of most employers are likely to limit the extent of PEL, and also its direction. While the NIAE study presents cogent arguments for a very broad interpretation of the purposes of PEL, employers are likely to continue to want to see some relationship between PEL and productivity. Studies of PEL in other countries have also identified various asymmetries in the provision and take-up of PEL: more large companies than small ones; more men than women; more high-level students (eg managerial or professional) than low-level; more urban students than rural; more young people than old people. Although the implications for higher education are difficult to foresee, it seems improbable that the level of provision will decrease in the next ten years; and it may well increase under the impact of technological innovation. However, it is difficult to imagine PEL becoming broader, and less specifically linked to production, except as a result of a direct government initiative: and this, again, is difficult to imagine in the present circumstances. Current government policy on post-school education suggests an increased emphasis on vocational aspects and some withdrawal of support for general or liberal education. Thus if PEL-related demand does increase, it seems likely to affect some departments, and even some institutions, more than others, and to benefit vocational, commercial and technical subjects in particular.

TABLE 5.7

Estimated numbers of students on paid educational leave: by type of institution*

Type of Provider	Adjusted Student Number
University Departments (Non EMDs)	18,023
Extra Mural Departments	4,195
Polytechnics	14,636
Colleges of Art	167
Colleges of Education	244
Colleges/Institutes of Higher Education	6,493
Colleges of Technology	9,458
Technical Colleges	13,844
Colleges of Further Education	13,235
Agricultural Colleges	2,103
Horticultural Colleges	282
Other Further Education Major Establishments	12,466
TUC/TU Colleges	1,857
WEA	2,971
All Other	35,258
Non-response − 223 courses (4.0%)	5,409
TOTAL	140,641

*Excluding degree courses and distance learning
(eg Open University and correspondence colleges)

Source
Killeen and Bird (1981).

Financial Factors
The financial factors affecting mature student demand can be analysed
either in terms of costs, or costs and benefits. Even the first is difficult. The
mature student is typically faced with a package of costs, each of which may
vary in its own right, and for reasons unconnected with other costs in the
package. Tuition fees are the most obvious cost, and these vary considerably
from one institution to the next. There is not even a standard university
policy, as yet, on fees for part-time degrees: they may even vary within
institutions. (But recent UGC guidance suggests that standard fees may soon
be prescribed.) In general, part-time fees are not high, compared to full-time
fees, but part-time degrees inevitably take longer.

Moreover, tuition fees may be met, or offset, by a grant, depending on
the type and level of course. Grants are discretionary for all except full-time
degree courses, and the chances of getting one depend on the policy and
finances of one's local authority. Charges for halls of residence also vary; as
will charges for private accommodation away from home. Two other major
items in the package of costs are materials and travel. The cost of books and
of essential equipment may or may not be offset by a grant; likewise with
travel. With the increases in the price of travel, this is a major consideration
for any commuting student. Finally, there are other possible costs associated
with childcare, loss of overtime or second incomes, social expenses associated
with studying, and extra heating and lighting.

The calculation of benefits to the individual student is even more
difficult. Rate of return analysis depends on the likelihood of getting a job at
the end of the course, which in turn depends on general levels of graduate
unemployment, and specific levels related to the type of institution attended,
and the subject studied. Moreover, the older the student, the fewer the
remaining years in which to benefit from the 'extra' return; and in many
cases the larger the amount foregone while studying, if study is full-time.
This implies an increasing disincentive to full-time study as one gets older.
However, the adult's disposable income will vary over the life-span, with
perhaps the greatest pressures on him or her in the late twenties and early
thirties when children are being reared, when a second income may be
reduced or absent, a mortgage has been taken on, and the salary has not
reached its peak or plateau.

With all these shifting conditions, can we say anything definite about
the financial aspects of demand? The current government is increasing
student grants below the rate of increase in inflation, and has also considered
(but has temporarily shelved) the introduction of a loan scheme. If extra
money does become available, it seems likely to be for Non-Advanced
Further Education, perhaps even channelled through employment not
education funding. There are also signs of a shift of policy emphasis as
regards levels of study — eg the encouragement of training for technicians
rather than technologists — as well as direction — vocational rather than
general. However, continued high unemployment rates could encourage

government support for retraining schemes at every level. Nor is there much chance of the other costs in the package being held down: they tend to be either energy-related (travel, heating), or labour-intensive (teaching, halls of residence, meals, child-minding, publishing). Moreover, the fact that a package of largely unrelated costs rather than a single, all-inclusive expense is involved makes control less easy and less likely. Without a detailed study of costs and trends, we can do no more than guess, but it seems unlikely that financial factors, as described above, will make it significantly easier for mature students to enrol, in the next decade. They may well make it more difficult.

Vocational Factors

By vocational factors, we mean the likelihood of a student getting a job, or a better job, or not losing a job, as a direct result of what he or she has studied. We have reviewed trends in graduate unemployment elsewhere (Squires 1981). Neither the general proportion of graduates unemployed, nor the trend, appears to be a major concern at the moment. However, there are considerable differences in the unemployment rates as between subjects, with the arts and social sciences faring worst; and the average unemployment figures for the polytechnics and colleges are significantly worse than for the universities. Several careers specialists have recently predicted a sharp worsening in all the higher education figures. On the other hand, they have predicted this for the last two years, and there may now be some signs that the recession is bottoming out. Trends in teacher employment and public service employment are already affecting figures adversely; on the other hand, a gradual technological upgrading of the economy would benefit many graduates. And there are signs that some institutions are taking steps to equip 'non-vocational students' with some marketable skills (in mathematics, computing, languages), in addition to the 'trained mind' which they are assumed to have developed. Graduate unemployment is thus a matter of uncertainty rather than serious anxiety, and in this the UK differs markedly from some of its continental peers.

The available statistics do not distinguish between young graduates and mature graduates. There are reasons for thinking that older, mature graduates who have taken a full-time degree find it more difficult to get a job than their young counterparts. Upper age limits, explicit or implicit, still exist in many employment sectors. Older graduates may have to be paid more. The stigma of 'instability' may attach to them, if they have thrown up a previous job to study. For the younger, mature student (say, in his late twenties), maturity is, however, a possible bonus. He has the work experience and savoir-vivre that young graduates, 'wet behind the ears', will not have; and he is still young enough to represent a good investment for a company. For the part-time mature student, the situation is different again, and less risky. Such a student will either have never left his job, or will be emerging from a household role. In either case, a qualification is likely to be a definite asset, in terms of promotion, or of getting into the job market.

A large question-mark, however, hangs over the trend of general unemployment. Is the current high figure of 2.5 million due to cyclical economic factors, or is there, in addition, a long-term trend towards structural unemployment, caused by labour-saving technology, and competition from low-wage developing countries? And if large-scale unemployment is here to stay, will it increase demand for higher education (either as a hedge against unemployment, or as leisure-filler) or decrease it, as people, especially teenagers, go directly into jobs rather than risk the uncertainties of higher education?

Whatever happens, part-time study would seem to benefit. The adult who gets a job as a first priority can then try to upgrade or re-orientate himself while still holding on to the job. Greater leisure, through a reduced working week, also facilitates part-time study. Unemployed adults can attend part-time courses (in the evening) and still qualify for benefit. (They may also be sent on full-time training courses.) Housewives can study part-time. The risks of full-time study would, by contrast, seem to increase. The eighteen-year-old no longer has a guarantee of a job at the end of a degree course, and the knowledge of that fact is perhaps spreading, even if the figures are not getting worse. The adult who gives up his job to study full-time is taking a major risk.

As with the other factors we have analysed, it is difficult to assess the impact of vocational trends. They may affect the balance and structure of higher education, rather than its overall size, leading to proportionately more part-time demand. Whatever happens to employment trends over the next decade, the individual adult is likely above all to perceive uncertainty: uncertainty created by technological, economic and political change. In those circumstances, the natural reaction perhaps is to hedge one's bets, and to see higher education not as an alternative, but as a complement to employment.

Institutional Factors

Finally, in this analysis of the factors which affect mature student demand, we must comment briefly on institutional factors: those aspects of higher education institutions which seem likely to have a direct influence on enrolments. Left to themselves, institutions would have every reason to want to attract more mature students in the 1980s. The polytechnics and colleges already have a tradition of mixed age entry; but the impending shortfall of eighteen-year-olds has also concentrated the minds of the universities wonderfully in this direction. In the minds of many lecturers, Model E would save higher education from the necessity of a painful contraction; and mature students are a key element in Model E. However, the signs are that institutions will not be left to themselves. We appear to be entering a period of unprecedented centralized control over higher education: through an increasingly dirigiste UGC; a new central body for funding PSHE; and beyond that (and even now), mechanisms for transbinary rationalization. This systemic centralization is likely to be paralleled by centralization within institutions in the face of contraction.

Despite these general developments, there are signs that both PSHE and the universities (somewhat tardily) are making deliberate efforts to attract more mature students. Alternative admissions requirements already exist in most institutions, though UCCA figures show them to account for only a small minority of cases as yet (UCCA 1980). These, combined with the flexibility of modular credit schemes, open up many more routes into and through higher education than existed previously. The Toyne Report on educational credit transfer has recommended the formalization of this process (Toyne 1979). As yet, we are some way from giving admissions 'points' for work experience, as the Swedes do, but the combination of *some* qualifications and *some* work experience seems likely to be increasingly attractive to admissions officers. (There is a considerable pool of the 'semi-qualified', ie adults who have one 'A' level or several good 'O' levels and thus fail to meet the full degree admissions criteria, but who nevertheless have some evidence of academic achievement. It is perhaps such students, rather than the *wholly* unqualified, who will provide the main pool of mature applicants.) Part-time degrees are also beginning to proliferate. The universities, in particular, are beginning to learn some of the flexibility in modes of attendance which has always existed in FE. Before long, part-time degrees provided by one institution may begin to compete with degrees offered by neighbouring institutions (and with the Open University) unless there are local agreements, or centralized arrangements. Finally, curriculum policy is beginning to reflect, in small ways, a desire to attract mature students, with courses which are likely to meet the presumed subject needs and preferred styles of teaching and assessment of adults. At this point, the line between higher and adult education is becoming increasingly blurred.

Instinctively perhaps, higher education institutions see student demand as a defence — perhaps their only defence — against cuts. It is likely, therefore, that whatever policy is imposed upon them, they will try to attract as many applicants as possible, even if only to demonstrate unsatisfied demand. We do not know what is going to happen to the APR among eighteen-year-olds; but for many institutions, mature students could be seen as, at the least, an insurance policy, and, ideally, a relief column arriving at the siege.

Conclusions
It is difficult to assess the combined effect on mature student demand of all the factors we have analysed. If the personal and institutional factors seem to point most clearly to increased demand, the occupational and vocational factors are decidedly ambiguous, and the financial factors look negative. Some of the increased demand may affect non-advanced further education rather than higher education, and part-time rather than full-time courses. In

any case, we cannot assume that either individuals or populations will go through even the quasi-rational calculus that we have attempted. In the final section of this paper, we will examine the role of policy in the demand equation. Demand, at least for higher education, is not a wholly manipulable or even explicable phenomenon: that is the policy fallacy. However, policy can do something to stimulate or damp down demand. Demand is also not purely a 'natural' phenomenon, which one can only observe; it is partly an *artefact*.

DEMAND, POLICY AND PROVISION

The general arguments for allowing adults access to post-school education are well known, and do not need elaborating here. They fall under three broad headings: socio-economic; developmental; and institutional. First the socio-economic argument stresses the need for adults to adapt to, or better, control, social and technological change. There is a narrower (vocational) and broader (socio-cultural) version of this argument. Secondly, developmental arguments depend on the notion that individuals' cognitive, affective (and, to a lesser extent psycho-motor) development continues, or should continue, throughout the life-span. Adults do not suddenly stop developing when compulsory schooling ends. Nor do their capacities necessarily decline in quite the straightforward manner once believed by some psychologists, such as Wechsler (1958). They may indeed develop new capacities and motivations as life goes on: adult capacities seem partly to reflect the opportunities given to use them (Labouvie-Vief 1977). Thirdly, adults need continuing access to education after school because the school system is an imperfect processor of human abilities. At the most basic level, this means providing remedial literacy and numeracy classes, but the argument applies at every level above that as well, where a person may have failed to do himself or herself justice, for whatever reason, while at school. And there is no immediate prospect that the school system, or the 16-21 provision that follows it, will attain a state of perfect efficiency. There are thus powerful and permanent arguments for providing adults with continuing access to educational and training opportunities throughout their lives. Some, though by no means all of those opportunities will be at an advanced level, ie in higher education.

When we consider mature entry to higher education, these three general arguments translate into rather more and different types of courses. The notion that there is such a thing as 'the mature student' or 'mature student provision' is too simplistic. It is possible to identify at least seven main types of courses to which adults may need access, and we do so below, commenting briefly on each type.

Type I: Full-time degrees

The number of students aged twenty-one to twenty-five at entry studying degree or degree-level courses on a full-time basis could probably be increased by altering grant regulations and admissions requirements. Beyond that age, family and financial responsibilities are likely to make entry more difficult, though not impossible, especially where there is a second income. Such students would presumably not be restricted as to what they could study, any more than other undergraduates are.

Type II: Part-time degrees

Both the Open University and, increasingly, other universities, polytechnics and colleges offer part-time degrees. Age and cost are less of a restriction in part-time study; distance, however, makes it more difficult to study subjects with a good deal of practical or laboratory work involved; and there is always the question of stamina.

Type III: Part-time AFE qualifications

Such qualifications are obtained after a number of years of part-time study, rising through various levels, and may reach Pass degree or near-degree standard. Students tend to be in their twenties, rather than older, having begun the 'climb' in their late teens. The courses are typically vocational, and well-established in AFE provision.

Type IV: One-year full-time vocational courses

Such courses are likely to attract adults who need to train or re-train themselves for a job, and who want to do so as quickly and intensively as possible. Some high-level TOPS courses fall under this heading, and they are probably more common in PSHE than in the universities. Admissions requirements vary a good deal, but can be quite strict. On the other hand, such students often have strong qualifications and experience behind them.

Type V: One-year part-time non-vocational courses

Some Open University associated student courses fall into this bracket. Such courses attract adults who want to engage in some serious study, but not too much, leading to a 'credit', which they may or may not see as a step towards a degree. Entry qualifications are typically flexible or 'open'.

Type VI: Non-certificated vocational short courses

Refresher or updating courses for professional and skilled personnel, lasting anything from a weekend to several months. Many such courses would be provided 'in-house' by companies and organizations, but some would be contracted out to, or arranged by, educational institutions. However, they are more likely to come under the heading of continuing education than of higher education.

Type VII: Non-certificated non-vocational short courses

Many, but not all, liberal adult education courses come under this heading. They deliberately eschew examinations and qualifications, and may last up to a year (or longer), though with only two hours contact per week. They can be seen as an end in themselves, or as a stepping-stone to more sustained study, and are typically in the domain of the arts and social sciences.

No classification like the above is entirely satisfactory; educational provision, especially post-school, has grown like Topsy in the past, and does not fall into neat categories. The distinction between vocational and non-vocational courses is not watertight, since different students can use the same course for different purposes. And the plethora of AFE courses and qualifications, though increasingly streamlined by BEC and TEC, is still very difficult to categorize. Interestingly, the DipHE falls into no category, and this tends to reflect the author's view that in a country where degrees typically take three years to get, a two-year qualification is not viable: students will usually go on to the third year while they are at it.

If we see an increased vocational emphasis in the 1980s, this would lead to an increase in Type III, Type IV, and Type VI courses, perhaps at the expense of contraction or at least non-expansion of other types. Type III courses are already an integral part of AFE, and many Type VI courses lie outside the formal educational system altogether. The scope for Type IV courses — one-year, full-time vocational — as a means of retraining adults in mid-career or mid-life could perhaps be explored further. Such courses are in some ways the antithesis of OU provision: intensive, strictly vocational, non-modular. Adults who need retraining may well put up with a lot of inconvenience (eg living away from home) and make a lot of effort if they know it is only for one year at most.

If Type IV courses point to a possible response to adult unemployment, Type V courses may be relevant to under-employment — either through a statutorily shortened working week, work-sharing, or generally increased leisure. The steady rise in OU associated student enrolments is worth bearing in mind in this connection; as are the Toyne report proposals for the facilitation of credit transfer, and the general growth of modular credit structures.

It may appear that we are under-emphasizing degree courses, and this is correct. While degrees are the core of higher education for those who work in the system, they may not occupy quite such a key position for mature students. Taken full-time they demand a considerable commitment in money; taken part-time a considerable commitment in years; and either way, a major investment of effort; any of which the mature entrant, with his or her multiple responsibilities, will think hard about.

Planned Stimulation of Demand
How can demand for the above types of courses be stimulated? How far is demand under policy control at all? Again, it is difficult to generalize, since conditions vary in each case. The main obstacle to demand may differ from course to course: in one case it may be money, in another time, in another distance, in another admissions regulations. It is more sensible for the organizers of each type of provision to ask the question: what discourages mature students from applying? than it is for us to pose such a question generally. Indeed the question should be broken down further, distinguish-

ing between types of students: men, women; adults in their twenties, thirties or older; urban, suburban, or rural adults; middle-class or working-class adults. Over and above such specific questions, however, a few general points can be made.

First, a more generous financial policy — either through student grants, loan schemes, paid educational leave, or control of fees — would obviously make the costs and risks of mature entry more generally tolerable. Secondly, the use of flexible admissions requirements, and modular credit schemes which permit both interruption and transfer of study, would benefit adult students in particular. Thirdly, facilities for part-time and/or distance study would overcome obstacles for those who are tied to employment either at work or in the home. Fourthly, more publicity about opportunities for mature students should increase inquiries, if not always enrolments. Fifthly, the actual content, teaching and assessment of courses can be modified to suit adult needs, whether in the form of 'Return to Study' orientation courses, special options for mature students, or modes of assessment more suited to people who may not have done examinations for a long time. (Obviously, dual standards have to be avoided here.)

Beyond such measures, some of which lie within the competence of individual institutions, others of which necessitate government initiatives, there are perhaps two other points worth raising. The first is the need for adequate information and guidance for intending students. Typically, each institution provides information only about itself, and the rapid growth of cross-institutional guidance services for adults points to a need here. At present, there are some twenty such services, most of them operating on a shoe-string. It is essential that adults are enrolled not just on any course, but on an appropriate course; the costs of a bad choice can be high. Guidance services could provide not only a comprehensive picture of all post-school provision (higher, further and adult education) but could also provide objective guidance at a time when institutions might be above all concerned with numbers.

Secondly, and related to this, it might be useful to allow adults to take aptitude or other tests related to entry, if they so desire. The problem with mature entry is often one of evidence, and such tests can provide *one* form of evidence, not only for admissions tutors, but for applicants themselves. Despite the general aversion to testing in this country, it is worth noting that it is widely used on entry to higher education in the USA, and that one guidance service for adults in this country (Belfast EGSA) uses such tests regularly, on a voluntary basis. For someone who has not gone through the normal hoops of 'O' and 'A' levels, or who has been away from formal education for a long time, such tests can provide useful information to weigh in the overall decision whether to apply or not.

Policy and Provision
However, a major question-mark hangs over the whole of the preceding

discussion, in the form of doubts about government policy on higher education, including mature entry to higher education. The impending cuts in higher education expenditure are a result not of an educational policy, but of an economic policy applied to higher education. The policy may be rationalized in educational terms (eg over-expansion, graduate unemployment), but there seems no doubt that the basic reason for the cutbacks is the belief that the country cannot afford the services that it has.

It is our view that these cuts in expenditure are likely to be implemented and to be translated into cuts in provision. Any general cut in provision, with its attendant publicity, is likely to damp down potential mature demand, and thus counteract some of the expansionary factors discussed earlier. This is not a foolproof prediction, but if people are generally aware that higher education is being cut back, they may hesitate to apply for it, especially in marginal cases. Secondly, the cuts are likely to institute a formal hierarchy (or triage) within the system, thus making the system more rigid and perhaps less responsive to mature students' needs. Thirdly, the process of implementing the cuts will lead to unprecedented centralization of control, both at system and institutional level. This is subject to the Hayekian criticism that, in higher education especially, the centre cannot know the system well enough to make sensible decisions; again there may be unfortunate implications for mature students.

There are signs, however, of an educational policy for higher education, even if it is currently being overwhelmed by the economic policy. This seems to contain the following elements:

1   A greater emphasis on the vocational and professional relevance of studies; an attempt to relate higher education more closely to working life.

2   An acceptance of the need for continuing education in relation to technological change, coupled with an unwillingness among governments and employers to pay for it.

3   A greater emphasis on non-advanced education and training in FE, perhaps at the expense of HE.

4   A general emphasis on cost-effectiveness in all post-school education, to be achieved in whatever way possible.

What do such policies portend for mature entrants to higher education? The main effects would appear to be a greater emphasis on vocational courses for mature students (because of their economic relevance) and (possibly) on part-time courses (because they are cheaper). Part-time studies could presumably develop in all types of institutions, but the vocational courses might be concentrated in non-advanced and advanced FE. Indeed, Rhodes Boyson is on record as saying that PSHE is better suited to vocational re-training than the universities (*Universities Challenged* BBC TV 2, 1 May 1981). We have already seen that PSHE has achieved both a much greater proportion of mature students, and a much greater recent increase in them, than the universities. It may be, therefore, that mature entry will be seen as one of the defining features of PSHE, but not of the universities.

A general growth in part-time studies has much to recommend it. As advocates of recurrent education have not been slow to point out, there are good economic, social and educational arguments for moving towards an alternating pattern of post-school studies; the main problem is the cost. However, there are two groups for whom a greater emphasis on full-time study might be apposite. First, those aged between twenty-one and twenty-five. Entry (to the universities at least) from this age group is currently low; yet they are in many ways in a good position to benefit from higher education, having had some work experience, but having not yet taken on the financial and family responsibilities which tend to accumulate in the late twenties. Such students might well show a greater sense of direction than some eighteen-year-olds, but they have not been away from formal education for so long that they find returning to study too difficult.

Secondly, there are those who need rapid, intensive retraining in mid-career, perhaps because of redundancy. Part-time courses are too long drawn out for such students: they need courses that are short, concentrated, and well targeted. They therefore need full-time support while they are studying, which can be justified on the economic grounds that they will be returning to productive roles sooner than otherwise, and contributing once more to the national wealth.

The other aspect of policy — greater vocational emphasis — is more problematic. There are powerful reasons in favour of it. It was illogical of the Robbins Committee to list four functions of higher education (including a vocational one) and then to go on to plan almost wholly on the basis of student 'rights'. Higher education has an irreducible plurality of functions: over-emphasis on any one of them leads to imbalance, and consequent damaging swings of emphasis. On the whole, I agree with the argument that the universities have been part of, and helped to maintain, an anti-industrial, anti-technology ethos which is at marked variance with the economic needs of the country, and thus may well have contributed to the UK's economic decline.

CONCLUSION
One's perception of the major issues and concerns in higher education during the next decade will tend to colour one's view of mature students. If one is concerned above all with the *size* of the system — numbers, demand, the problems of expansion or contraction — then one is likely to be interested above all in the trends in mature entry, whether these are increasing or decreasing, and what might be done either to stimulate or depress demand. Mature students thus come to be seen primarily against the backdrop of a falling eighteen-year-old intake.

If one is more concerned with the *type* or nature of the system, then one will perhaps see the enrolment of mature students as evidence of a greater diversity or plurality in higher education: a diversity of students which may, in turn, lead to a greater diversity of courses, course structures, teaching methods, types of assessment, and modes of attendance. Implicit in this view is the interesting question: how far do the students adapt to the institution; and how far do the institutions adapt to the students? Much of the latter adaptation is of a very practical and pragmatic kind: changes in timetabling, in library hours, provision of crèche facilities, and so on. But at a more fundamental level, one can surmise that higher education might become or have to become more responsive to market pressures than it was in the days of a carefully-selected, assured eighteen-year-old intake. Market pressures, however, have their dangers as well, as the United States experience shows (Chapter 3).

Finally, if one believes that the main problem facing higher education in the 1980s is that of finding a successor to the Robbins *principle*, mature students will raise questions about the relationship between higher education and recurrent/continuing education. After a long succession of false dawns, the idea that education should have a lifelong dimension now seems to have arrived, in both public and policy circles. Yet there are hard questions to be asked, not only about priorities but about finance, and about some of the wilder claims made by advocates of recurrent education. If one might hazard a guess, it is that giving higher education a lifelong dimension might in the end steady up the system, not only demographically (avoiding a purely cross-sectional intake) but also in terms of aims, by avoiding excessive swings of emphasis and priority. Recurrent education implies the recognition of a permanent and irreducible plurality of educational aims; a permanent conflict model which can never allow any one principle or function to dominate completely.

REFERENCES AND SELECT BIBLIOGRAPHY
Australian Vice-Chancellors' Committee (1975) *Special Admissions* Canberra: AVCC
Barrett, E., and Powell, J.P. (1980) Mature age unmatriculated students and the justification of a more liberal admission policy *Higher Education* 9 (4) 365-381
Becher, T., Embling, J., and Kogan, M. (1977) *Systems of Higher Education: United Kingdom* New York: ICED
Bourner, T. (1979) The cost of completing a part-time degree by full-time study *Higher Education Review* 12 (1) 54-69
Burns, R.B. (1979) *The Self Concept* London: Longman
Carley, M. (1980) *Rational Techniques in Policy Analysis* London: Heinemann, pp.10-20
Conference of University Administrators (CUA) Group on Forecasting and University Expansion (1978) *Final Report* Norwich: CUA
Cross, K.P. (1978) *Adult Learners: a data-based description* Berkeley: Centre for Research & Development in Higher Education

Department of Education and Science (1978) *Higher Education into the 1990s*

Department of Education and Science (1980) *Continuing Education: post-experience vocational provision for those in employment* London: HMSO

Finniston, Sir M. (1980) *Engineering our Future: report of the committee of inquiry into the engineering profession* (Cmnd. 7794) London: HMSO

Gordon, A. and Williams, G. (1977) *Attitudes of Fifth and Sixth Formers to School, Work and Higher Education* Report to the DES. University of Lancaster

Grainge, P.R.W. (nd) *The Mature Student in a College of Education* Mimeo

Harnqvist, K. (1978) *Individual Demand for Education: analytical report* Paris: OECD

Hopper, E. and Osborn, M. (1975) *Adult Students* London: Frances Pinter

Jones, H.A. (1977) *Adult Access to Post-Secondary Education in the United Kingdom* SME/ET/77. 31. Paris: OECD

Killeen, J. and Bird, M. (1981) *Education and Work; a study of Paid Educational Leave in England & Wales 1976/77* London: National Institute of Adult Education

Labouvie-Vief, G. (1977) Adult cognitive development: in search of alternative interpretations *Merrill-Palmer Quarterly* 23 (4) 227-263

Locke, M. and Pratt, J. (1979) *A Guide to Learning after School* Harmondsworth: Penguin

McIntosh, N.E. and Calder, J.E. (1975) *A Degree of Difference: Vol. 1 Research Findings* Milton Keynes: The Open University (SRHE, 1976; Praeger, 1977)

McIntosh, N. (1974/5) Open admissions; an open or revolving door? *Universities Quarterly* 29 (2) 171-181

Nisbet, J. and Welsh, J. (1977) The mature student *Educational Research* 14, pp.204-207

OECD (1981) *Mature Age Students in Australia* SME/ET/81.02/23

Pike, R.S., McIntosh, N., and Dallhof, U. (1978) *Innovation in Access to Higher Education* New York: ICED

Scott, R. (1978) Open admissions: a reply to critics *Higher Education Review* 11 (i) 51-70

Squires, G.T.C. (1978) *New Groups in Post-Secondary Education* SME/ET/ 78.42. OECD: Paris

Squires, G.T.C. (1979) Innovations in British higher education and their implications for adult education. In Lowe J. (Editor) *Learning Opportunities for Adults, Vol. II* Paris: OECD

Squires, G.T.C. (1981) *Higher Education and Working Life: reform of studies in the UK* Paris: OECD (forthcoming)

Tapper, E. and Chamberlain, A. (1970) *Mature Students at the University of Sussex* Mimeo

Tough, A. (1979) Fostering self-planned learning. In OECD *Learning Opportunities for Adults* 2. Paris: OECD

Toyne, P. (1979) *Educational Credit Transfer: feasibility study; final report* Funded by the Department of Education and Science

UCCA *Statistical Supplement to the Seventeenth Report 1978-9* Cheltenham: Universities Central Council on Admissions

Wechsler, D. (1958) *The Measurement and Appraisal of Adult Intelligence* (3rd edition) Baltimore: Wilkins & Wilkins

Whitburn, J., Mealing, M., and Cox, C. (1976) *People in Polytechnics* Guildford: SRHE

White, T. (1975) *Non-Transitional Forms of Post-Compulsory Study* SME/ET/74.85. Paris: OECD

Williams, G. (1977) *Towards Lifelong Education: a New Role for Higher Education Institutions* Paris: UNESCO

Woodley, A. and McIntosh, N. (1976) *People who Decide not to Apply to the Open University* Survey Research Department, The Open University

Woodley, A. (1980) How open is open? *Higher Education Review* 13 (1) 3-18

Wynne, R. (1979) *The Adult Student and British Higher Education* Amsterdam: European Cultural Foundation

6

POSTGRADUATE STUDY

by Ernest Rudd

INTRODUCTION by Oliver Fulton

It is extremely difficult to write in general terms about the demand for and access to postgraduate study, since postgraduate courses are now so varied. They range from the traditional research for a doctorate in the sciences to short courses of training or retraining for vocational purposes. Ernest Rudd's chapter gives some indication of the wide range of types of course called 'postgraduate'. It may once have been possible to think of a distinction between postgraduate work as providing specialized training for highly selective professions and undergraduate courses as providing general and non-vocational education, but even this apparently clear demarcation is a thing of the past (if it was ever valid). Many postgraduate courses provide general education of a sort also obtainable at undergraduate level; many undergraduate courses are highly specialized. The boundaries are often arbitrary, and have more to do with the accidents of historical tradition or the amount of knowledge that can be communicated in three years than with the 'level' or 'standard' of teaching or the modes of study. The results of this multiplicity are frequent confusion and discussions at cross purposes about the policy issues.

However, two general points can be made. The first is that if there is no clear distinction between undergraduate and postgraduate courses, then policies for postgraduate study should not automatically be different from those for first degrees. If we accept that demand is an appropriate planning criterion for undergraduate places, we should not rule it out across the board in principle for postgraduate places. If it is desirable for the state to subsidize undergraduate higher education, there is nothing in the nature of postgraduate courses which decrees that they should necessarily be funded differently. In both cases, equity (between subjects with different traditions, for example) may well demand that the principles should be the same. The second point is more obvious: it is quite unlikely that policies can be devised for application to postgraduate education as a whole. The costs alone of providing postgraduate places have such a wide range that it probably does not make sense to aim even for uniform pricing policies, let alone for uniform criteria for provision, for selection and so on. It is essential to disaggregate postgraduate courses.

Once we do so, then in a sense (and fortunately, given the space available here) the problem of postgraduate study disappears. Research degrees, for example, become largely a matter of research policy. It is perfectly sensible that the Research Councils are responsible for distributing government funds to research students and to research projects: the chief importance of postgraduate research in many subjects (in the sciences, for example) is to secure the future supply of research workers (or even the present supply where students immediately join in collaborative research with their supervisors). There are still difficult problems — in determining the size of the cake for individual subjects, for example — but these are problems of science policy, not of the supply of courses.

Similarly, much of postgraduate coursework is better regarded as continuing or recurrent education. It is here that the nominal 'level' is of least significance; there is often little difference in content or in difficulty between a nominally postgraduate course provided as training or retraining for those with a first degree earned some years earlier and an undergraduate course provided for those about to graduate and start their first job in the same profession. Here again, therefore, the problem of finding a policy for postgraduates disappears, to be replaced by policy for recurrent education. One can perform similar conjuring tricks for other types of course — and, indeed, at a much greater level of specificity.

However, the most difficult issue is finance. There is evidence that there is unsatisfied demand, perhaps considerable, for postgraduate education. As Ernest Rudd shows, a reduction in numbers of grants has been associated with a reduction in numbers of full-time students; but the demand seems insensitive to the low or negative rate of return to postgraduate study. There may be good policy reasons for partly discounting the results of rate of return studies; employers could well be misguided in their assessment of the value of postgraduates. But if we were to decide to respond as far as possible to demand, there must still presumably come a point when the strong intrinsic interest of students in pursuing their chosen subject further ceases to be something which the state should support even at a minimal level. As Rudd concludes, there is nothing in any of the usual arguments to tell us when that point is reached.

The answer suggested in Chapter 1 is that as far as individual students are concerned that point would be reached well before the beginning of postgraduate study. Four years of post-16 education will not enable many people to reach postgraduate level. If so, subsidies will need to be provided not on social criteria, but on the basis of science, manpower or general economic grounds.

A final quite different reflection is that the present custom is for state subsidies to graduate students to consist of full-time grants, fee subsidies, or combinations of both. However, we may here be less imaginative than we might. The very large number of part-time graduate students (who do not appear sharply different in kind from their full-time contemporaries) suggests that this is a mode which might be exploited further. Part-time fee levels have of course been kept low as a matter of policy. However, it might in many cases be possible to improve the efficiency of part-time teaching if students had more time to spend on the course. A grant in lieu of a fraction of salary (paid either to the student or to the employer) might produce a better result in numbers of completed degrees than the policy of concentrating grants on full-time students.

There might be other ways of encouraging part-time study. For example, there is little or no chance of distance learning on postgraduate courses. Even the Open University has found it necessary to provide residential courses for postgraduates. However, although not all types of course would lend themselves to distance learning, some could. In addition, despite their obvious qualification, we use postgraduates for teaching far less than do some other countries, such as the United States. At a time of apparent oversupply of teaching staff this suggestion may not be popular with the academic profession; but it is a method of subsidizing postgraduates with much to commend it.

DEMAND FOR AND ACCESS TO POSTGRADUATE STUDY

At undergraduate level virtually all full-time home students can obtain a grant for full-time study. Thus their numbers are largely determined by the extent to which potential students want to enter higher education, and the ability and willingness of the universities, polytechnics and other colleges to take them. At graduate* level there is a third determinant — the availability of finance.

In Britain the main sources of finance of full-time graduate students have been (a) grants from central and local government (including the Research Councils), (b) grants from other sources, (c) salary as an employee doing research that will be used for a thesis, (d) salary from an employer who seconds the student for study, and (e) family or savings. In recent years government studentships have grown in importance and they now support roughly two-thirds of home full-time graduate students.

Studentships — and indeed admission to research degrees — are in general available only to graduates (and holders of comparable qualifications) who have achieved 'good' degrees — first class or upper second class Honours. It is this which gives graduate study its special importance. It takes a substantial proportion of our best graduates. They are the élite of an élite.

Most full-time students studying for higher degrees are in the universities; in 1977 there were 36,800 there compared with 2,300 in further education, who were almost entirely in the polytechnics (1,400 in polytechnics were working for universities' higher degrees, so there may have been some double counting). Most of the issues relating to these students are the same, regardless of whether they are in a university or a polytechnic, so both groups are discussed together.

---

*For various reasons I exclude students on postgraduate teacher training courses from the coverage of this chapter, although it is not always possible to do so from the statistics.

There are many other graduate students, but for some of the other groups the numbers are lacking or inexact. The universities had 12,000 students on full-time non-degree postgraduate courses lasting at least a year, of whom about half were studying for a school-teacher's qualification. They also had 23,400 part-time graduate students on courses lasting at least a year, of whom 19,000 were working for higher degrees (the residue here includes a very small number of full-time students on courses lasting less than a year but more than a term). There are no comparable data for the polytechnics.

There are also substantial but unknown numbers of students attending shorter courses of postgraduate study, full-time or part-time, at universities or polytechnics. Some recent studies I have made (not yet published) to aid a policy review by the SRC (now the Science and Engineering Research Council) give a substantial amount of information about such students within the SERC's field.*

For part-time and short-course study too I shall discuss the problems affecting the universities and the polytechnics together.

FULL-TIME STUDY

Over half the full-time graduate students in the universities (excluding those in teacher training) are working for research degrees, and a third are following taught courses leading to higher degrees. Many of the remainder are working for higher diplomas or certificates, especially in social work. However, the division between research and courses is not sharp, and indeed many advanced course students give as a reason for studying that they felt drawn to research. Research students are increasingly required to attend lecture courses; and in virtually all taught courses the students complete small pieces of research. The difference is partly of emphasis but more of length. Generally one year of postgraduate study is a course; two years or more are research.

Similar data for the polytechnics are not available.

The period of the most rapid expansion of studentships began in 1957 and the effect of this on the numbers of full-time graduate students can be traced in Table 6.1. By 1967 they had increased threefold since 1957, while other full-time students had only doubled in number. Since 1938 the graduates had increased tenfold, the others three and a half times. The cuts in government expenditure of the early 1970s severely affected the research

---

*These surveys were of (a) all part-time courses and short full-time courses (in the SRC's field) in universities and polytechnics, and (b) part-time advanced course and research students; related studies were of (c) part-time courses at Brunel University, their students and their employers, by Wendy Keys, and (d) a general sample of industrial employers, by Anne Izatt and David Parsons of the Institute of Manpower Studies. It is hoped that all four studies will be published together.

councils, and, for the first time since 1957, the number of their new awards fell slightly. Since then the numbers of studentships have fluctuated a little from year to year according to the vicissitudes of government funding. On the whole, research council awards in the sciences and social sciences have shown a downward trend, from a peak of 6,700 new awards in 1971, 1972 and 1973 to 5,800 in 1979, and those of the DES, in the arts, an upward trend, from 1,600 to 2,100 new awards (for England and Wales) in the same period.

TABLE 6.1
Numbers of full-time home and overseas graduate students in universities in Great Britain compared with numbers of awards for postgraduate study made by the research councils and the Ministry of Education/Department of Education and Science (Thousands)

	Awards(a)		New students(b)	All home students(b)	All overseas students(b)	All students (excluding education students)
	New	Current				
1938	–	–	–	–	–	3.0
1950	–	–	–	–	–	8.0
1957	1.1	1.8	–	–	–	10.5
1960	1.7	3.5	–	–	–	13.6
1965	4.0	7.8	–	20.2	8.2	23.2
1966	4.5	8.8	–	22.9	9.1	26.2
1967	5.0	9.8	20.7	26.2	8.8	31.5
1968	5.5 (c)	10.6 (c)	21.7	28.6	9.1	30.9
1969	7.3	12.9	22.4	29.4	9.8	32.0
1970	8.2	14.6	24.1	31.3	10.8	34.5
1971	8.3	14.9	28.0	32.7	11.8	36.6
1972	8.4	15.3	27.9	33.0	13.1	38.0
1973	8.4	15.6	28.8	32.2	14.6	38.5
1974	8.3	15.5	29.4	31.8	16.0	39.4
1975	8.0	15.6	30.7	32.6	17.2	41.0
1976	8.2	15.7	30.8	32.3	18.0	42.0
1977	8.6	16.1	29.6	30.8	18.1	40.6
1978	8.6	16.5	29.9	30.7	18.5	41.0
1979	7.9	16.1	29.3	30.2	17.5	39.4

(a)   Does not include a small number of awards given by other government departments principally the Scottish Education Department, or, up to 1968, by LEAs
(b)   Including students in education departments
(c)   In 1969 the DES and SSRC took over responsibility for certain awards previously made by LEAs

– = not available

Source
Statistics of Education Vol. 6. UGC annual reports. Research Council reports. Unpublished tabulations.

Correspondingly the numbers of full-time home graduate students in the universities have been going down, even though the numbers of first degrees awarded to home students have been rising. This means home students' opportunities for full-time postgraduate study have been reduced.

The number of overseas students in the universities, as Table 6.1 shows, has risen most rapidly since the increase in home students' numbers ended. Over the decade 1968-78 they doubled in number. But this upward trend has twice been reversed — the first time temporarily — by rises in fees — in 1967 and again in 1979.

Altogether the number of graduate students in the universities — home and overseas — reached a peak in 1976 and has since slightly declined.

The complexities of the systems of departmental quotas by which most studentships are allocated make it difficult to discover how much unsatisfied demand there has been for full-time postgraduate study. On the whole, the information available suggests that, at any time since 1945, except in two areas, if there had been more studentships there would have been more students. The two areas in which in most, but not all, years there have been spare studentships have been advanced (taught) courses in science and technology and the schemes developed to encourage scientists to do industrial research. The number of advanced course studentships awarded in science and technology rose to nearly 1,900 in 1971 and has since fallen to a little over 1,600 in 1979. This fall does not seem to have resulted from a shortage of awards.

Table 6.2 shows the distribution of university students between the main subject groups and forms of study. In science (in 1979) over four times as many students were working for research degrees as were following courses. In other fields the balance was less heavily tilted towards research — in arts subjects and in engineering and technology there were about one and a half research students for every one advanced course student; while in social, administrative and business studies the balance was reversed, there being almost two advanced course students for every one doing research.

Women and working-class postgraduate students
Fewer women than men enter full-time postgraduate study, although the proportion has increased substantially in recent years. In universities, women constituted 35 per cent of all full-time postgraduates in 1979, compared with 23 per cent in 1966; in 1977 they were 26 per cent of part-time students, compared with 14 per cent in 1966. Comparable figures for full-time undergraduates are 39 per cent for 1979 and 29 per cent for 1966. In other words, not only are there fewer women than men in postgraduate study, but women graduates are still somewhat less likely than men graduates to go on to postgraduate work. Some explanations of the difference are clear. Women are less likely than men to gain first class Honours degrees. They are less likely to graduate in science or engineering, where a higher proportion of graduates than in the arts continue their studies, and where a higher

TABLE 6.2
Graduate students in universities: by subject group and type of study: men and women: Great Britain (1977) (Percentages)

	Education	Medical subjects	Engineering and technology	Science	Social studies	Arts	Other subjects	N = 100 %
Full-time								
Men								
Research for degree or qualification	1.3	6.4	20.1	40.3	15.2	12.7	3.9	18,818
Degree courses	7.6	4.1	23.2	17.5	31.1	9.0	7.5	9,769
Other courses (incl. teacher training)	50.3	9.1	5.1	3.0	19.7	5.7	7.1	6,727
Women								
Research for degree or qualification	3.2	11.1	4.7	32.3	19.6	24.7	4.3	5,190
Degree courses	12.2	7.1	5.1	12.0	35.0	20.6	8.0	3,024
Other courses	62.1	4.1	0.1	0.1	21.5	5.2	5.1	5,343
Part-time								
Men								
Research for degree	9.9	7.7	13.0	21.0	21.7	22.5	4.1	9,745
Other research	5.9	24.1	10.2	17.0	17.7	20.6	4.3	693
Degree courses	38.9	4.5	13.3	16.2	19.4	4.7	1.8	4,585
Other postgraduate	35.9	27.5	9.8	6.7	5.0	2.3	5.2	2,307
Women								
Research for degree	12.3	10.0	2.2	16.2	20.8	34.5	4.0	3,095
Other research	5.2	28.4	1.1	14.8	14.4	32.8	3.3	271
Degree courses	45.0	8.7	1.1	12.4	16.1	14.1	2.7	1,535
Other postgraduate	59.7	16.6	1.4	6.0	6.1	5.2	5.0	1,210

Source   *Statistics of Education* Vol. 6, 1977.

proportion of those that do continue do research rather than follow taught courses. These factors do not, however, explain the whole of the difference. It seems that those influences that result in fewer women than men entering higher education at all are at work to a small extent here too. There are plenty of hypotheses for what these are, but little hard data.

The Robbins Report (and others) mentioned that the general tendency for working-class youngsters to drop out of education is reversed at postgraduate level, in that a higher percentage of graduate students than of undergraduates are from working-class families. Our 1966 data, with that of Kelsall et al., showed that this was the result of the higher proportion of arts students and women students who came from middle-class homes (compared with students in science and engineering and men students) coupled with the relatively low percentages of arts students and women students going into graduate study. Once these factors had been allowed for, the proportion of working-class students continuing their studies was the same as that of the middle-class students (Rudd 1975, pp.37-39).

PART-TIME STUDY
Part-time study (other than with the OU) is far more important at graduate than at undergraduate level; in 1979 there were 4000 part-time under-graduates in the universities and 25,900 part-time graduate students (on forms of study lasting a year or more). It has a long history, but serious defects in the statistics make it inadvisable to try to compare the growth of full-time and part-time study before the present definition was adopted in 1972. From then to 1979 the number of part-time graduate students in universities increased by a third whereas home full-time students fell by a tenth.

Our recent surveys of part-time postgraduate study in science and technology (referred to above) found very roughly twice as many students in the universities as in the polytechnics. For part-time students, proximity to their place of work and home is one of the most important considerations in deciding where to study, so they are heavily concentrated in those universities and polytechnics that are in large towns.

We found that more of the polytechnic students than of those in the university were following courses rather than doing research. Most of the polytechnic courses were for part-time students only, whereas the universities generally provided for part-time study within a course that was primarily for full-time students. The completion rate for the part-time students on courses in the universities was higher than in the polytechnics, though whether this was due to the difference in the form of course provided or to other factors it is impossible to tell.

This study and the earlier study of part-time students (Rudd 1975, Ch.9) have shown that, although many of them have deliberately chosen to study part-time, preferring this to full-time study, many others would have preferred to be full-time students but could not gain grants. It is tempting, therefore, to explain recent growth as resulting from the reduction in grants for, and increase in the expense of, full-time postgraduate study. However, to be sure of this we would need to know more about the reasons for the growth of part-time study in earlier periods.

Relatively few part-time graduate students persevere long enough to gain a higher degree (Rudd and Hatch 1968, Ch.2). Where they do, and often too where they do not, the cost in money, effort, loss of family life and leisure, and in many other ways, is considerable.

The subject groups of the university students and their forms of study are shown in Table 6.2. Fewer of the part-time than of the full-time students do research in science; it is difficult for anyone who does not work in a laboratory to study part time for a research degree in science, and many of these students are using research done for their employers to gain themselves a degree. There are two other striking differences between the distributions of part-time and full-time students: firstly, substantial numbers of school-teachers follow part-time taught courses, especially in education, for higher degrees and diplomas. Belief in the value of these seems to be stronger amongst school-teachers than elsewhere, and it is easier to gain a higher degree by a taught course than by research. Secondly, part-time study is especially common in medical subjects, where many of the students do research or follow courses that lead either to a diploma or to no qualification at all.

There are substantially fewer women amongst the part-time students, in spite of more of the students being in fields in which more women graduate: 28.5 per cent of the part-time compared with 38.0 per cent of the full-time students. Perhaps within the whole field of postgraduate study the most important need for which there is too little provision is study facilities and finance to help women graduates to resume their careers after raising families.

REASONS FOR POSTGRADUATE STUDY

When graduate students are asked why they entered postgraduate study they are likely to stress expressive reasons rather than instrumental ones; they talk of feeling drawn to research, and of wanting to take their undergraduate studies further, and of gaining knowledge for its own sake. Beyond this, research students and those following the more academic taught courses part company from those following courses in applied fields, of whom a substantial proportion also mention the wish to get a better job and a higher salary, while those who have had a period in employment are likely also to mention a wish to make better progress in their chosen career. Part-time students' motivation is surprisingly like that of full-time students with, if anything, more emphasis on expressive reasons. A reason for entry to a PhD so obvious that it gets forgotten is that it is expected to lead to a job that will be (in the student's view) well-paid and interesting — preferably university teaching or research. Amongst the reasons which, as they are less creditable, are mentioned more rarely than they occur is a tendency to prefer the known world of the university to the unknown outside. The wish to cover up a weak first degree is mentioned by only a small fraction of those having such a degree. PhD students hardly ever say that they would like to be called Dr. instead of Mr.

The reasons that the universities and their staff put forward for providing the more vocational forms of graduate study are clear enough — a Masters course in clinical psychology is intended to produce clinical psychologists. At the next level, where graduates who already have a profession are being given more advanced knowledge and training in a section of their field — where, for example, civil engineers are being given further knowledge of soil science — the purpose is still clear, though one can then sometimes question the recruitment to the course of new graduates without work experience.

The justification for providing postgraduate education becomes far less clear-cut when its vocational application is less likely — for example a Masters in the sociology of religion or a PhD in geography. Then the university teacher may talk of the intellectual gains likely to accrue from studying — the ability to think clearly, to plan one's own work and carry it out, and generally, to stand on one's own feet. For the individual teacher, there is greater prestige in teaching and supervising graduates than undergraduates. Those who are themselves active researchers get the opportunity to exercise and demonstrate their research skills in the supervision of students' research, and more chance to talk about their own research to graduate students than to undergraduates. Most academics regard the advancement of their subject as important, and setting graduate students to work in it is a way of advancing it. Also, in some fields, notably chemistry, the staff actually do a large part of their research through students, a high proportion of published articles being in the joint names of students and their supervisors.

The reasons why the various government agencies provide the finance that so largely shapes graduate study cannot be regarded as totally independent of the reasons why academics want to have graduate students; through their share of the membership of the UGC and the research councils, and of the sub-committees of these bodies, academics participate in the decisions on this. The key considerations, however, are those arguments that actually persuade the Treasury to disburse funds. In the late fifties and the sixties an important argument was the need to produce teachers for the expansion of the universities. In science and the social sciences, and especially the more applied fields, arguments were also based on the needs of other employers for graduates who are trained in research and/or in those advanced and highly specialized branches of subjects that cannot be covered in the undergraduate syllabus. (There is often confusion between a normative sense of need, meaning that employers ought to use them, and a market-place definition based on employers' wishes and intentions as expressed in hiring graduates.) One finds occasional references to manpower planning. Also there are references from time to time to Britain's need for pure scientists (who, it is argued, can be produced only by the universities) based on the argument that developments in applied science and technology spring from the progress of pure science. More rarely, it is argued that research done by research students contributes to the development of academic disciplines.

Certain counter-arguments can also be found. In 1966 the Interim Report of the Swann Committee (Committee on Manpower Resources 1966) drew attention to the relatively small share of the graduates with first class Honours in science and technology who went into industry and the schools, and to the role of graduate study in bringing this about. It also said '. . . patterns have been set and the expectations raised of careers in research which are unlikely to be satisfied in this country.' In 1967 and again in 1972 the UGC called on the universities to slow down the rate of growth in postgraduate study on the grounds that priority should be given to undergraduates, the Robbins figures for postgraduates had been exceeded, the numbers staying on were more than the country could afford, and there would in future be less need for new university teachers (see also Rudd and Hatch 1968).

Since 1972 the rate of growth in government expenditure, not only on higher education expansion but also on research, has been hit increasingly severely, implying that the arguments for ever increasing numbers of graduate students are now less convincing.

Employers' views on the value of postgraduate study vary widely. They are frequently mere opinions, no objective assessment of its value within the firm having been made. Actions are more important than expressions of opinion, and so to look at this issue properly requires a study of the functions, career paths, salaries, etc. within a large number of firms of people with varying qualifications. This has not yet been done, but in the meantime there is some evidence from salary data.

In our 1966 study of graduates who entered postgraduate study in 1957 (Rudd and Hatch 1968, Ch. 6) we found that where it could be expected that a PhD would be most valued — in scientific research and technological development — industry put scarcely any more monetary value on a PhD than on a Masters plus two extra years experience in employment. More recently, the Department of Employment's 1977 survey of 1970 graduates (Williamson 1981) indicates that on average each extra year of postgraduate study, coupled of course with one fewer year's experience in employment, produces a reduction in salary. Over a surprisingly wide range of specialities, and types of work and employer, graduates who have done no postgraduate study are paid more than PhDs. Masters degrees are sometimes in an intermediate position, though in a few fields, notably engineering, they do command a premium. It is clear that a high proportion of employers put more value on years of experience in employment than on years of full-time postgraduate study.

This finding implies either that postgraduate students are not seeking a higher salary through their studies, or that they are ignorant of the effect of these studies on their likely incomes. Both explanations could be partly true. As data on the incomes of graduates with higher degrees have not been easy to find, it would be surprising if students knew precisely what income they could expect; though they have probably been aware that the occupations recruiting PhDs are not amongst the best paid. However, students enter graduate study more for expressive than for instrumental reasons; they see themselves as choosing to enjoy being what they find most interesting for a few years before getting down to the serious business of earning a living. In as far as they are looking to a future career, their concern is to find a way into work they will enjoy rather than that which pays well.

POST-EXPERIENCE STUDY

Certain forms of graduate study must follow immediately after the first degree — a mathematics graduate who wishes to be a statistician needs immediately to gain a Masters in statistics. Others come best after a gap — a new graduate should not need an up-dating course. Others, again, may be taken either immediately on graduation or after a gap; in many of these cases a gap allows the graduate a better opportunity of deciding more precisely in what he wishes to specialize. Although a gap may be desirable, graduates rarely return to the university or polytechnic as full-time students; both employers and employees are generally opposed to the idea. For the employee, full-time study can mean not only a year's separation from his home and family, but also the risk of being left behind in the race for promotion. The employer is often unwilling to lose the services of a useful employee for a whole year. Both believe that there is too much academic and theoretical content in many courses to meet their needs.

A way round some of these difficulties might be thought to be part-time study. However, the recent surveys* for the SRC have thrown doubt on the vocational usefulness of part-time study for a Masters or PhD. A few (very few) employers use Masters courses for graduate trainees. A tiny percentage of the other students are sent to study by their firms. Most, however, are studying with the consent of their employers, or at least a lack of opposition, rather than at their employer's instance; and the reasons they give for studying are, again, expressive rather than instrumental — only a minority say that their decision to study was influenced to the slightest extent by vocational considerations.

The kind of postgraduate study of which both employers and employees do approve is the short full-time course lasting from a week-end to three or even six months, but generally about a week. In science and technology the number of these is booming. They generally cover a narrow field of

---

*See above.

knowledge or a particular technique or skill. They can be fairly quickly arranged, with a minimum of academic red tape, so they can be used to put over the latest research results. They enable the student to acquire precisely the amount of knowledge he needs, without having to cover extraneous material; there is, after all, no reason why the natural module for knowledge should be the quantity that can be absorbed in an academic year. And, in particular, they do not require the student to be away from home or work for a long period. A succession of such courses, taken over a number of years, can sometimes form the study period for a Masters degree. Our recent surveys found that 88 per cent of the short full-time and 66 per cent of the short part-time courses were in polytechnics and Scottish colleges. Nine universities provided over 70 per cent of the short full-time courses.

The main gap here is in the dissemination of information about what is available, which at present generally takes place in a rather restricted way. As the interval of time between the course being arranged and being held is often quite short, and many of the courses are never repeated, or are repeated only once or twice, any general listing would have to appear at frequent intervals.

SELECTION OF STUDENTS
More attention has recently been paid to the success rates of graduate students, which are low, especially in the arts and social studies. In science and engineering they are lower in the polytechnics than the universities. Many of the issues here lie outside the scope of this book; but the question of selection is relevant. At present, selectors for places in graduate study and for studentships make little effort, and in any case lack the means, to discover whether the student has any aptitude for or any strong motivation towards research — there is a research element in most higher degrees. It is simply not enough to assume that anyone with a good first degree will make a good graduate student.

CONCLUSIONS
Though the forms which postgraduate study and research take are many and various, for overall policy it makes sense to regard them, across subject boundaries, as coming into three groups:

(a) Those essential to a graduate who wishes to enter a specific occupation — eg social work, or university teaching. Even allowing for human inability to foresee the future accurately, it ought to be possible to predict the likely vacancies in the chosen occupation sufficiently well to base numbers of home students on manpower projections.

(b) Those related to the job and best studied after an interval. Here there seem to be strong reasons to encourage the continued expansion of short full-time post-experience courses, which have the flexibility to meet the changing needs of both employers and employees. These courses are largely self-financing, but there are needs for relatively small amounts of finance to set up arrangements for circulating information about them and perhaps to overcome various impediments to their expansion, such as the lack of residential accommodation appropriate to the kinds of students attending. There is also a case for exploring the combination of some short full-time courses with an element of distance learning.

(c) Other courses and forms of study. These are by definition less vocational. Often it is not that they are irrelevant to any vocation but that they are not relevant to any one specific vocation or are relevant to vocations in which the students can have little realistic expectation of finding employment. They include most PhDs as well as non-vocational Masters degrees. Most of these courses and forms of study are of so little value to employers that they would prefer their staff not to have followed them; and if the return on investment were the sole criterion deciding the numbers of students, there would be very few entering for or given grants for these higher degrees.

There are, however, other arguments for such study. One is that through it Britain is able to make a contribution to the advancement of science and international scholarship. Another is that, by giving selected graduates an enjoyable educational experience, it adds to the quality of life and the quality of our civilization. Graduate students, like art galleries, opera and orchestras, are something that a wealthy country, and we are still a wealthy country, ought to be able to afford. But there is nothing in this argument that tells us how many.

REFERENCES

Committee on Higher Education (1963) (Robbins Committee) *Report* Cmnd. 2154, London: HMSO

Committee on Manpower Resources for Science and Technology (1966) *Interim Report of the Working Group on Manpower Parameters for Scientific Growth* Cmnd. 3102, London: HMSO

Rudd, E. and Hatch, S.R. (1968) *Graduate Study and After* London: Weidenfeld and Nicolson

Rudd, E. (1975) *The Highest Education* London: Routledge and Kegan Paul

Williamson, P. (1981) The careers of graduates — earnings and unemployment *Employment Gazette* 220-222

7

OVERSEAS STUDENTS

by Maureen Woodhall

INTRODUCTION by Oliver Fulton
In many respects, overseas students constitute an even more special case for demand and access policies than do postgraduates. Here at least, the arguments in favour of total 'nationality-blindness' in selection and admission are fairly weak, while the case for policies which differentiate both between home and overseas students and among foreign nationals is quite convincing. (This is not to say that it is one-sided: there are good arguments both for positive and for negative discrimination.) The possible lines of argument are laid out very clearly by Maureen Woodhall (below), and at greater length in Williams (1981); it is not necessary to anticipate or to retrace them here. Many of them, in any case, range well outside the primary area of concern of this book, into problems not only of foreign policy, overseas aid and foreign trade, but also (for example) of the international labour market, the research and teaching process and so on.

However, this is not an adequate reason to dismiss overseas student policies as irrelevant to our more general concerns. For one thing, home and overseas demand are interdependent. In some institutions the recruitment of large numbers of overseas students has ensured the viability of courses which might otherwise have been too small to sustain: as a result, drastic reductions in overseas numbers as a result of high fees could well reduce the opportunities available to home students. (Whether recruiting overseas students at subsidized rates is the most desirable or efficient way of sustaining diversity is another matter.)

The changeover to 'full-cost' fees in 1980, whatever its possible economic or other justification, was widely, and quite fairly, interpreted as a policy not only for dealing with the foreign student 'problem' but also for modifying the behaviour of British institutions. A major attraction to government was that it served the simple financial purpose of reducing the cash support for higher education without altering (on paper) its support for British students. But given the competitive international market and the sudden huge increase in fees which was required, the effect has, not unexpectedly, been less straightforward. The Robbins Committee scarcely distinguished between home and overseas students; and during the 1960s the principle of response to demand was generally applied to both without distinction. The introduction first of quotas and then of differential fees is the only experience we yet have of central government interference with that principle, and it should be possible to learn from it.

One lesson which might be drawn concerns the process of policy change. The Conservative government was widely criticized in 1980 for the abruptness with which the change to full-cost fees was introduced, and for the lack of consultation which preceded it. However, there had been frequent warnings to higher education institutions (from governments of both political parties) since the late 1960s, in effect inviting them to develop their own alternative policies, and these had largely been disregarded. The principle of differential fees and the introduction of quotas had already been accepted, if reluctantly, some years earlier. Much of the indignation was not really about the new principle but its financial implications. Nevertheless, the policy was introduced with great suddenness, and without adequate consideration of its implications for any of the range of issues spelled out by Woodhall. On the other hand, the consequence turned out to be a searching examination of the issues, with reports from two House of Commons Select Committees and a definitive review of evidence and analysis of the issues sponsored by the Overseas Students Trust (Williams 1981). Whether the politer democratic processes of 'consultation' before the event would have produced such a wide-ranging examination is an interesting question. It also remains to be seen what use will be made of the criticisms and proposals which have resulted from it.

The second lesson is substantive, not methodological. The governing principle for the supply of places for overseas students is now a market principle, modified and limited by a very wide range of policy considerations. In effect, and with important differences (notably the low level of state subsidy) this is an extreme case of an experiment with the kind of policy alternatives proposed in Chapter 1. It will provide a test, therefore, both of how British higher education responds to market pressures; and of whether the multiple criteria for subsidy proposed by Williams (see below) can actually be translated into effective principles of financial support. As an experiment in modifying the behaviour of institutions and of central government it will be worth watching.

THE OVERSEAS STUDENT QUESTION

Throughout the world there are now estimated to be approximately one million students taking part in higher education in a foreign country. The number has quadrupled since 1960, when there were about 240,000 foreign students studying outside their own country. This world-wide growth in demand for foreign study has caused a number of problems in some countries, and the question of access to higher education for students from overseas is being actively studied or discussed in a number of countries as well as in Britain. At present, foreign students are heavily concentrated in five countries: the USA, Canada, France, Germany and the UK. These five countries take approximately 60 per cent of all foreign students and thus have been most affected by the rapid increase in demand, but in recent years other countries have also become concerned about the increase in foreign students, and have introduced or strengthened measures to limit foreign student admissions, either through numerical restrictions, such as quotas, or through imposing or increasing tuition fees. The question of admissions policy for overseas students has therefore become a major issue in a number of countries, and 1980 and 1981 have seen various national conferences, commissions or research studies on the subject, which have served to emphasize the need for governments to adopt coherent policies towards foreign students, rather than rely on ad hoc measures to control access to higher education.

In Britain, the number of foreign students in all forms of higher education trebled between 1958, when there were 42,000 and 1978, when there were 120,000 (Table 7.1). In universities the number of overseas students more than doubled between 1968 and 1978, and in the same period the numbers in all publicly financed higher or further education almost trebled. The result of this rapid expansion is that in 1978-9 overseas students accounted for over eleven per cent of all students in higher education, compared with only 5.6 per cent in 1971. This very rapid increase in overseas student numbers gave rise to mounting concern in Britain in the 1970s. At the same time, in other countries too, there was a growing recognition that the admission of foreign students should be controlled in some way. This reflected two concerns about the cost of subsidizing overseas students and also about the appropriate balance between home and foreign students. In some countries restrictions on the admission of foreign students have been introduced in order to prevent home students from being virtually swamped by foreign students, particularly in certain faculties. For example, both Austria and Switzerland have introduced strict, numerical quotas because in the 1960s foreign students accounted for more than twenty per cent of all students in higher education and the introduction of 'numerus clausus' policies in neighbouring countries caused a sharp increase in the number of foreign student applications in the early 1970s. As a result of these measures the proportion has fallen to ten per cent in Austria, but is still around twenty per cent in Switzerland. Numerical quotas governing the admission of foreign students now exist in Denmark, Germany, the Netherlands and Sweden, and a number of restrictions were introduced in France in 1979.

In Britain, the government has adopted the alternative policy of controlling foreign student admission through differential fees, partly because it was believed that a policy of numerical quotas, introduced by the Labour government in 1976, had failed to stem the tide of rapidly increasing numbers, and partly because the costs of subsidizing overseas students were seen as a major problem by the Conservative government in 1979. The Robbins Committee estimated the costs of subsidizing overseas students as £9m in 1963. By 1979 this had risen, according to Treasury estimates, to £102m for higher education and a further £25m for non-advanced further education. Thus, the policy of 'full-cost fees', introduced in 1980, when universities were required to charge a minimum of £2,000 a year for arts

TABLE 7.1
Overseas students in Britain 1950-1978

	Universities	Other advanced higher education (polytechnics, colleges of education and other HE and FE establishments)	Total higher education	Non-advanced further education (polytechnics and other HE and FE establishments)	Total publicly financed HE and FE	Private sector institutions	Grand total
1950-51	8242	—	—	—	—	—	12500
1958-59	10672	—	—	—	—	—	42100
1963-64	14014	7028	21042	10425	21113	20987	64169
1968-69	15975	5554	21529	8744	31467	32702	69819
1973-74	25318	9755	35073	18091	30273	39546	95209
1976-77	34454	21473	55927	26847	53164	42045	124942
1977-78	35888	22675	58563	27544	82774	42168	123759
1978-79	37140	22485	59625	27154	86107	37652	119559
			10441	4258	86779	32780	

Source
British Council *Statistics of Overseas Students in Britain, Annual Reports.*

courses, £3,000 for science and engineering and £5,000 for medicine, dentistry and veterinary science, was primarily designed to reduce the cost of the public subsidy of overseas students.

TABLE 7.2
Proportion of overseas students in UK higher education

	Total enrolment	No. of overseas students	Proportion of overseas students
	(000s)	(000s)	(per cent)
1971-2	464	26	5.6
1972-3	473	30	6.3
1973-4	481	34	7.1
1974-5	487	40	8.2
1975-6	505	48	9.5
1976-7	515	55	10.7
1977-8	509	57	11.1
1978-9	508	58	11.4
1979-80 (provisional)	509	56	11.0

This policy was challenged on two main grounds. First, that the government had miscalculated the costs of subsidizing overseas students, by looking only at crude figures of average costs of educating overseas students, and secondly that it failed to take account of the economic benefits derived by the British economy from the presence of overseas students. These questions were examined in a study, by Blaug et al., of the economic costs and benefits of overseas students, which was published, together with a number of studies of the wider implications of British policy on overseas students, in Spring 1981 by the Overseas Students Trust (Williams 1981).

It is extremely difficult to measure precisely either the costs or the benefits of overseas students. It is certainly true that the marginal costs of enrolling additional students are usually lower than average costs in higher education; in arts and social science marginal costs are probably about half average costs, and in science and engineering about two-thirds (Verry and Davies 1976). However, overseas students are heavily concentrated in the most expensive subject areas, namely postgraduate courses in science and engineering where both average and marginal costs are well above the average for all British higher education. Thus Blaug estimates that in 1979-80 the total marginal costs of overseas students in all public sector higher and further education were £266m. On the other hand, it is clear that a reduction in the number of overseas students will not bring about marginal savings equivalent to the marginal costs of enrolling additional students, at least in the short run. Thus, it remains to be seen how much saving of public funds will arise as a result of the new policy on 'full-cost fees,' and at the same time it must be admitted that the so-called 'full-cost fees' do not represent the actual costs of different courses, since they are based on crude estimates of average costs, rather than actual marginal costs, which vary considerably between institutions.

However, the cost of subsidizing overseas students must be seen in relation to the benefits they bring. It is even more difficult to measure these in monetary terms, but there are a whole range of possible benefits which have been recognized, although not measured. Peter Williams, in his introduction to *The Overseas Student Question* (Williams 1981) suggests the following list of British interests and obligations to be taken into account in formulating a policy on overseas students:

'(A) British interests
  (1) Educational
      (i)   Attracting bright scholars;
      (ii) Value of international element in educational institutions;
      (iii) Research output of overseas students;
      (iv) Reciprocal access for British scholars to overseas institutions.
  (2) Economic
      (i)   Spending on goods and services;
      (ii) Balance of payments;
      (iii) Future export orders for goods and services.
  (3) Political
      (i)   Direct influence and goodwill towards Britain;
      (ii) Promotion of democratic values.
(B) British obligations
  (1) Formal obligations
      (i)   Treaty obligations;
      (ii) Cultural exchange agreements;
      (iii) Pledges under international schemes of cooperation.
  (2) Informal responsibilities
      (i)   Assistance to developing countries;
      (ii) Countries educationally dependent on Britain;
      (iii) Students already on course;
      (iv) Refugees.'

The presence of overseas students does bring a number of benefits, but unfortunately it is impossible to quantify them in any precise way. For example, it is often suggested that one of the main economic benefits gained from the presence of overseas students in Britain is a stimulus to trade, and an inquiry in 1980 by the Overseas Students Trust produced many very positive statements from representatives of about fifty major British exporting companies about the links between trade and education or training in Britain. However it has proved quite impossible to measure the extent of the impact of overseas study on future exports or other commercial interests, and Blaug (in Williams 1981) concludes: 'There is some connection between exports and overseas students but we refuse to indulge in spurious precision by assigning a number to the connection.'

One attempt to quantify the economic benefits, by the London Conference on overseas students in 1979, estimated that the benefits exceeded the costs of subsidizing overseas students, but Blaug questioned both the assumptions and the method of calculation that produced this estimate and concluded that in 1978-9 'the net costs of overseas students exceed their economic benefits.'

This does not mean that it is in the British interest to discourage overseas students, but simply that a large-scale subsidy of overseas students cannot be justified on purely economic grounds. There are, of course, other grounds for encouraging or subsidizing foreign students. The subsidy can be regarded as a special form of foreign aid, or as a way of promoting British political interests or achieving other objectives of foreign policy. William Wallace, in a discussion of the foreign policy implications of overseas students in Britain (Williams 1981) argues that:

'Policy towards overseas students, and expenditure incurred under that policy, can make at best only a marginal contribution to the achievement of foreign policy objectives. . . . But much politics, much commerce and much more diplomacy, is a matter of margins.'

He suggests that expenditure on subsidizing overseas students should be regarded as an element within the external relations budget, rather than within the education budget, and that then 'it is for ministers to decide how far the intangible benefits gained justify the expenditure.'

Apart from general questions of foreign policy, it is clear that two important issues in any consideration of policy towards overseas students are the needs of developing countries and the significance of expenditure on subsidizing overseas students in the overall foreign aid budget. About eighty per cent of overseas students come from developing countries and in the past, subsidized fees have been a significant form of financial assistance for them. But a system of subsidized fees involves an indiscriminate subsidy, equally available to all overseas students, regardless of origin, and not confined to developing countries. In fact in recent years there has been a shift in overseas student numbers away from the poorer commonwealth countries, in favour of richer countries, particularly the oil producers. Table 7.3 shows the changes that have occured since 1969 in the origins of overseas students. One advantage of a policy of full-cost fees for overseas students is that it is possible to link it with a policy of selective aid which channels assistance where it is judged to be most needed. However, one of the problems with the introduction of full-cost fees in 1980 was that it was not so linked. The

TABLE 7.3.
Countries with more than 1,000 students in publicly financed and further education in the UK in rank order

1969-70			1974-75			1978-79		
1	USA	2,360	1	Malaysia	7,010	1	Malaysia	13,308
2	Malaysia	1,713	2	Iran	5,222	2	Iran	9,095
3	India	1,668	3	Nigeria	3,533	3	Nigeria	5,896
4	Pakistan	1,577	4	USA	3,248	4	Hong Kong	5,133
5	Nigeria	1,473	5	Hong Kong	2,931	5	USA	3,720
6	Kenya	1,275	6	Greece	2,735	6	Greece	3,148
7	Cyprus	1,179	7	Kenya	1,946	7	Iraq	2,482
8	Sri Lanka	1,153	8	Cyprus	1,892	8	Sri Lanka	2,068
9	Iran	1,074	9	India	1,881	9	Jordan	1,875
10	Canada	1,057	10	Sri Lanka	1,659	10	Singapore	1,786
11	Hong Kong	1,053	11	Pakistan	1,311	11	Cyprus	1,587
			12	Iraq	1,287	12	Rhodesia	1,534
			13	Turkey	1,178	13	Turkey	1,463
			14	Canada	1,097	14	Kenya	1,166
			15	Singapore	1,010	15	India	1,162
						16	Canada	1,061
						17	Germany	1,023
						18	Libya	1,014

Source
British Council *Statistics of Overseas Students in Britain, Annual Reports.*

government now appears to be convinced of the value of selective aid, and in an answer to a parliamentary question in May 1981 Mr Mark Carlisle, Secretary of State for Education, said: 'My basic criticism of the plan that we inherited is that it did not attempt to discriminate in any way in the assistance given. If and when resources become available, we should be more discriminating in the aid that we give' (reported in *Times Higher Education Supplement* 22 May 1981).

If such a policy is to be adopted, it raises the question of the basis for discrimination. Ideally, any system of selective aid should take account of both British interests and British obligations. At present, the government provides selective subsidies in the form of reduced fees, or financial assistance in the form of scholarships to the following groups of students.

i   Students from member countries of the European community, who pay the same fees as British students.

ii   Refugee students who also pay 'home' rates of tuition fees.

iii Students admitted to British institutions under full reciprocal exchange schemes.

iv   A small number of postgraduate students who receive postgraduate research scholarships designed to attract overseas students of high research calibre.

v   A small number of students who receive scholarships provided by the ODA.

vi   Students already enrolled on courses prior to October 1980.

Apart from these categories, all overseas students must now pay 'full-cost fees', with considerable differentials introduced for the first time between different subjects, which meant that some students who enrolled in 1980 paid fees four hundred per cent higher than overseas students taking similar courses in 1979. A full assessment of the impact of the fee increase is not yet possible, but in 1980, on the basis of an analysis of the effects of previous fee increases, Mark Blaug and Richard Layard predicted that the overseas student numbers would decline by about ten per cent in universities in 1980-81 and by more thereafter, and that the reduction would be greater in polytechnics and non-advanced further education (Williams 1981). Preliminary information available early in 1981 broadly confirmed these predictions, and suggested that admissions in 1981 would be at least a third lower than in 1980.

The impact in individual institutions and departments will in some cases be much more marked. Overseas students have tended, in the past, to be heavily concentrated in certain geographical and subject areas. In 1979 overseas students represented seven per cent of all undergraduates but thirty-six per cent of all postgraduates. In some universities and polytechnics overseas students in 1978-9 accounted for more than a third of all students but only about three per cent in some other institutions. A survey of overseas students in 1980 revealed that they were heavily concentrated in science, engineering and technology courses, and that more than half of all the postgraduate students were taking courses in which overseas students outnumbered British students (Blaug and Woodhall in Williams 1981). In the case of some postgraduate courses, more than three-quarters of the students were from overseas, which means that a fall of forty to fifty per cent in overseas student numbers might make it impossible for such courses to continue.

In the future, therefore, policy on admission of overseas students must take into account the possible effects of reductions in overseas student numbers on the viability of courses, and therefore on opportunities for British students, and also on the balance between home and overseas students in different institutions and courses.

Recent experience and debate on overseas student policy, and particularly the introduction of 'full-cost fees', has served to emphasize that policy on admissions and in particular the question of selective financial assistance for overseas students, must take account of many different issues and objectives. At present, the Overseas Students Trust is embarking on a study of the possible implications of various options, which could form the basis of a policy of selective scholarship assistance. The present government has offered help and assistance with this project, although no funds, and the Foreign and Commonwealth Office has promised to co-operate, and provide any necessary information. However, before selective programmes can be introduced there must be agreement about the criteria for awarding scholarships or fee remissions. Financial assistance could be awarded on the basis of a combination of any of the following criteria.

1   The academic quality of overseas students.
2   The needs of sending countries, particularly developing countries.
3   The balance between different countries of origin.
4   The balance between home and overseas students in different courses or institutions.
5   The financial means of individual students, which are by no means identical with the state of development of the country of origin.
6   Possible links with British trade or other commercial interests.
7   Historical or other obligations.

In the past, some of these issues have been largely ignored, as overseas student numbers increased in response to outside pressures rather than an assessment of priorities. A policy of 'full-cost fees' combined with selective assistance for certain overseas students can provide the means of developing a coherent policy, based on specific criteria, for the future. Before this can be developed, however, there must be informed debate about what these criteria and priorities should be.

REFERENCES

Verry, D. and Davies, B (1976) *University Costs and Output* Amsterdam: Elsevier

Williams, Peter (Editor) (1981) *The Overseas Student Question: Studies For Policy* London: Heinemann, for the Overseas Students Trust